GENDER, CHANGE AND IDENTITY: MATURE WOMEN STUDENTS IN UNIVERSITIES

Gender, Change and Identity: Mature Women Students in Universities

BARBARA MERRILL

Ashgate

Aldershot • Brookfield USA • Singapore • Sydney

© Barbara Merrill 1999

Published by
Ashgate Publishing Ltd
Gower House
Croft Road
Aldershot
Hants GU11 3HR
England

Ashgate Publishing Company
Old Post Road
Brookfield
Vermont 05036
USA

British Library Cataloguing in Publication Data
Merrill, Barbara
     Gender, change and identity : mature women students in
     universities
     1. Women - Education (Higher) - Great Britain
     I. Title
     378.1'9822'0941

Library of Congress Catalog Card Number: 99-72663

ISBN 1 84014 993 0

Printed in Great Britain by
Antony Rowe Ltd, Chippenham, Wiltshire

Contents

Preface

Learning sociology at school and university enabled me to articulate, understand and politicise my life experiences as a working-class woman. Sociology, more than other subjects, made me aware of the power of knowledge and learning. I learned to question the 'taken for granted' in the social world. Moving into adult education after several years working in secondary education I began teaching adult students and talked to many more about their learning experiences, in my capacity as a research and development officer. The transition from initial to adult education led me to reflect upon my teaching experiences in both sectors, and thereby compare the teaching of adults with the teaching of children. In doing so I began exploring and questioning the concept of andragogy. Starting in a new field I was eager to examine adult and continuing education from a sociological perspective. Reading a wide range of literature on adult education and working in the field raised many questions that I wanted to investigate further about the relationship between theory and praxis. Interest in interactionism, feminism and Marxism shaped my theoretical perspectives. I wanted to understand the world of adult education from the viewpoints of the learner, particularly women adult students, within a framework of gender and class relationships.

Gender, class and race inequalities have been central concerns throughout my life. Being female and of working-class origin I soon came to experience initially class, but later gender, discrimination and inequalities in society. Later as a teacher in a multicultural comprehensive school I quickly became conscious of the pervasiveness of racism in society through the lives of the black pupils.

As a working-class undergraduate in the 1970s at Warwick I was overwhelmed by the middle-class culture of both other students and the institution. As an undergraduate I found it difficult to adjust to the middle-class culture of the institution. This occasionally undermined my confidence despite my sociological and political background. I was, therefore, interested in how working-class adult students, who had been out of the education system for a long time, coped with the middle class environment of a 'traditional', although young, university like Warwick.

Many of the pupils at the school where I taught had been alienated by the white middle-class school system and left school having underachieved Did the adult students at Warwick share similar life histories? If so why had they chosen to return to learn, and why at this particular moment in their lives?

My development and research work brought me into contact with mature women students, and with concerns about access. However, it was gender issues that stimulated my interest and thinking about mature students the most, although I could not ignore the links between gender and class. I was struck by the women's enthusiasm and determination to learn despite the problems they faced both within and outside the University. My experiences as a teacher were reinforced by the literature that I read: girls experienced schooling differently from boys. I wanted to find out whether or not this situation was applicable to the experiences of female and male mature students in universities. Underlying this was a theoretical concern: to what extent are there continuities and discontinuities between initial schooling and adult education in relation to gender?

In recent years the widening of access to higher education has been high on the political and policy agendas. Although we are now in a period of consolidation in British higher education the policy of widening access has enabled non-traditional adult students, particularly women, to enter higher education. Universities are characterised by a more diverse student population. Access policy and practice has largely been aimed at getting adults into the system. The entrance of adult students into universities like Warwick and onto special degree programmes, such as Part-time and 2+2, is evidence of institutional change. However, it is a limited change as they enter on the university's terms. Policy-makers have, on the whole, not seen the need to foster institutional change to meet the needs of mature students, especially within the 'old' universities. 'Old' being the term now used to refer to those institutions that were universities in the former binary higher education system. If non-traditional students are mostly having to adapt to existing structures, what are the implications for the quality of their educational experiences? Mature women students are having to cope with studying and domestic responsibilities, delicately balancing their public and private lives. To mature women students, universities such as Warwick may appear inflexible in relation to their learning needs.

The biographies of mature women students are valuable in revealing the educational and gender links between initial and adult education; but above all adult educators can learn a great deal from them about what institutions need to do to meet the needs of non-traditional adult students. We can learn from the learners. In the absence of planned institutional change mature students learn to act upon their social world by initiating small-scale strategies that make their lives at university easier to manage at the micro and meso levels. For certain adult students the student experience is a different one now as they have successfully put pressure on some departments to change practices. A minority of lecturers have responded to the increasing presence of adult students in their teaching groups by reviewing and modifying their teaching styles. Other lecturers and departments have not succumbed to change. Adult students at Warwick, however, have only managed to change the institution's culture and practice by a small number of degrees. As a group they lack the power to challenge the core values, ideology and policy of the institution as a whole. Although critical of the organisational arrangements that makes studying problematic for those with domestic and employment responsibilities, adult students do endorse the academic culture. Learning is perceived as an enjoyable and motivating experience. Knowledge opens up new ways of viewing the world. In the process the self is redefined, adult students become changed persons. Learning empowers adult students. Studying also enables many mature women students to reflect upon their past lives and reinterpret how they perceive themselves as women.

Although beyond the scope of this study, another aspect of widening access for non-traditional students that has not been addressed by research is the question, 'access to what?' The focus of attention has been, and still is, on the access of adults into higher education. The empowerment of mature students may be short-lived if there are no opportunities for them to make progress in relation to employment or further study, resulting in women returning to domesticity, something which many wanted to escape. Is higher education in this situation merely reproducing and reinforcing existing gender, class and racial inequalities?

1 Gender Issues in Adult and Higher Education: Concepts, Perspectives and Research

Despite such empirical and theoretical advances, it is clear that we need to understand more fully the differential access to adult education according to sex and class and the ways in which adult education could respond to the interests of not just the working-class, but women. By doing so, we will understand better the role of adult education in society, and in particular, how it is related to the position of women (McLaren, 1985:22).

Background

An examination of women's lives, past and present, public and private, as an approach to understanding the experiences of mature women students in universities provides the central framework for this study. Micro and macro sociological theories are integrated to look at how past biographies and gender, class, age and race have impacted upon women's present social world of university life, family, and in some cases, employment. In doing this I am interested in how the women in this study perceive the student world and how they perceive themselves as students in a middle-class university like Warwick. The world of the university is explored through women's attitudes and relationships towards, for example, learning, assessment, lecturers, departments and other students. Are the student experiences of adult women distinct from those of adult male students and younger students? To what extent are their lives as mature students constructed by gender? This last question is explored further and problematised by enlarging the scope of this study to assess the impact and inter-relationship between gender and other factors such as class, age and race. As Seidler maintains: 'It means recognising that, for instance, men and women face different difficulties and situations in their lives, and that these are mediated by relations of class, race and ethnicity' (Seidler, 1994:91).

1

While recognising that structural forces such as gender, class and race have played a central role in shaping their lives and experiences in initial schooling, work and marriage, this study examines how, within these constraints, women were able to construct and change their lives in a positive way through learning at degree level. To what extent, therefore, does learning as a mature woman student result in fulfilment, self-realisation and a changed identity? The dialectic between structure and agency becomes a crucial dimension in analysing how women's lives are both shaped by structural forces and their own actions.

This study offers one paradigm for understanding the lives of mature women students in universities. There was not scope to document in depth other approaches, such as the influence of departmental and institutional cultures: parameters had to be set. Brief references, however, are made to lecturer and institutional perspectives as the actions of the mature women students cannot be divorced from these factors. For example, the women's participation and experiences at departmental level provide an insight into lecturers' attitudes and institutional cultures. This study draws on a comparative United Kingdom (UK)/ Belgian research project on the access of adults to universities.

Although this study centres on women, a small sample of men was included in the research to see how far issues and experiences were gendered ones. The inclusion of men necessitated a discussion of masculinity, albeit briefly. Such a dialogue helps to clarify our understanding of femininity. Maynard (1990) forcefully argues that: 'it is also the case that women and femininity cannot be understood without reference to men and masculinity also. In fact literature written about women which has the most analytical depth is precisely that which has also included an analysis of male privilege and power' (1990: 283).

In recent years the numbers of adult students in British universities has increased as access and educational opportunities have widened. Those aged 21 years and over consisted of approximately 33% of full-time first year undergraduate students in 1996 compared to approximately 24% in 1980. Mature students, however, are not a homogeneous group. Differences can be identified in terms of mode of study, age, gender, class and ethnicity. Being a young, unmarried mature student is qualitatively different from being an older, married mature student with family responsibilities. These differences are explored through focusing on participants' life histories by looking at their initial schooling, family, employment and university experiences. Reasons for returning to learn, admissions procedures, learning experiences as mature students, and attitudes towards assessment, lectures and seminars, are also considered. Being a mature student is an important aspect of women's lives but they also have other commitments. This study locates the experiences of being a mature student within the wider context of their lives by looking at the dynamics between women's public and private spheres.

This study is sociological. Theories of action and structure; feminism, Marxism and interactionism, are combined and modified in order to obtain a fuller understanding of the experiences of mature women students. In doing this I am drawing on adult education theory and sociological theory.

The bulk of this research draws upon interview and biographical materials. Three categories of mature students at the University of Warwick were studied; part-time, full-time and 2+2. Part-time degree courses at Warwick attract mostly adults who are in either full- or part-time employment as courses are available in the evening. Adults who opt for the traditional three year full-time undergraduate degree have either, for example, gained credits from an Access course or studied for A levels prior to entry. A 2+2 degree is aimed at non-traditional adult students who have been out of the education system for a long time. The first two years of the degree course, equivalent to year one of a traditional three year degree, are taught in local Further Education (FE) colleges. Adults can enter a 2+2 degree course without formal qualifications but they must show that they are capable of degree level study. 2+2 degrees are broader in terms of subjects than a single honours degree at Warwick.

The names of the thirty interviewees have been changed to ensure confidentiality. A summary profile of each participant is outlined in the appendix. References and quotes are also included in the text from questionnaire data taken from a wider sample of mature students at Warwick. The questionnaires were anonymous and in these cases participants are referred to by gender and degree course.

The Invisibility of Women in Adult and Higher Education

This first chapter explores current research and literature on mature women students within adult and continuing education. Higher education has been largely excluded from the research field of gender and education in Britain. At school level the picture is different; gender and education inequality is well documented, mostly by feminist educational researchers such as Spender, Weiner, Arnot, Deem and Sharpe, both empirically and theoretically. Gender inequality, however, does not stop at the end of schooling as higher education is not isolated from the rest of society. Higher education also plays a role in perpetuating and reproducing gender relations as all educational institutions are integral to the culture and structure of society. Parallels can be drawn here with race and higher education.

Gender and higher education in the UK is an under-researched area. Several factors may account for this. Some feminist educationalists, concerned with disadvantaged women, do not appear interested because the girls who make it to university are successful in educational terms and mostly middle-class. They will become the future elite (Wolpe, 1977, Bryne, 1978). Another factor could be the reluctance of academics to investigate their own institutions. Research in this field indicates that women who enter universities as either students, academics or researchers experience sexism and marginalisation (Coates, 1994).

Even though women now account for about fifty per-cent of the university student population in England and Wales, this gender balance is not reflected in the academic and administrative hierarchies within universities. Data collected by the Universities' Statistical Record (USR) paints a grim picture concerning the position of women academics, including research staff, in universities. Within the 'old' universities for 1993-94, 23% of all full-time staff were women. Only 5% of professors, 12% of senior lecturers or readers and 27% of lecturers were women. This virtually excludes women from the decision-making machinery in universities. Full-time female staff are more likely to be on the research side (53%) than males (32%). As Acker asserts, 'among academics in Britain, women are not only a minority but are found in less secure posts' (Acker, 1994:135).

Female academics, particularly those in male-dominated departments, experience isolation, marginalisation and exclusion from informal networks (Kanter, 1977, Fogarty et al., 1971):

> The barriers to equality encountered by women academics have their roots deep inside the structure of higher education, itself influenced by norms and values of the wider society (Acker, 1994:132).

While the staffing structure remains male-dominated and hierarchical with little sign of change in the near future, there are grounds for more optimism in relation to equal opportunities and the access of adult students. Widening access into higher education has encouraged women, both working and middle-class, to return to study. Reflecting upon this we may find in future that working-class people are more likely to gain entry to university as adults than 18 year olds, particularly as student loans may be an inhibiting factor for younger students. While grant loans are also detrimental to the recruitment of working-class adult students, studying and taking out a loan may still be more appealing than unemployment or returning to low paid unrewarding jobs after a period in the home childrearing. With increasing numbers of women entering universities, as younger and mature students, it is time to address the issues of gender relationships, experiences and inequality within higher education.

Clarifying Terms and Concepts

A wide range of terms and concepts is applied in discussions about the education of adults such as: adult education, lifelong learning, continuing education, recurrent education, non-traditional student. This is not an exhaustive list but it illustrates the complexity and, sometimes, confusion within the field of adult education. Writers frequently refer to these concepts without being precise about their meaning. There is an assumption that the reader has a shared understanding of the language and jargon used. Language, however, is cultural and concepts are not value-free. Concepts may be interpreted differently, depending upon the perspective of the writer or reader.

A difficulty arises, therefore, in defining concepts associated with adult and continuing education, such as lifelong learning, recurrent education, the learning society. Defining the concepts is problematical because the language has become part of a political discourse. Different groups and organisations, nationally and internationally, claim ideological ownership of a particular concept. In order to understand the concept the reader needs to have knowledge of the context in which it is being used and who is using it.

In broad terms, the concepts of lifelong learning and the learning society imply that learning occurs throughout life, replacing the notion of continuing education. Adults can return to learn in educational institutions at different periods in their lives. The dichotomy between initial and adult education is broken down as learning is viewed as a lifelong process. However, lifelong learning is generally discussed in terms of formal rather than informal learning. A closer examination reveals that these concepts are used in a political sense. They originate largely from policy makers in national governments and organisations such as the United Nations Educational, Scientific, and Cultural Organisation (UNESCO), the Council of Europe, the Organisation for Economic Co-operation and Development

(OECD) and more recently the European Commission (EC). While appearing liberal, and even radical, they are frequently linked to the economic and political values and needs of a market economy.

In Britain the concepts of lifelong learning and the learning society are used by the Government to promote a specific economic policy which was put into practice by the former Department of Employment. In common with other European countries, Britain's rapidly changing industry and technology requires different types of skills from its workforce and more frequent upskilling if the economy is to survive and advance. In political terms these concepts relate to the needs of the economy and industry through the provision of vocational education. Lifelong learning is viewed as a cure for economic problems (see the Green Paper, 1998). In educational terms, therefore, the policy translates into a narrow view of learning and education for adults. In 1994 the Economic and Social Research Council (ESRC) launched a research initiative entitled 'The Learning Society' which provided scope for adult education research. An examination of its aims and objectives reveals an interpretation of lifelong learning that favours vocational and accredited learning.

In this study these concepts are used in broader and more radical ways. First, it should be remembered that learning is not confined to formal educational institutions. Learning occurs informally throughout one's life in the home, workplace and in leisure. Educationalists and employers are now formally recognising this process through Accreditation of Prior Experiential Learning (APEL), although it is still largely restricted to learning in the workplace. This may exclude some women who acquire a range of skills and knowledge through motherhood and childrearing.

Lifelong learning in an ideal world should be recognised as an entitlement for all adults should they wish to return to learning at whatever level of study. Unfortunately economic, educational and political barriers make it difficult for certain social groups and classes to participate (McGivney, 1993). Education has the potential to empower adults (Freire, 1972), particularly those disadvantaged by the inequalities of initial education. Many of the 2+2 degree students in this study failed to achieve their potential in initial schooling because of educational, class, gender and race inequalities. Adult education offers such adults the opportunity to fulfil ambitions and realise their educational potential. Adult education, however, remains largely accessed by the middle-classes who may already have achieved high levels of education (Cross, 1981 and Woodley, Wagner et al., 1987).

This study focuses on mature students and, in particular, non-traditional adult women students. The research concentrates on adult students in universities and more specifically, on women taking degree courses. At university level the definition of a mature student is clear: 21 and over at undergraduate level and 25 and over at postgraduate level. Non-traditional students form one element among mature students. The term, 'non-traditional student' refers to adults who enter university without the traditional qualification of A levels but have alternative entry 'qualifications'. These may include Access course credits, one A level, vocational qualifications, APEL or, as in the case of Warwick's 2+2 degrees, evidence of recent study or the capacity to study for a degree. Many non-traditional students have been out of the formal education system for several years. I also use the term in a wider sense to include particular social groups such as: working class women, working-class and black people who are under-represented in higher education. Like Weil (1989) I have misgivings about the term 'non-traditional student'. While it is helpful in pointing out inequalities in relation to class, gender and race and the need to redress the balance there is the danger that non-traditional students become stereotyped or marginalised, particularly within 'old' universities. Labelling them as non-traditional implies that they are different to other students in a negative sense. By categorising them as a separate group, prejudices may arise on entry with admissions tutors acting as 'gatekeepers'. Although the discourse of non-traditional adult student has been criticised for its negativity (Williams, 1997) nothing has been forthcoming to replace the term.

The final concept pertinent to this research is access. Early debates about widening access for adults into higher education centred around student numbers and concern to fill courses. 'Current rhetoric about access to HE (higher education) is concerned with securing adult students for institutions rather than adapting institutions' (Percy, 1988: 119). Economic pragmatism, rather than a desire for social equity, resulted in the entry of adults to certain higher education institutions, largely the new universities. The rapid increase in student numbers of both young people and adults has led to the British higher education system as being described as a mass one. While this may be the case in terms of numbers it is not the case in terms of social class: the student population remains overwhelmingly the preserve of the middle classes. As Parry points out: 'the achievement of "mass" levels of participation in a system retaining and rewarding "elite" characteristics has been one of the distinctive features of the rapid expansion of British higher education in recent years' (1997: viii). Widening access should be about opening up and making higher education institutions more accessible to social groups who were previously largely excluded.

Working on a UK/Belgian comparative research project made me aware how frequently we take the meaning of concepts for granted not only within but across cultures. Discussions at research meetings soon made it apparent that we interpreted concepts such as adult, access and non-traditional students differently. Being clear about key concepts is, therefore, essential for research and understanding.

Adult Education Research: What Happened to Gender?

Adult education literature is diverse, reflecting the wide range of adult education traditions, practices and perspectives. This diversity can be confusing. Moving from a career in initial and community education to adult education I wanted to inform myself as quickly as possible about my new field of study but it was difficult knowing where to start. Initial reading raised a range of questions. Some of the literature was American, for instance, Cross (1981). Would this translate to a British context? Reading adult education literature begged a more fundamental question; what is adult education? It cannot be described as a discipline in its own right, as the study of adult education employs a plethora of, mostly, social science disciplines; sociology, education, psychology, social psychology, philosophy, history, politics, management studies and economics. While a multi-disciplinary approach is enriching and interesting it can also be frustrating and lacking in coherence. The employment of several disciplines may partly account for the paucity of theory within adult education while, according to Gooderham (1993), the high priority given to the practice of adult education also explains the absence of theory. The lack of an identifiable discipline raised the following question: am I a sociologist studying adult education or an adult educator drawing on sociology to make sense of how adults experience higher education?

Literature on women adult students in universities is sparse but expanding. British research on adult education, until recently, has been predominantly by male researchers. A growing and significant number of female writers are establishing themselves within the field such as Benn, McLaren, Thompson and Withnall. Discourse has until now, focused on a male view of the world. As a result empirical research largely discusses adult students as a homogeneous group or deals superficially with class, gender and race. Woodley, Wagner et al. (1987) disregarded ethnicity as a factor in their study as they did not want to risk antagonising respondents. This was an omission as one of the aims of the study was to look at the characteristics of mature students. By largely ignoring variables such as age, ethnicity or gender there is the danger of assuming that mature students in universities experience 'being a student' in similar ways. This could result in the stereotyping of mature students' behaviour. Others have made this observation:

> The large scale studies have not been especially concerned with gender experience of higher education and have not therefore been especially grounded in theories about women's education or about women's lives (Pascall and Cox, 1993: 19).

To draw on an analogy with Spender's (1982) research on gender in schools, women have been rendered invisible. McLaren forcefully states:

> Without an understanding of women's experiences and aspirations the field of adult education will continue to suffer from major misconceptions. A feminist perspective has a great deal to offer adult education (McLaren, 1985:18).

Does this paucity of gender research in adult education reflect the dominance of male academics in university Continuing Education Departments? Or is this an outdated image? (A survey would be required to clarify the picture.) While it is likely that the number of female academics in Adult and Continuing Education has increased over the past few years, Heads of Department are still more likely to be male. In some departments the Head of Department may play a strong role in encouraging or even influencing areas for research.

Signs of change are apparent but it is difficult to gauge whether this is superficial, or whether changes are being embedded within the culture and practices of Adult and Continuing Education Departments. The Universities' Association for Continuing Education (UACE) national conference on gender in 1994 marked a significant step forward. The conference attracted a large number of mostly female adult educators. It gave recognition to the importance of gender issues as a field of study and practice. At other conferences it is noticeable that seminars or workshops focusing on gender attract an overwhelmingly or sometimes all female audience. Even if men are largely absent this does indicate that the demand from women to discuss gender and adult education is high.

Searching For Gender: Adult Education Literature

Feminist adult educators in the UK, notably Edwards, Hughes, Kennedy, McLaren and Thompson, have responded to the invisibility and marginalisation of gender research through the development of empirical and theoretical work. This research is overwhelmingly confined to women participating in non-university adult education. Much of the research focuses on women returners, (Sheridan, 1992, Kennedy, 1987) women on Access courses (Hughes and Kennedy, 1985), women's studies courses (Thompson, 1983) and women's experiences of continuing education (Benn, Elliott and Whaley, 1998).

Such research literature is important in putting gender on the agenda of adult education and establishing a feminist research tradition. Research in this area is an acknowledgement of the existence of sexism and gender inequality within adult education as it stresses the particular issues and experiences faced by women adult students at cultural and structural levels. Discourse on gender, however, remains confined to a small circle of mostly female academics and does not appear to be penetrating literature produced by male academics. The paucity of research on women cuts across all academic disciplines. Mies emphasises there is a 'virtual exclusion of women, of their lives, work and struggles from the bulk of research' (1991: 65).

Empirical research on women in universities needs to be more widespread. Pioneers in this field are, for example, Acker, Edwards, McLaren, Pascall and Cox. Acker (1984) writing since the late 1970s, was one of the first to highlight gender differentiation within higher education and put the issues on the academic agenda. She has drawn attention to the sexism experienced by both female students and academics, culminating in an important study: *Is Higher Education Fair to Women?* (1984) edited, interestingly, with a male co-editor, Warren-Piper. More recently the issues have been reviewed in a study edited by Davies, Lubelska and Quinn (1994) and another edited by Morley and Walsh (1995) which looks specifically at feminist academics.

McLaren's study: *Ambitions and Realizations - Women in Adult Education* (1985), argues for a feminist analysis of women in adult education, including universities. She stresses that her 'interest in the subject of women in adult education stems from a belief that women's experiences need to be made visible and that the attempt of women to change their lives is an important issue that must be documented' (McLaren, 1985:14).

Over the past few years the widening of access has enabled adult students, many of whom are women, to enter university through a variety of routes such as Access courses and franchised or 2+2 degrees. There is a growing body of literature addressing the field of access and institutional change (Woodrow, 1988, Fulton, 1989, Woodley, Wagner et al., 1987, Parry and Wake, 1990, Williams et al., 1997). Much research on mature students discusses and measures their experiences in impersonal terms using statistical data. A more interesting approach is employed by a small but increasing number of researchers, such as Weil (1986), Pascall and Cox (1993) and Edwards (1993). In their writings mature students are presented as actors in a social context: experiences, attitudes and perceptions are central to understanding.

Surveying the Field: Studies on Women Adult Students in Higher Education

The pioneering and valuable study by McLaren (1985), *Ambitions and Realization* is included here although it does not look at mature women in universities. McLaren (1985) carried out a longitudinal study between 1974 and 1982 of the experiences of mature women students at a female residential adult education college and their futures after leaving the college. These were second-chance working-class students hoping to obtain a qualification which would enable them to enter higher education. Many were married, some with children, and all had made a critical decision to return to learn at a residential college to improve their chances on the job market and fulfil personal ambitions. For McLaren, (1985) the aim of her study was to look at how women struggled to achieve:

> My interest in the women...stemmed from my concern with the larger problem of how women struggle to make something of their lives...They (students) shared a strong belief that education was a viable route by which to reach their objectives... They hoped that a return to education would improve their status, income, conditions of employment, knowledge, autonomy and sense of well-being (McLaren, 1985: 149).

Her study is influenced by two theoretical perspectives; theories of social reproduction and Weber's idea of subjectivity. However, the two theoretical perspectives are dealt with superficially and remain largely unconnected to each other and to the findings of her research. Despite the lack of integration of theory with the research findings McLaren's study provides a comprehensive outline of mature women's experiences in an educational institution. Their past lives of family, schooling and work are related to their educational ambitions as adults, and more importantly, how studying impacted upon their domestic and family life. Her findings parallel in many ways the studies of mature women in universities (Pascall and Cox, 1993, Edwards, 1993).

In contrast Edwards' (1993) study focuses on a narrower aspect of mature women in higher education; the separateness and connectedness between education and the family. The key question for Edwards is: 'what is it about gaining a higher education that means it is viewed as so potentially disruptive to relationships between women and the men with whom they live?' (1993:1).

Her research sample consists of thirty-one women from different classes and ethnic backgrounds. All were at varying stages of studying for a social science degree in one of two universities and one polytechnic. The research was conducted during 1988-89 using in-depth interviews. From a feminist perspective Edwards (1993) explores the way in which the public and private lives of the women interacted and impinged upon each other. Her interest in this subject area stems from being a mature student when taking her first degree although her autobiographical experiences are not related to the lives of the women in her study.

Edwards uses the research data to:

> ...construct an overall typology and continuum of the ways in which education and family can coexist in women's lives. I then draw out the links and interactions between the women's place in the typology and positioning on the continuum, and their relationships with their partners (1993:128).

She identifies three main patterns of behaviour in relation to separating or connecting family and student life for her typology. Firstly, women who strove to connect and integrate family and education; secondly, those who wanted to separate the two and lastly, those in the middle who connected some aspects but not all. The first group saw themselves as one person, acting and feeling the same at home as at university. In practice they wanted their family to visit the university, to see other student friends socially, feed their work and family experiences into their studies and discuss and share their studies with partners. The women in this category were more likely to experience conflict with their partners. The women's gain of knowledge and power was perceived as threatening by partners.

Those who separated home and university acted out different roles in the two institutions. Family life was left unaffected by their academic commitments. These women lived two separate lives. The third, ideal type, fell between the first two as there were some separations and some connections. With this group:

> There were no particular patterns to these women's separations or connections except in one aspect. Crucially, the women who mixed connections and separations shared with those who separated education and family a sense of having two different parts to their lives (Edwards, 1993:131).

Sixteen of the women were placed at the connecting end of the typology, six at the separating end and nine in the middle. Several of the women in my study spoke about increasing conflict with partners since beginning their studies and this is becoming a growing problem for 2+2 students at Warwick. It would, however, be wrong to claim that conflict does not occur between male mature students and their partners, as my research did find evidence of this.

Pascall and Cox's (1993) study offers a comprehensive and significant account of mature women students in higher education. However, the women were studying for their degree during the late 1970s and early 1980s so in this respect the sample is not a recent one. Their sample is not non-traditional as most of the women had attended grammar school and left with qualifications, some with A levels. Since the early eighties policy changes encouraging access has resulted in new types of degree study and new modes of entry enabling higher numbers of non-traditional students to enter higher education. Despite this, their study is an important contribution to the field on several counts. Firstly, the text is co-authored by a male academic, Cox. It is rare and refreshing to find a male academic who places gender at the centre of his research. Many feminists, however, would not enthusiastically embrace the notion of men working in this field. For them this research domain belongs to women as only women can grasp the meaning of women's experiences and 'weltanschauung'. Men, because they have not experienced gender inequality can only achieve a partial insight into the reality of women's lives.

Secondly, by using a longitudinal approach Pascall and Cox (1993) are able to consider whether or not obtaining a degree has fulfilled the women's aspirations in career terms and other aspects of their lives. Lastly, the research contributes to the growing debate on the widening of access by focusing on a small but growing sector within universities; mature women students. Employing qualitative methods, Pascall and Cox (1993) interviewed a sample of forty-three women studying in two higher education institutions in the East Midlands. A biographical approach was used. Most were taking social sciences or arts degrees. Tracing about half of their original sample the women were re-interviewed about ten years later in 1991 to discover what impact returning to education had had on their lives.

In attempting to explain why the women had returned to education as adults Pascall and Cox (1993) consider a spectrum of factors; experiences in initial schooling, domesticity and employment within a framework of gender and class relationships. The women had high expectations of education: they wanted education to move them out of domesticity and unfulfilling paid work. Interviews ten years later centred on whether or not education had changed their lives and fulfilled ambitions and career goals. Education is discussed in terms of outcome. While the study provides an interesting and useful account of women's biographies describing their reasons for returning to education there is little insight about the experiences and processes of change during their years of study at university. Pascall and Cox (1993) are interested in looking at how the self is changed yet it is the processes of learning and being a student in a higher education institution which impact upon the self. It is difficult to assess how the self has changed and developed if the university years are not fully taken into account.

Pascall and Cox (1993) draw on the theories of Boudon (1973), Hopper and Osborn (1975), Bernstein (1973) and Abrams (1982) in respect to why the women returned to education, their experiences in initial schooling and in paid and unpaid work. Theories of gender reproduction are largely dismissed. Comparison of the women's accounts of their lives with theories of reproduction highlighted a rift between the two, according to Pascall and Cox (1993). For them, reproduction theories are too deterministic and pessimistic in assuming that women have little control over their lives, forcing them into a life of domesticity and low-paid work. The women in their study, they argued, were more positive about their lives:

> They reviewed life histories in which domesticity and poor opportunities in paid work had knotted them together to tie them down, they saw education as the way to untie the knot (Pascall and Cox, 1993:5).

Pascall and Cox (1993) argue that their research highlights a contradiction between theory and practice. For them education is not an oppressor of women, rather it offers the opportunity for women to change their lives. The theories they discuss relate to initial schooling. The contextual and cultural situation is different from that of adult education. For example, attitudes towards education will differ; adults choose to learn while many working-class pupils dislike school because it is compulsory (Corrigan, 1979). Willis (1977) and McRobbie (1978) maintain, however, that working-class pupils do not passively accept the forces of education but engage in behaviour of resistance.

Pascall and Cox's (1993) study is an optimistic one. Education is held in high esteem as a means of potentially changing women's lives and undermining gender oppression they experience in society:

> The extension of education for women and by women is a concession with real potential for destabilizing traditional notions of femininity and the dependence they sustain (Pascall and Cox, 1993:143).

A more pessimistic view of women in university adult education, degree and non-degree courses, is expressed by Usher (1982). She accepts the argument that:

> University adult education does play a vital part in sustaining the dominant culture, ideology and social relationships of production in capitalist Britain and in so doing contributes to the sexual division of labour and opportunity which undermine the pursuit of genuine equality for women (Usher, 1982:4).

According to Thompson (1982) women participate highly in non-degree university adult education but find it difficult to gain entry to other university departments and degree courses. Adult Education Departments have a low status within the university hierarchy and their courses and students are viewed as non-academic and, therefore, not suitable to be allowed entry to the high status knowledge delivered by other departments. For Usher (1982) participating in university adult education is not enough to emancipate women from traditional gender roles. Liberation through education lies in the content of the curriculum and in particular a curriculum which challenges the sexist and elite knowledge of existing university courses. Such a curriculum would enable women to value the contribution of women's experiences:

> There is a real job of learning to be done here because it means that women cannot accept meanings and values which all men and women have inherited. It means that they must work out their own values which

may well be different from the values of men. This is clearly a political process because if it is recognised that the balance of power between the sexes lies with men, and if education is to be associated with increasing genuine equality between the sexes, then education must involve itself in a process through which women can construct their own knowledge and evaluate their own achievements (Usher, 1982:11).

Sperling's (1991) study looks at the issues of gender inequality in relation to mature students' access to higher education. McGivney's (1992) comprehensive text refers to non-university adult education. Sperling (1991) maintains that women, compared to men, are at a disadvantage in gaining entry to higher education because of structural and attitudinal barriers. Admissions tutors act as gatekeepers. Prejudiced attitudes mean that women are viewed as being less reliable than male adult students because of domestic commitments. Cultural ethos and attitudes, therefore, vary from institution to institution and from department to department.

Universities, according to Sperling (1991), are geared to meet the needs of eighteen year olds, not non-traditional students. To provide women with a more equal chance of entry and success at degree level in higher education, institutions need to adjust their practices:

> Not only is it necessary to provide adequate and affordable child care, suitable timetables, student-friendly teaching and assessment methods and educational guidance and counselling, it is necessary to change the content of higher education to include the experiences of women as relevant bases of knowledge (Sperling, 1991:212).

Such issues have implications for institutional change which is not always easy to achieve, particularly in 'old' universities. Sperling, while raising the question of whether or not 'male decision-makers would be willing to make changes' (1991:212), fails to address how this objective could be achieved.

Although Weil (1986, 1989) does not confine her research to women her studies offer a welcome departure from most adult education research. Her research documents the learning experiences in forming the 'learner identity' of non-traditional adult students, women, working-class and black people, from the perspectives of the students. Weil stresses that:

> There is the disjunction between non-traditional learners' expectations and their actual experiences of higher education. There are also disjunctions between the different values and beliefs adult learners and lecturers bring

to their interpretations of what it means to generate and validate knowledge and to inhibit and facilitate learning (Weil, 1986:232).

Weil (1986) concludes that class, gender and ethnicity shape the experiences and perspectives which non-traditional students bring with them to higher education, but that these are not accommodated within the institution.

Other, smaller scale research has been undertaken, notably by Arksey, Marchant and Simmill (1994) and Sanderson and French (1993). Another recent study examines mature women studying by distance learning with the Open University (Lunnebourg, 1994) while Benn et al. (1998) look at the experiences of women in a wide range of continuing education. Research is growing but still not extensive. In particular there is an absence of research which looks at women studying different modes of degree courses such as 2+2 degrees, part-time and full-time degrees. Do particular groups of women study a particular mode of degree? Does the mode of degree impact upon their experiences as a student? To what extent are these experiences individual or collective ones? How do women define their situation as mature students? How do their experiences compare to those of mature male students? To what extent are they similar or different? In theoretical terms is it possible to combine macro and micro sociological approaches to understanding mature student experiences within a higher education institution?

Sociological perspectives have been applied to the study of adult education by, for example, Jarvis (1985) and Jones (1984). The following section examines the contribution of work in this field and discusses how it could be applied to understanding the experiences of mature women students.

The Sociology of Adult Education: A Useful Starting Point?

Connelly (1992), in an article which critically overviews the sociology of adult education, asks the question 'why there is not a sociology of adult education with a similar range and depth of theory as its initial education counterpart?' (1992:251). He concludes:

> that an independent sociology of adult education does not exist. That sociology which does exist is primarily derived from theories of initial education. Where it can be argued that a non-derivative sociological study of adult education has been attempted it is only at an embryonic stage (Connelly, 1992:252).

Connelly (1992) was not the first to argue this point. Jarvis emphatically stated that: 'despite its long history, no sociology of the education of adults exists in the same manner as there are sociological studies of initial education' (1985:3).

Both Jarvis (1985) and Jones (1984) argue that a sociology of adult education is limited because of the diverse range of practices within the field. Jarvis (1985) extends his argument by pointing out that another problem is the absence of a clear definition of adult education. Gooderham continues in a similar vein:

> As a result, adult participation research has largely been atheoretical, descriptive rather than explanatory and, above all, almost exclusively concerned with the psychology of participation (1993:28).

The explanation for Gooderham (1993) lies in the fact that adult education is a 'normative discipline'. Adult education practice, he maintains, is viewed as the overriding concern of adult educators, including some in universities.

Jarvis's text, *The Sociology of Adult and Continuing Education* (1985), represents one of the early attempts to introduce a theoretical approach through a sociology of adult education. His book covers a wide range of adult education issues, drawing on sociological theory from sociology in general and the sociology of initial education. Jarvis argues for the need for a sociology of adult education but his critics maintain that he fails to develop one (Keddie, 1986, Connelly, 1992) as his study reads more like a comprehensive student textbook. Jarvis outlines the different perspectives and philosophies within adult education and refers to the debate concerning the two sociologies (macro and micro), highlighted by Dawe (1970). A distinction is made between two sociologies and two types of education, the classical and romantic curriculum:

> The two sociologies are, thus, correlated to the two educations, each having similar sets of presuppositions about man in society. Each sees man as either the product of society or society as the product of man (Jarvis, 1985:50).

The romantic curriculum is equated with the liberal tradition in adult education and the action approach in sociology. Jarvis's macro/micro typology, therefore, places Marxism with functionalism despite the ideological differences between the two perspectives. Keddie (1986) is critical of Jarvis's typology and claims that his work is grounded in functionalism rather than a humanist approach. There is no attempt to introduce a sociology of adult education which looks at the issues from the perspectives of the actors. Above all Keddie (1986) is critical of Jarvis's assertion that his book provides a sociology of adult education. Another study of the same era by Elsey (1986) also offers an extensive review of sociological theory and its relationship to education and adult education. Unlike Jarvis (1985), Elsey (1986) applies social action theory to an understanding of how adults become students and their subsequent experiences as students.

Jones (1984), in contrast, offers a radical approach to the sociology of adult education by linking Marxism and phenomenology. For Jones (1984) the education system is socially constructed and related to political ideology:

> Knowledge has too easily in the past been aligned with systems of control and authority in society rather than seeing it as socially constructed and arising out of the process of social interaction. Knowledge is socially defined and embodied in individuals and institutions (Jones, 1984:105).

He draws on the works of Bourdieu, Althusser, Gramsci, Bowles and Gintis, Braverman and Bernstein in asserting that education reinforces phenomenology to look at how knowledge is constructed and used as a mechanism for selection and control:

> Educational systems not only reflect ideologies but in turn help to create ideologies. The self-perpetuation of both is broken only by the advent of innovation which itself is not arbitrary but a reflection of sociological conditions (Jones, 1984:94).

Connelly (1992) criticises Jones for omitting reference to the theory of Freire:

> While Jones usefully refers to the important sociological perspectives of Marxism and phenomenology he is not successful (indeed does not even try) in integrating the two to demonstrate how they can be seen to comprise the theory of the new sociology (Connelly, 1992:237,238).

Youngman in *Adult Education and Socialist Pedagogy* (1986) is clear about his theoretical position: 'there has been very little writing in English on the theory and practice of adult education from a Marxist perspective' (Youngman, 1986:9). He views adult education as firmly part of the education system: initial and adult education are integrated and interrelated:

> To see the unity of adult education and to locate it within a national system is to understand why adult education must be regarded sociologically and politically as part of the single social institution that is education. Consideration of adult education has to take into account that it is part of the organisational processes in society which systematically shape consciousness, develop knowledge, impart skills and form cultures (Youngman, 1986:2).

The integration of initial and adult education contrasts with the perspectives of other adult educators who stress a clear distinction between the two. However, my experiences of working in both sectors support the view of an overlap between initial and adult education, for example, in the way that children and adults learn.

In orthodox Marxist style Youngman (1986) maintains that:

> Education under capitalism plays a key role in reproducing this separation, so that the working-class is denied knowledge and skills it requires to take control of production (Youngman, 1986:200).

Youngman (1986) attempts to develop a socialist education theory and practice from Marxist theory. He is critical of Marxist educationalists like Bowles and Gintis (1976) for being too deterministic in their interpretation of Marxism. Using the work of Giroux (1983) on resistance in education, he interrelates the economic and political infrastructure to culture and ideology.

Thompson (1980) has played an important role in advocating, developing and now reasserting a radical sociological and theoretical approach to adult education. Westwood (1980) also presents a Marxist analysis of adult education by stressing the importance of both the reproduction of production and ideology in education, again drawing on the theories of Bourdieu, Bowles and Gintis and Althusser. She points out the dominance of the middle-classes in adult education. More recently Allman and Wallis (1995) make a plea for the development of 'a dialectical theory of consciousness and a critical concpt of ideology' (1995: 31), in order to challenge 'the postmodern condition'.

Gooderham's (1993) work on developing a sociology of adult education is different as it concentrates on one specific aspect of adult education, participation of adults, to draw up a conceptual framework of perspectives on participation in higher education.

From this brief review of the field of research it is clear that the sociology of adult education remains at an embryonic stage. The groundwork has been carried out but a distinct conceptual and theoretical framework has yet to be developed, although Youngman's (1986) work attempts this. The sociology of initial education, Marxism, feminism and interpretive sociology are valuable starting points.

2   Drawing on Theory: Combining Action, Structure and Feminism

> The conflict between objective and subjective approach is not to be construed as radical or totally irreconcilable dichotomy but rather as suggesting a need to integrate two focuses of analysis ... both the objective and subjective focuses ought to be indispensable components of a holistic and dialectic approach because they refer to two facets of organisation and functioning of symbolic systems (Rossi, 1983:7).

Introduction

This chapter examines and draws on various strands of sociological theory; feminist sociology, action and structural theories. No one theoretical perspective is adequate for gaining an understanding of the experiences of adult students in universities as such an approach would be one-dimensional. Mature women students' experiences of and interactions within the university, family and work are complex and sometimes contradictory. A multi-theoretical approach combining micro and macro or action and structure sociologies provides a fuller and more realistic picture of the complexities of social life. The task, however, is not an easy one. Historically, sociology has consisted of competing perspectives, ideologies and methodologies, often conflicting, and with little dialogue between the varying 'sides'. After all, one essence of sociology is that there is no one world view but multiple realities:

> The initial impression one has in reading through the literature in and about the social disciplines during the past decade or so is that of sheer chaos. Everything appears to be 'up for grabs'. There is little or no consensus except by members of the same school or subschool - about what are the well-established results, the proper research procedures, the important problems, or even the most promising theoretical approaches to the study of society and politics. There are claims and counterclaims, a virtual babble of voices demanding our attention (Bernstein, 1979:X11).

Sociology, despite its internal conflicts, remains a valuable tool for making sense of the social world. The value of sociology and particular theoretical approaches for understanding the experiences of mature women students in universities are reflected upon in the following sections.

Discovering Sociology

When I decided to study sociology at A level in 1971 it was a relatively new subject. Few schools included it within its curriculum. People studying sociology at that time were subject to comments such as: 'it's not a real subject,' 'it's easy', 'it's just common-sense'. Sociology appealed to me because it appeared, unlike other subjects, to be relevant and not abstract and alienated from my own life and everyday experiences. It was a subject which I could relate to because it connects with life in a very real way. Sociology made my life experiences understandable. Sociological reflection helped me as a working-class woman to stand back, reflect and become more aware about myself and society.

Studying sociology soon imbued me with a 'sociological perspective'. I became conscious that I was looking at social situations in a different and often critical light. As Berger so aptly stated in his study, *Invitation to Sociology*: 'The fascination of sociology lies in the fact that its perspective makes us see in a new light the very world in which we have lived all our lives' (Berger, 1963:33). As someone starting sociology another memorable and fascinating comment by Berger (1963) became imprinted upon my mind:

> It can be said that the first wisdom of sociology is this - things are not what they seem. This too is a deceptively simple statement. It ceases to be simple after a while. Social reality turns out to have many layers of meaning. The discovery of each new layer changes the perception of the whole (Berger, 1963:34).

Studying sociology helped me to conceptualise and demystify my life experiences in a meaningful way. Individual experiences of class and gender inequality were transformed into a social and group context. Micro and macro experiences became interrelated. At undergraduate level I became interested in three sociological perspectives; Marxism, feminism and symbolic interactionism, in particular the works of Goffman and Becker. I did not accept the deterministic interpretation of Marxism as I believe that

Marxism combines, in a dialectical way, action and structure theory. Goffman focuses on individual action within an institution but he does not ignore the institutional or macro context. The actors are situationalised within a social context. What Goffman and Becker fail to do, however, is to take adequate account of power relationships within society. Integrating Marxism, feminism and symbolic interactionism enables the dynamic relationship between micro and macro behaviour to be studied within a critical framework. The researcher can probe deeper with enquiry. A range of questions can be asked. What experiences and perceptions did the mature women students bring with them to Warwick? How were these shaped by past life experiences? To what extent are their experiences gender or class based? How do they perceive their experiences at Warwick? How has the self changed? To what extent has the institution shaped their behaviour and attitudes? How have adult students impacted upon the institution's culture? Do their private and public lives interrelate or conflict? What are their hopes and aspirations for the future? What can these three sociological perspectives contribute to the field of adult education?

The Two Sociologies

Macro or structural theory, and in particular the work of Marxists and Marxist feminists, provides a framework for analysing the impact of gender and class upon the lives of women in this study. To what extent does education as an adult offer a means of emancipation from gender and class oppression? Micro or action theory, such as the work of Goffman and Becker, are valuable in looking at how the women's identities changed as a result of being socialised into a student career and academic culture.

Combining macro and micro theories is not an easy exercise. The two paradigms explain behaviour in opposing ways. Early debates in the late 1960s and 1970s assumed the two approaches, structural and action theories, to be irreconcilable:

> Originally the dispute concerned ontological epiphenomenalism (the assertion of the primacy of either structure or agency as the ultimate constituents of a society) and methodological reductionism as the means of explanations in terms of whichever of the two was held to be primary (Archer, 1998:74).

For macro theorists structural forces are the key to understanding behaviour. Individuals/groups' behaviour is shaped by the culture and structure of institutions and society. Actors internalise their expected roles through socialisation. Human beings create institutions which then assume an objective force over and above them. As Berger and Luckmann emphasise 'the institutional world is objectivated human activity' (1966:78). Critics argue that structural theory is too deterministic: humans are portrayed as having no free will; their destiny is mapped out for them by social, economic and political forces. Individuality is denied as the actors' definition of the situation is defined by the central value system. Consciousness and action are, therefore, derived from structures.

Action theory emerged partly as a response to dissatisfaction with positivist functionalism. The starting point in explaining behaviour is diametrically opposed to that of structural theorists. In action theory the individual plays a central role in shaping her/his behaviour and consciousness. People socially construct their own reality which implies that they have a free will. Subjectivity is central to understanding social reality if actors define their own situation. Institutions, structure and ideology are created and changed by human action. The two perspectives, therefore, tackle the question of control from different and opposing angles. Structural theory maintains that institutions control human behaviour. In contrast action theory argues that actors make and shape institutions by defining their own situation. The individual social actor and the social interaction with others becomes the focus of analysis while the institutional structures and central value system are at the heart of the structuralist approach.

Moving Forward: Unifying Macro and Micro Sociology

Most sociologists are locked into either a structuralist or social action paradigm. This dualism is also reflected in methodological approaches. A minority are making attempts to unify the two theoretical paradigms. This, I would argue, is beneficial as people do not live their daily lives in either a macro or micro world; the two are intertwined. The women in this study were consciously trying to change their lives by becoming more educated despite being constrained by family lives. The concepts are tools constructed by sociologists to help them analyse the social world but in doing so they have artificially dichotomised human behaviour.

Marx's writings combine macro and micro approaches. Critics of Marx argue that his writings are too deterministic as people are portrayed as puppets responding to the social, economic and political forces which bear down upon their lives. Giddens (1971) argues that this interpretation is misguided as Marx stressed that consciousness is rooted in human praxis. Others, Schaff (1970), Lewis (1972), responded to this criticism by highlighting the humanism of Marx's early writings. Marx's thesis on historical materialism developed in the *German Ideology* (1846), centres on the dialectical and dynamic relationship between the subjective individual and the objective social world. People actively create the society in which they live but at the same time the social world shapes the individual. The dynamic interaction between action and structure is apparent in the lives of the mature women students in this study. The women left Warwick changed persons. Their attitudes and behaviour were shaped by individual action in choosing to learn and also by the influence of the academic institution. As Marx states: 'while society is produced by men, society itself produced man as man' (Marx, 1844:157). By acting upon the social world humans change it.

Berger and Luckmann's, *The Social Construction of Reality* (1966), was one of the first attempts to synthesise systems and action theories. Using a 'humanistic' phenomenological approach they looked at how knowledge in society is constructed as a dialectical process between objective and subjective reality:

> It is important to emphasize that the relationship between man, the producer and the social world, his product, is and remains a dialectical one. That is, man (not, of course, in isolation but in his collectivities) and his social world interact with each other. The product acts back upon the producer. Externalization and objectivation are moments in a continuing dialectical process (Berger and Luckman, 1966:78).

Three concepts are central to the understanding of this process; externalisation, objectivation and internalisation. Berger and Luckmann (1966) succinctly summarise their analysis in three key points: 'society is a human product. Society is an objective reality. Man is a social product' (Berger and Luckman, 1966:79). Dawe's *The Two Sociologies* (1970) epitomised and publicised the debate:

> There are, then, two sociologies: a sociology of social system and a sociology of social action. They are grounded in the diametrically opposed concerns with two central problems, those of order and control. And, at every level, they are in conflict. They posit antithetical views of human nature, of society and of the relationship between the social and the individual (Dawe, 1970:551).

Nearly twenty years later Alexander (1987) argued that: 'the perennial conflict between individualistic and collectivist theories has been re-worked as a conflict between micro-sociology and macro-sociology (1987: 289). The problem of structure and agency has been central to many key writers such as Boudon, Bourdieu, Giddens, Habermas and Touraine.

Giddens (1976) attempted to unify the two strands within sociology using the concepts 'duality of structure' or structuration. He points out that 'structures are created, transformed and reproduced by human action but the relationship is two-way as structures also impose constraints upon actors' (Giddens, 1976:138). Giddens believes that it is not possible to study society by focusing only on one approach. Only a few empirical studies have synthesised systems and action approaches within their research and theory. Paul Willis's (1977) text, *Learning to Labour* is frequently cited as a study which incorporates what Giddens calls the structuration approach.

Layder explains:

> The notion of a duality here refers to two continuously interrelated aspects of social life. First, it indicates that society exists simultaneously both inside and outside individuals in the sense that while individuals deeply internalize the social world in order to become social beings, society is, of necessity, a system of reproduced social relationships which stretches beyond the power and influence of specific individuals and groups and so on (Layder, 1998: 88).

Cicourel (1981) makes an obvious but important point that the distinctions between micro and macro sociologies are a construction of the researcher. Actors unconsciously integrate micro and macro activities in their everyday encounters and interaction:

> Micro and macro levels of analysis are integrated in everyday settings as a routine feature of all cultural or social organization. The members of a group or society have created their own theories and methodologies for achieving this integration (Cicourel, 1982:65).

Sociology remains largely compartmentalised at the levels of theory, methodology and the categorisation of research topics. However, macro and micro activities cannot be isolated from each other; they are interdependent. To utilise only one approach does not give a full representation of social reality. The actor's definition of their situation has to be located within an institutional and national context. Individuals act out their lives in macro and micro worlds. Their thoughts at the micro level, in this study, about their degree subject, teaching and learning approaches, or the department may well be shaped by departmental and institutional policies. In turn, the voiced opinions of mature students about their teaching and learning experiences may influence and generate new policies by the institution, such as more flexible approaches to learning. Gender and class, as this study shows, are macro factors which impact upon the consciousness and actions of mature students at macro and micro levels. Integrating macro and micro approaches enables the sociologist to put all the jigsaw pieces together.

Interpretive Perspectives: Drawing on Microsociology

Interpretive sociology contains several strands. One element is shared in common; the subjectivity of individuals in constructing and defining their social world in a meaningful way. Human beings are active and doing, not passive and responsive. To use Cicourel's (1972) phrase humans are not 'cultural dopes'. In this respect the interpretive paradigm breaks away from the traditional social sciences. My aim is to draw on the perspectives of symbolic interactionism and adapt them to the context of this study by linking interpretive perspectives to feminist sociology and structural theories of reproduction.

Symbolic interactionism developed from the individualistic approach to understanding behaviour within American sociology at the beginning of the twentieth century. The key founders of symbolic interactionism are Mead, Thomas, Cooley and Dewey; more recently Goffman and Becker have been influential in the study of deviant behaviour and education.

Central to symbolic interactionism is the belief that: 'human beings are capable of making their own thoughts and activities objects of analysis, that is, they can routinely, and even habitually, manipulate symbols and orient their own actions towards other objects' (Denzin, 1974:153). Consciousness, not social forces determines action. Social structure becomes secondary to human agency. The self develops through interaction with others; it is a social construction. Language, learnt within a social context, gives meaning to a symbolic world. Blumer (1956) reminds us:

> We can and I think must, look upon human life as chiefly a vast interpretive process in which people singly and collectively, guide themselves by defining objects, events and situations which they encounter (Blumer, 1956:686).

A person's identity is created through the response of others to our actions. In any social situation we present our self to others, define the situation in terms of expected norms and rules, and adopt a role which we perceive is expected of us. This research looks at how adult students had to present the self in a new social situation and quickly learn how to act out the student role:

> Fundamentally, group action takes the form of a fitting together of individual lines of action. Each individual aligns his action to the actions of others by ascertaining what they are doing or what they intend to do, that is, by getting the meaning of their acts... In taking such roles the individual seeks to ascertain the intention or direction of the acts of others. He forms and aligns his own action on the basis of such interpretation of the act of others (Blumer, 1964:184).

This is referred to by Cooley (1922) as 'the looking glass self' which consists of three stages; presentation, identification and subjective interpretation. Goffman's work also employs the definition of the situation as a key concept but he differs slightly in his interpretation to other symbolic interactionists:

> Presumably, a 'definition of the situation' is almost always to be found, but those who are in the situation ordinarily do not create this definition, even though their society often can be said to do so; ordinarily, all they do is to assess correctly what the situation ought to be for them and then act accordingly (Goffman, 1974:1-2).

Goffman's approach uses dramaturgy to describe and understand the behaviour of the self. Interaction, or encounter, is defined by Goffman as being: 'The reciprocal influence of individuals upon one another's actions when in one another's immediate physical presence' (Goffman, 1959:26).

In face-to-face interactions the individual puts on a 'front' in her/his performance to others. Goffman makes an analogy with actors on a stage: individuals stage a performance to produce and manage their interactions to gain respect from others within a social context. For the women in this study seminars were arenas where they acted out the student role in public to younger students and lecturers.

Common perspectives and shared understandings are produced through interaction. This approach is useful in looking at how mature women students define their situation in taking on the role of student. To what extent do they perceive and present themselves as students, particularly part-time students? How do they think they are perceived by younger students and lecturers? Shared experiences and understanding created the formation of subcultures among adult students at Warwick. The concept of career, as used by Becker (1961, 1963) in his study of deviants and medical students, and Goffman (1961) in his study of mental patients, is also applicable to studying the student career of non-traditional adult students. Goffman defines career as: 'any social strand of any person's course through life... The concept of career, then, allows one to move back and forth between the personal and the public' (Goffman, 1961:119).

The self is an object defined by the self and others but through interaction it has the potential to change. The self is defined and redefined. This is an important point in relation to the lives of mature women students. Has the self-identity of the mature students changed as a result of being a student? Has the change of self amongst women students produced a greater gender awareness? People act out different roles in different situations. To what extent does the role of student encroach on their private lives in the family? Does it conflict or complement?

Symbolic interactionism and other social action perspectives have developed a distinct methodological approach. Researchers view the world from the point of view of those they are studying to 'tell it like it is'. As a result, symbolic interactionists, such as Becker and Goffman, appear to be 'sticking up' for the underdog by illustrating individual resistance to the power of institutions. Again this has implications for non-traditional adult students. How far, for example, do women students try to resist the regulations, such as seminar times, imposed upon them by an institution which they may regard as inflexible in relation to their domestic commitments? The women's lives as students are characterised by struggles both at university and, for some, with partners at home. Lecturers teaching adults need to be aware of the complexities and struggles of the women's daily lives.

Symbolic interactionism has been heavily criticised, particularly during the 1970s, for ignoring concepts of power, institutions and structure (Gouldner, 1971, Birkett, 1991). Interactionists, however, do not totally ignore issues of power and structure but they do not take the issues far enough. For example, Becker (1963), Cicourel (1976) and Goffman (1961) implicitly and explicitly raise issues of power inequality without asking how and why power and social inequalities exist, or how they are reproduced. Their approach is liberal rather than critical and radical. The women in this research lacked power in their lives, particularly in the family. Studying for a degree was an attempt by the women to change their lives and hence challenge the power inequalities they experienced.

Musolf (1992) reviewed symbolic interactionist literature to assess the claims made by critics. He maintains that since 1975 symbolic interactionism, 'has focused on both constraint and human agency' (Musolf, 1992:171). Concepts of power, structure, institutions and ideology are considered. The reconstruction of symbolic interactionism, Musolf (1992) argues, has brought it closer to the perspective of the British School of Cultural Studies (BSCS). According to Musolf (1992), interactionists locate power in the process of everyday interaction and communication thus making a link with macro sociology. Rogers, in discussing Goffman's work, confirms that a 'careful study of his work reveals insights into power, hierarchy and status' (Rogers, 1980:101). A central concern of symbolic interactionism is how actors in organisations manage to subvert power, manifested by rules and roles, through negotiation. Thomas (1984) maintains that negotiation equips actors at the bottom of the hierarchy with, 'mechanisms for altering the asymmetrical hierarchical power relations' (1984:217). The women in this study used negotiation to change certain departmental rules to their advantage.

Goffman's work takes into account the structural elements of organisational life. In *Asylums* Goffman (1961) is concerned with how mental patients secure a 'space' for the self within a constraining institution. Ignatieff (1983) succinctly summarises Goffman's (1961) description as, 'how these selves manage to find an asylum from the asylum' (Ignatieff, 1983:95). Although the contexts are different the approach is useful for looking at how women adult students establish themselves, make sense of, and adjust to life in an elite university. Of key concern is the dialectical relationship between micro and macro behaviour. To what extent does the university as an institution change the values, attitudes and behaviour of mature women students? How do they, as individuals and as a group, adjust to the educational environment? Becker's (1964) concept of 'situational adjustment' offers a useful approach as he applies it to adult socialisation. Adults move in and out of new social situations, each situation requiring a different role and adjustment. This in turn affects personal development.

Gender, a key element of this study, is to be found within interactionist discourse (Goffman, 1979). Symbolic interactionism, however, is inadequate on its own for an explanation of class, gender and race issues. For this purpose theories of reproduction and feminist theory need to be referred to. Interactionism, however, is not completely redundant in this field. By concentrating on human consciousness and subjective experience, interactionism is helpful in understanding how participants perceive their class, gender and ethnic positions and experiences. What interactionism fails to do is endorse a theory of social change. Goffman (1974) makes clear that his work does not allude to Marxism and issues of social change:

> The analysis developed does not catch at the difference between the advantaged and disadvantaged classes and can be said to direct attention away from such matters. I think that is true. I can only suggest that he who would combat false consciousness and awaken people to their true interests has much to do, because the sleep is very deep. And I do not intend to provide a lullaby, but merely to sneak in and watch the way people snore (Goffman, 1974:14).

Musolf (1992) emphasises that symbolic interactionism has moved a long way since the 1970s, developing its paradigm to accommodate and recognise the macro influences on human behaviour:

> Clearly symbolic interactionism is attempting to explore the dialectical features of constraint and human agency in social life. As it attends power, structure, institutions, and ideology it furthers a more comprehensive and critical view of social life (Musolf, 1992:185).

Interpretive perspectives such as symbolic interactionism are, therefore, valuable in looking at the processes of how students, individually and collectively, creatively act to shape and change their world.

Feminism and Sociology: Redefining Sociology

Since the 1970s feminist sociologists have been voicing their criticisms of sociology for its male perspectives and views of the world. As Jessie Bernard expressed: 'practically all sociology to date has been a sociology of the male world' (1973:774). Ribbens and Edwards (1998) 'became conscious of how far social theories, concepts and models had been overwhelmingly developed around male activities in the public sphere'. The invisibility of women within sociology, both as producers and subjects of knowledge, is perceived as a structural problem (Oakley, 1974, Roberts, 1981, Reinharz, 1992). Sociology's subject matter is about the understanding of interaction between individuals and groups in society so why has the discipline largely failed to include women among its studies? A similar history exists within adult education (Thompson, 1980).

Feminist sociologists are implicitly raising interesting questions about the construction of knowledge and distribution of power in society. According to Smith (1978) and Spender (1981), women's thoughts have largely been ignored throughout history because men have only regarded the work of other men as being significant: only men's views of the social world are endorsed as valuable and valid knowledge. For Spender (1981) the dominance of white males in sociology has serious implications for the type of knowledge produced:

> Most of the knowledge produced in our society has been produced by men...They have created men's studies (the academic curriculum), for, by not acknowledging that they have 'passed off' this knowledge as human knowledge (Spender, 1981:1).

Who defines knowledge and who is excluded from access to knowledge raises questions about who has power in society (Bernstein, 1971, Young, 1971, Bourdieu and Passeron, 1977). Bernstein explicitly states:

> How a society selects, classifies, distributes, transmits and evaluates knowledge it considers to be public, reflects both the distribution of power and the principles of social control (Bernstein, 1971:17).

Women's subordination in society is partly a reflection of their lack of access to and control of knowledge. The women in this study recognised that their education was 'unfinished'. Returning to education and having access to knowledge would, they hoped, give them greater power to compete for a more fulfilling and professional occupation within the labour market. Some also realised that learning gave them greater control and power within the private sphere, something that several partners disliked.

To summarise, sociological concepts, methods and theories reflect the male view of the world (Smith, 1987). For Spender the task confronting feminist sociologists is to reconceptualise 'female experience from a female perspective' (1981:3). A fundamental criticism of sociology by feminists (Spender, 1981, Smith, 1987,1989) is aimed at the objectification of knowledge, the researcher and the researched. Smith (1989) traces this discourse back to Durkheim's (1938) study, *The Rules of Sociological Method*, where he establishes his argument on the existence of social facts or social phenomena existing externally to the individual. The social world is an objective one. Knowledge is presented as the 'truth' and hence is used to justify sexist discourse on women in society. This tradition is still dominant:

> The ethic of objectivity and the methods used in its practice are concerned primarily with the separation of the knower from what he knows and in

particular with the separation of what is known from any interests, 'biases', etc., which he may have which are not the interests and concerns authorized by the discipline (Smith, 1989:88).

Feminist sociologists, like interactionists, phenomenologists and ethnomethodologists, argue for the centrality of subjectivity within sociology. Feelings, thoughts, experiences and emotions enter into the theoretical and research processes. Sociologists are not detached from the real world, and neither are the participants in their research 'objects' without consciousness and feelings:

> Reading sociology, we are reading about a world we are part of and active in, a world that situates exactly the actualities that we live. We are, also, of course, reading in that world as that in which our reading is going on (Smith, 1989:43).

For Smith (1987, 1989), asserting subjectivity in sociology is not an easy task.

Feminist sociologists find themselves in a contradictory position because of the nature of the discipline and academic life. Oakley (1981) and Reinharz (1992) have developed research strategies which locate the researched as a subjective participant (see chapter 4). Problems arise in maintaining subjectivity at the stage of producing research results as 'the research product will be located in the ongoing textually mediated conversation of sociology' (Smith, 1989:53). In writing a sociological text researchers, even interpretive sociologists, according to Smith (1989), interpret their subject's narratives as these are the rules of sociological discourse and academic acceptability.

One strategy to locate the study of women within sociology has been the introduction of Women's Studies. This has been popular at undergraduate and graduate level and also within adult education (Thompson, 1980). Two women, Helen and Avril, in this research were motivated to study for a degree after completing a Women's Studies course. Another, Pamela, gained the confidence to learn after attending a Women's Return to Learn course.

Feminist Solutions To Male Sociology?

What solutions do feminist sociologists offer for advocating a non-sexist sociology for women; or do they merely proffer a critique of existing sociological theory and methodology? How useful and transferable is this approach for understanding gender issues within adult education? Influenced by the rise of the women's movement and feminism in the late 1970's many feminist sociologists claim that they have established a space within sociology which firmly locates women and gendered issues as a research and theoretical concern (Smith, 1978).

Feminist sociologists were optimistic in the 1970s that a paradigm shift would occur within sociology. Stacey and Thorne (1985) and Acker (1989) maintain that there is little evidence of this but rather: 'a vast accumulation of new empirical and theoretical work about women existing in relative isolation from a world of sociological theory that continues in a prefeminist mode' (Acker, 1989:65). Stacey and Thorne (1985) and Acker (1989) identify a number of factors that may have inhibited the development of a feminist paradigm in sociology. These include the failure to view gender as a main theoretical concept, the prominence of positivism, the marginalisation of feminist empirical work, the lack of development of a feminist theory and the 'social organisation of the discipline'.

According to Acker (1989), feminist sociologists have not managed to break away from the power of the discipline of sociology as an academic pursuit. To survive within an academic institution means to conform to the pressures of funding agencies, publishers and the institution which as Acker (1989) points out are ruled by men. For Acker, 'to do sociology still means emersion in the established ways' (1989:71). Feminist theory remains underdeveloped because feminist sociologists continue to discuss gender within existing conceptual frameworks (Acker, 1989). For Ribbens and Edwards (1998) feminist sociologists are continually confronted by the dilemmas of social research and academic writing:

> Dilemmas occur at every stage of the research process. From the outset, there is a difficulty in 'letting go' of established academic bodies of knowledge, theories and methodologies...The dominance and authority of academic discourses and conventions also extends to how we write up our research. In utilizing and going along with academic conventions we can gain authority and credibility, but again we risk silencing, mutilating or denigrating the voices of the subjects of our research (Ribbens and Edwards, 1998: 16).

What would a feminist paradigm engender? Is a new paradigm possible when feminism does not consist of one approach but rather a number of feminisms? There is not one coherent body of feminist knowledge but a variety of often conflicting perspectives. For Acker a feminist paradigm would: '...place women and their lives, and gender, in a central place in understanding social relations as a whole' (Acker, 1989:67).

Specifically this would include an improved understanding of class, the state, sexual division of labour, sexual violence and male dominance in the family. For Stanley and Wise: 'a feminist social science should begin with the recognition that 'the personal', direct experience, underlies all behaviours and actions' (1993:164). Besides creating a new epistemology a feminist paradigm would produce a new methodology, 'for', not of women.

Sociologists need to recognise that they cannot distance themselves and the subject matter from those they research and the society in which it is situated. The experiences of the researcher are not divorced from their research or conceptual and theoretical discourse. My life experiences, past and present, influenced the choice of my research. I shared a similar gender and class background to many of the women in this study. This helped me to understand why they wanted to change their lives through education. Smith (1987) calls for a 'reorganisation' of sociology:

> This reorganization involves first placing the sociologist where she is actually situated, namely at the beginning of those acts by which she knows or will come to know; and second, making her direct experience of the everyday world the primary ground of her knowledge... The only way of knowing a socially constructed world is knowing it from within. We can never stand outside it (Smith, 1987:91,92).

By focusing on the subjectivity of the sociologist and the researched, Spender (1981), predicates that feminists have altered the process of knowledge construction. For Spender (1981) an alternative to men's sexist knowledge about women and society is being developed such that women are gaining power through the politics of knowledge. Many of the women in this research studied courses on gender in various disciplines. In Spender's (1981) terms they gained awareness about women's position in society. This led them to reflect upon and conceptualise their life experiences and reassess their location within the family, employment and university.

Unlike 'mainstream' sociology, feminist sociology shares with Marxism in proposing a sociology that will bring about social change. Theory and practice are dialectically linked as theory develops out of experience and practice. At the same time theory can change practice. Stanley and Wise (1993) advance this idea one step further by advocating a similar relationship between theory, experience and research. Experience refers to the experiences and consciousness of the researcher feeding into and being a central part of the research process. A sociology for women engages with the world of women, acting as a potential liberating force helping women to understand and change their lives. A similar analysis is applicable to adult and community education and, in particular, the work of Freire.

Feminist Theory: A Contradictory Term?

Arguing for a feminist sociological theory or feminist methodology obscures the fact that there are many feminisms. Feminists are not united; there are numerous and complex divisions: liberal feminism, radical feminism, Marxist feminism, socialist feminism, existentialist feminism, psychoanalytic feminism and postmodern feminism. Within these categories further theoretical divisions exist. It may also be misleading to talk about 'women' as if they are a homogeneous group. Doing so conceals class and race inequalities. Despite the common factor of gender white middle-class women experience the world differently from white working-class women. Black women have criticised the feminist movement for representing the interests, in theory and practice, of white women only. Feminist theories, according to black feminists such as Carby (1982), are white and ethnocentric yet assume that their discourse is universal to all women including black women and women in third world countries. The small number of black women in this study talked about the impact of racism, as well as sexism, upon their lives.

Despite the different perspectives feminism does have one overarching aim in common: the development of a feminist consciousness to identify the causes of women's oppression and implement strategies to overcome it. However, the causes of oppression and the processes of liberation will differ according to the particular feminist perspective.

In this next section a brief outline of feminist theories relevant to this research are presented, although this is not an easy task because of the multifaceted nature of feminist perspectives. Three perspectives which Arnot and Weiner (1987) identified as having influenced educational research and theory; 'Equal Rights in Education' (liberal feminism), 'Patriarchal Relations' (radical feminism), and 'Class, Race and Gender: Structures and Ideology' (Marxist/socialist feminism) are included. I draw on aspects of these theories in later chapters and relate them to the lives of the women in this study. However, the theories of Marxist feminism and, to a lesser extent radical feminism are the dominant ones used in this text. I do not, therefore, discuss psychoanalytic, existentialist or postmodernist feminisms.

Liberal Feminism

Friedan in *The Feminist Mystique* (1963) talked about the 'problem with no name' in relation to the role of housewives in post-war society. Society expected women to gain fulfilment through domesticity and motherhood, not employment. Being efficient and competent with housework were viewed as life's goals for the suburban housewife. For Friedan (1963) the traditional role of housewife meant drudgery and boredom for most women. She maintained that society could no longer ignore the voice of women saying: 'I want something more than my husband and my children and my home'(Friedan, 1963:29). The women with families in this study experienced 'the problem that has no name' as outlined by Friedan (1963). They found spending time in the home looking after children isolating and boring. The women wanted more out of life than serving the needs of husbands and children.

Several voiced their opinions within the perspective of liberal feminism. The women did not want to be confined to the role of housewife. They wanted the same choices as men in society. Education was thus viewed as an important institution for the achievement of equality of opportunity for women.

Radical Feminism

The origins of radical feminist thought are generally attributed to the works of Kate Millett's (1970) *Sexual Politics* and Shulamith Firestone's (1970) *Dialectics of Sex*. Radical feminism argues that patriarchy, the domination and control of men over women, is the root cause of women's oppression. For radical feminists women's oppression is universal. According to Millett (1970) all men oppress all women. Women are an oppressed class while men are the ruling class. Gender oppression is the main form of oppression in all societies.

One important aspect of radical feminist theory is that it challenges traditional notions of power and politics. Power and politics are no longer viewed as being confined to the public world; politics also invade the private lives of the family and sexuality. This theoretical approach is useful in examining the power relationships between the women and their partners in this study.

Millett (1970) argues that sexual relationships are political as they are the means by which men exert power over women in both the private and public domain. Patriarchy is maintained through the processes of ideology and socialisation in the family and other institutions. The family, therefore, plays a central role in maintaining the power of patriarchy. Women and men internalise the cultures of femininity and masculinity. For the women in this study entering the public sphere of university gave them a greater degree of control over their lives. However, within the family several had to struggle, often failing, to achieve greater co-operation from partners with housework and childrearing. Power in the family continued to reside with the husband. Challenging this power was perceived as a threat by some men, causing domestic conflict. Politics from this perspective is about individual men exerting political power over individual women. Relationships between men and women are political or what Millett (1970) calls 'sexual politics'.

Radical feminists have, therefore, made a significant contribution to political theory by demonstrating that politics and power extend into the private world of the family. Criticisms of their theories have been put forward by other feminists, notably Marxist/socialist feminists. Radical feminism, in viewing all men as oppressors, ignores the concept that masculinity is also a social construct as men have been socialised into a male role. The older working-class men in this study were aware that the interaction of class and gender factors had limited their choice of occupations and shaped their role and relationships within the family.

Marxist/Socialist Feminism

Like many women in the 1970s and 1980s I was involved in many aspects of the women's movement. The following are impressionistic and personal reflections upon those experiences. Women talking and working with other women felt powerful and special, giving women strength and a voice. Consciousness-raising groups did, as outlined by radical feminists, make women aware that the 'personal is political'. Women discovered that they shared common problems and inequalities as a result of male dominance and sexism but this could be tackled by women campaigning and working together in the 'struggle'. Women learnt that women-only groups do have a different atmosphere compared to mixed groups; they are less competitive, individualistic and aggressive.

While recognising that sexual oppression and patriarchy played a significant part in the subordination of women in society I could not agree with radical feminists that it was the fundamental reason. I believe men are also constrained and oppressed by their gender role. Not all men can be classified as 'sexist' or 'chauvinist'. Some men do support the feminist cause, others have the potential to change.

My personal involvement in the Women's Movement, particularly through a women in teaching group, stimulated my interests for wanting to examine women's lives through theory and research. What role can education play in liberating women in society? The women in this study talked about their lives as mothers, wives and students to each other in seminars and as they socialised in the coffee bars. To what extent would this sharing of experience result in consciousness-raising about their position as women in society?

Marxist/socialist feminist thoughts were articulated academically by feminists such as Mitchell (1971), Barrett (1980) and MacDonald (1981), although Barrett has now moved on to postmodernism. Marxist feminists base their theories on the writings of Marx and Engels while socialist feminists attempt to combine Marxism with the ideas of radical feminism. Much of the debate centres on the relationship and interaction between class and gender within capitalist society. Mitchell (1971) and Hartmann (1981) argue that society is both capitalist and patriarchal. This is the essence of the 'dual systems' theory. Others attempt to merge the two concepts to develop a 'unified systems' theory (Young, 1980, Jaggar, 1983). Marxist/socialist discourse centres on debates concerning domestic labour, women and the labour market, alienation and class and gender relations. One unifying theme is their belief that gender relations, like class relations, have a historical and material basis within capitalist society. Women's oppression cannot be understood without reference to the socio-economic relations and structure of society. The root cause of oppression is the capitalist system, not men. Men are also oppressed and alienated under capitalism.

Gender and class relationships shaped the lives of the women in this study. Initial education and the family reproduced gender and class relationships, restricting their employment horizons and constraining their role within the family. However, they discussed their oppression mostly in terms of being women rather than working-class. The interaction of gender and class inequalities are examined by Marxist-feminists:

> What we need is a theory that is at once large enough and yet is capable of being specific. We have to see why women have always been oppressed, and how they are oppressed now, and how differently elsewhere...We should ask the feminist questions, but try to come up with some Marxist answers (Mitchell, 1971:99).

One strand within Marxist feminism relates women's position in the economic sphere to their role within the family. Women's subordinate position within the home is replicated in the labour market:

> It is clear that on the one hand the wage relation characteristic of capitalism, and the accompanying separation of home and workplace, have historically made a substantial contribution to the present sexual division of labour in which women's position is located primarily in relation to responsibility for domestic labour and financial dependence on a male wage-earner (Barrett, 1980:57).

Using Marx's concept of the reserve army of labour this theory illustrates how women's economic dependence on the male breadwinner in the family has resulted in their low status in the paid economy (Beechey, 1977). It is a circular argument. Employers pay women low wages which reinforces their dependency upon husbands and marriage. In this way, Barrett (1980) argues, gender, to a large extent, becomes separate to class. Most of the women in this study were in low-paid female jobs. Economically they were dependent upon their husband's income and felt trapped by this. Kate, for example, disliked the lack of economic freedom. She hoped that a degree would enable her to obtain a better paid job as she was considering leaving her husband to live as a single parent.

Mitchell (1971), Hartmann (1981) and Jaggar (1983) maintain that the family is the root cause of women's oppression in society. Jaggar's (1983) theory on alienation relates closely to the experiences voiced by the women in this study. She extends Marx's theory of alienation from the workplace to the family. Women's needs are subsumed to the emotional and material needs of men within the family. Women do not realise their creative potential; family life is unfulfilling and dehumanising. However, the women in my research became conscious of the alienation they were experiencing as housewives and took active steps to emancipate their lives.

Marxist/socialist feminists have extensively introduced and developed gender into traditional Marxist theory. What has not been fully resolved is the relationship between capital and patriarchy and hence class and gender. Marxist feminist educational theory (Barrett, 1980, MacDonald, 1980) has gone further along this road.

Looking to the Future: The Feminist Debate Continues

Compared to the late 1960s, 1970s and early 1980s, feminism and feminist issues today appear to have disappeared from public consciousness. Over a decade of right-wing Conservative rule has wiped feminism and left-wing politics off the public arena. Some would even argue that we are now living in a post-feminist era; equality between the sexes has been achieved. A glance at statistics and data on employment and roles within the family soon indicates otherwise. Housework and childrearing continued to be the responsibility of the women in this study once they became students. Many were critical of their husbands for failing to share in these roles and, thereby, help ease the pressures of their studies.

Feminist scholarship is flourishing with recent theoretical divergence into postmodernist theory. What feminist discourse does illustrate by its numerous perspectives and theories is the complexity of gender oppression and the solutions to it. In reflecting upon the theories it is important to ask the question; how do they help us to understand the everyday lives of women? How do they relate to the public and private lives and experiences of women adult students?

Men should not be excluded from the debate. We need to raise men's awareness and consciousness of how women are oppressed by men and structural forces in society. Masculinity, as well as femininity, has to be challenged if oppression is to be tackled. For this reason I was interested in examining how gender affected the lives of the men in comparison to the women. As Seidler points out, ' A significant strain in the response of men to feminism has been a negation by men of their own masculinity' (Seidler, 1994: 98). The ivory towers of academia, dominated by a male hierarchy and a male view of the world is a good starting point.

Structuralism: Theories of Reproduction and their Utility for this Study

Marx and neo-Marxists have constructed theories of reproduction. However, Marx's theory, as noted earlier in this chapter, is not purely deterministic. Marx's writings integrate macro and micro sociology in a positive way. This study draws on the influence of Marx in combining structure and action theories.

For Marx a dialectical view of history is essential as human beings are both the products and producers of the social world as the experiences of the women in this study illustrate. Fundamental to Marxist thinking is the notion that people are potentially creative. Under capitalism the economic and social relations of production constrain human action through exploitation and class relationships, alienating people from their essence. The adults in this study believed that they had not achieved their educational potential at school. This was one reason why they experienced alienation at work. Dominant ideology and institutional structures result in the working-class experiencing a false class consciousness. In turn this leads them to accept their subordinated class position. The concept of false class consciousness can be transferred and applied to gender and the position of women in society. In this sense women experience false gender consciousness as well as false class consciousness. The concept of false gender consciousness is discussed in relation to the position of non-traditional working-class women students. Participants redefined their role as women. How applicable is the concept of false gender consciousness in this context?

Within the Marxist view of the state the education system forms part of the superstructure alongside other key institutions. The superstructure supports, reinforces and reproduces the infrastructure, the economic system, through the production of ideology and a central value system which reflects the interests of the ruling class. The curriculum, knowledge and culture of the education system, therefore, represents those of the bourgeoisie or middle-class. Some participants from a working-class background found the middle-class culture of the grammar school alienating and thus rejected it.

Theories of reproduction are taken up and extended by various Marxists writers. Of particular value is the contribution of Marxists such as Bowles and Gintis, and Bourdieu and feminist Marxists such as MacDonald and Barrett to the study of education and the role of the state in capitalist society. Some of these theories will be integral in discussing the mature students' class and gender experiences of schooling.

Moving Away From Dualism: Towards a Unification of Macro and Micro Sociology

Integrating interpretive, feminist and structural theories offers a powerful approach to understanding the social world. Adult students are both consciously attempting actively to change their lives 'for the better' while also being constrained by structural forces of gender, class and race. Structure and agency continually interact to shape and reshape their lives. The micro and macro worlds are a part of their everyday lives at university, work and in the family and cannot be separated out. The challenge is for sociologists to represent the social world theoretically as one which results from both human action and cultural and structural forces. For Weiler this means a theory: 'That will recognize both human agency and the production of knowledge and culture and will at the same time take into account the power of material and ideological structure' (Weiler, 1989:7, quoted in McCall and Becker).

3   Researching Women's Lives: Interviews as Life Histories

...interviewing offers researchers access to people's ideas, thoughts, and memories in their own words rather than in the words of the researcher. This asset is particularly important for the study of women because in this way learning from women is an antidote to centuries of ignoring women's ideas altogether or having men speak for women (Reinharz, 1992: 19).

Moving from Theory to Method

In undertaking research the method chosen (in this case interviews) and how this is carried out reflects the theoretical perspectives of the researcher. But the research process is more than this. As feminists have highlighted the researcher also brings with them a personal history which subjectively influences and becomes part of the research process.

Social research is a difficult and perplexing task, whatever its focus and topic. One of its fascinations is that it requires sensitivity to issues on many different levels. On the one hand, we need to think through our theoretical frameworks and assumptions. On the other hand, research is also an intensely practical exercise, requiring us constantly to make detailed, concrete decisions. But these layers within research cannot be distinguished in actuality in quite this way, since theory and nitty-gritty decisions do not occur in different places but are constantly intertwined within the research process (Edwards and Ribbens, 1998: 1).

My interviewing approach attempted to synthesise and combine two sociological perspectives; feminism and interactionism. The two perspectives are not poles apart. Feminist researchers (Stanley and Wise, 1983 and Fonow and Cook, 1991) recognise the parallels, relationship and influence of interactionism, ethnomethodology and phenomenology within feminist methods. Both pursue a humanistic approach to interviewing by valuing the interviewee as a person and not an object. A central unifying theme is their opposition to postivism. Interactionists, like feminists, are concerned about avoiding the exploitation of interviewees by researchers for their own means:

> Interviewing as exploitation is a serious concern and provides a contradiction and tension in my work that I have not fully resolved...at a deeper level, there is a more basic question of research for whom, by whom and to what end... All too often the only interests served are those of the researcher's personal advancement. It is a constant struggle to make the research process equitable (Seidman, 1991: 24 - 25).

The interview is an interaction between researcher and researched. Research itself is a process of symbolic interactionism. Through research the sociologist is acting upon and constructing the world:

> Interviews must be viewed, then, as social events in which the interviewer (and for that matter the interviewee) is a participant observer... interview data, like any other, must be interpreted against the background of the context in which they were produced (Hammersley and Atkinson, 1983:126).

Feminism and interactionism allow the participant to 'tell her/his story' by defining the world through her/his own perspective and experience. This process is facilitated by unstructured interviews and biographical method. An interview from feminist and interactionist perspectives is a powerful methodological tool. What participants have to say becomes important and valued. Meaning is constructed by the stories they tell as participants define their past, present and future situations to reconstruct their social world. We, as researchers, are privileged to be let into their private worlds and need to consider this when making these private worlds public. Interviews are a valuable method because behaviour is put into context; socially, politically and historically.

> We argued that the researcher is an active presence, an agent, in research, and she constructs what is actually a viewpoint, a point of view that is both a construction or version and is consequently and necessarily partial in its understanding (Stanley and Wise, 1993:6,7).

For feminists a prime goal is to use social research to change women's oppressed lives. Research is, therefore, closely linked to social change. Central to feminism is the belief that research is 'for women' and many feminists are adamant that feminist research can only be undertaken by women:

> ... we see an emphasis on research by women as absolutely fundamental to feminist research. We reject the idea that men can be feminists because we

argue that what is essential to 'being feminist' is the possession of 'feminist consciousness'. And we see feminist consciousness as rooted in the concrete, practical and everyday experiences of being treated as, a woman (Stanley and Wise, 1993:31,32).

Quantitative and Qualitative Research: The Debate Continues

Research in adult and continuing education is characterised mostly by descriptive approaches largely because research, until recently, has been policy and programme driven. Concern has also been with producing statistics showing, for example, the number of adult students, reasons for returning to learn and types of courses chosen (Woodley et al., 1987, Fulton, 1989, Smithers and Robinson, 1989, Sperling, 1991). While statistical information offers a useful insight and background it does not provide a full picture. Statistical data fails to engage with the interesting issues and questions of how adult students experience being a student; what it means to them, their perceptions, attitudes and behaviour as a lived experience.

A theoretical and conceptual framework is largely lacking in adult education research. As Ruddock eloquently summarises, research: 'has been characterized by a pedestrian pragmatic empiricism' (Ruddock, 1971:19). Little progress has been made since Ruddock's statement in the early 1970s. Could this be a result of the eclectic nature of the discipline? Drawing upon several disciplines and epistemologies may make it difficult for a clear and coherent conceptual and theoretical framework to develop. Thompson adds:

> There are a number of reasons to explain why adult educators seem to underestimate the value of theory. Most of them are to do with the ramifications of being 'practical people' who judge credibility in terms of action. ... In our discussions with adult educators, consequently, we have sensed a preference for descriptive rather than analytical accounts of practice (Thompson, 1980: 220).

A growing number of adult education researchers in the UK, such as Weil, Benn, Thompson, are addressing the human aspects across the spectrum of adult education. Weil (1989) clearly states her preferences for qualitative approaches:

> Qualitative research helps to expose a new language - the language of genuine lived experience. It is a mode of research that does not pre-define the nature of learning and adult learners' experiences. ... Research that is

grounded in a concern with meaning and relevance rather than measurement and typology can shift the ground from which we seek to understand the experiences of adult learners. It has the capacity to enrich - and to re-define - theory and practice related to adults learning (Weil, 1989:18).

There is a need for more extensive qualitative research in this field, related to a critical and theoretical sociological framework. This will not be an easy task for adult educators as the field lacks a theoretical tradition. There is little to build upon. Sociological research on initial schooling offers a useful starting point as parallels exist between initial and adult education. Theories on initial education are transferable if adapted and modified to the world of adult education. Other fields of sociological theory will need to be synthesised to develop a theoretical framework within adult education: gender, class, race, family, employment. As a discipline, sociology provides a useful tool for demystifying the social world and raising critical questions by using qualitative approaches for research and establishing a theoretical framework. As Denzin explains: 'Order is given to theory, methodology and research activity through the use of what Mills termed the 'sociological imagination' (1978 :6).

For as Becker (1967) argues: 'There is no position from which sociological research can be done that is not biased in one or another way'(1967:245). The biography of the researcher influences not only the choice of research study but also the type of research methods employed and the presentation of the research data. Feminist researchers, such as Reinharz (1983), argue for the disclosure, acknowledgement and discussion of researchers' attitudes and values in their writings.

Subjectivity: The Human Element of Research

Interactionism and feminism provide a framework for analysing the causes and meanings behind people's behaviour in a given social situation. 'Research is not...a disembodied agent of pure logic, but a social encounter' (Rock, 1979:182). Research is about attempting to understand the subjective meaning of human behaviour and locating those subjective experiences within the context of people's lives and social situation. Douglas (1970) posits a similar stance: 'concrete human events are always to some degree dependent on the situational context in which they occur and can adequately be explained only by taking that context into account' (Douglas, 1970:37).

Following Denzin's (1971) argument for a 'naturalistic enquiry', I wanted to understand the behaviour of mature women students in particular social situations, at university and life outside, by entering their social world and understanding their behaviour from the actor's perspective. At the same time I was anxious that the research findings should not become shrouded in 'sociological mystique' saturated by sociological language and theory as this would remove it from the people I was studying. Corrigan stresses the importance of keeping sociological writing accessible to the layperson. 'Whether sociology is a science or a philosophy, it is nothing if it fails to discuss the experienced problems of ordinary people; and it is nothing if it fails to do this in a way which people can understand' (Corrigan, 1979: 16). Presenting and writing research in a way which does not exclude others outside the academic community is an important concern for many feminists:

> There is no reason why academic language should be different from - it is just a convention, but it is a convention that excludes others from taking part in academic discourse. It is also a convention that serves a particular purpose - to uphold notions of knowledge as abstract, rational and detached from women's everyday lives... For feminist researchers in higher education a further dilemma arises - not only must the research be written up in 'standard English', but, with the growth of an academic theoretical 'meta - language', also written in a style that is acceptable to male-stream academia, even if the style and language is inaccessible to the people who take part in the research (Standing, 1998: 194, 195).

The women in this study were interested in the outcomes of my research. Many enquired whether the findings would be published in academic journals or as a book. They were interested in reading about research in which they had made an active contribution.

Interviews are a social process involving social interaction between both researched and researcher. Interviews yield a dynamic insight into the lives of the interviewees: how they experience, interpret and act upon their lives. To obtain this understanding the interviewer must be prepared to share her/his thoughts and life experiences with the interviewee. Interviewing is not a one-way process with the researcher exploiting the researched for their own ends. In carrying out my interviews I was anxious to avoid this situation. I wanted the interview to be more like a conversation with an exchange of information from both sides. Conducting interviews in this style is more in tune with the philosophy of adult education.

Moving to the Interview Stage

Interviews were the dominant method in this research. This approach encouraged participants to draw on their life histories. Seidman (1991) succinctly summarises the value of interviews:

> The purpose of in-depth interviewing is not to get answers to questions, nor to test hypotheses and not to 'evaluate' as the term is normally used. At the root of in-depth interviewing is an interest in understanding the experience of other people and the meaning they make of that experience...Being interested in others is the key to some of the basic assumptions underlying interview technique...At the heart of interviewing research is an interest in other individuals' stories because they are of worth (Seidman, 1991:3).

Adopting a life history approach to interviewing enabled me to build up an understanding of the past and present life experiences of the adult students in a fuller way than other methods would allow. Knowledge about their family, schooling and employment background proved critical to an understanding of why they had decided to enter university as a mature student at that particular moment in their lives. Interviews offered an insight into the inter-relationship and interactions between their public and private lives. As an 'insider researcher' I was also a participant observer within the organisation.

Interviewing as a Subjective Experience

Interestingly, although there was a gender mix in terms of numbers on the part-time and three year degree (full-time) programmes the overwhelming majority who responded to being interviewed were women. Many of these women besides coping with being students also had domestic responsibilities and in the case of part-time students, full-time jobs as well, yet they found the time to participate. One reason for the higher response rate from women may be the fact that the interviewer was also female. Male students may be less willing to open up and discuss their public and private lives with a female researcher. This begs the question whether men would 'open up' if interviewed by a male researcher in a non-exploitative manner? Feminists, such as Reinharz (1992) and Oakley (1981) argue that for a fuller understanding of women's lives it is necessary for women to be interviewed by female researchers. Black sociologists indicate similar findings in relation to ethnicity. Earlier research by Labov (1973) indicates that factors such as the interviewer's gender, age and ethnicity may be critical to the way the interviewee defines the situation and hence how they respond in the interview.

Gender differences in interview responses may relate to gender socialisation. It is socially more acceptable for women to talk about their private lives, emotional issues and problems than men. Finch (1984) identifies several reasons for women being more forthcoming in interviews with women. One related factor discussed by Finch (1984) is the assumption that women are more used to 'outsiders' such as doctors, health workers and other professionals probing into their private lives.

Students on the 2+2 social studies programmes are predominantly women but one of the few male students was willing to be interviewed. A sample of thirty mature students was drawn up from the questionnaire for interviewing. This quota consisted of ten students from each of the three types of degree programmes available to mature students at Warwick: full-time 'traditional' three year degree, part-time and 2+2 degrees. In terms of gender 21 women and 9 men were interviewed.

The Mechanics of the Interview Process

The adult students were interviewed twice during the research programme: once in the third term of their second year (1994) and again towards the end of their final year of study (1995).

A smaller sample of fifteen was identified for the second interview; five full-time, five part-time and five 2+2. Two in-depth interviews separated by a year enabled the researcher to establish a relationship with the interviewees. It allowed the students to reflect upon their experiences and perceptions as students and highlight any changes over a period of time. One interview would provide limited information and a snapshot view of the students' lives:

> Multiple interviews are likely to be more accurate than single interviews because of the opportunity to ask additional questions and to get corrective feedback on previously obtained information. As time passes, the researcher also can see how thoughts are situated in particular circumstances (Reinharz, 1992:37).

Getting the students to talk was not a problem; many of them did so for a long duration. The interviews were not structured. Instead I had a list of areas I wanted to discuss. Some areas were explored with some interviewees in more depth than others as each 'story' was different. Significant factors and experiences in their lives varied, for example, in relation to why they decided to study for a degree. However, common elements of gender, class and educational experiences could not be ignored: all had significantly impacted upon their lives. Talking about these issues opened up both public and private areas of the women's and, to a lesser extent, the men's lives. Making public the private lives of women is problematical:

> It is the particular topics under consideration - aspects of private, domestic and personal lived experiences - that so clearly draw these issues out and present us with dilemmas. Social researchers concerned with domestic and initimate issues are involved in the social construction and material production of knowledge within the domain of public, and academic, discourses. Amibiguity thus arises when we seek simultaneously to serve an academic audience while also remaining faithful to forms of knowledge gained in domestic, personal and intimate settings (Edwards and Ribbens, 1998: 2).

Before beginning the second interview I invited each participant to read the transcribed notes of their first interview. All did so. They were asked if the notes, as far as they could remember, were an accurate portrayal of the interview. On reading their transcripts many were surprised at the depth and breadth of the material covered. Kate's comment echoed those of others: 'Gosh, did I really say all that? It seems more like counselling. It's amazing how things change over a year'.

None of the feedback was negative. On the contrary, reading the transcripts was an illuminating experience as they could see how they had developed and changed as individuals. A small number asked if they could keep a copy of the transcription. Some researchers may be critical of this approach, considering it too 'dangerous', as it leaves the researcher exposed and vulnerable. I, however, would argue that it is an essential process with multiple interviews. In this particular situation it helped to quickly re-establish a relationship between interviewer and interviewee and one which was less exploitative. Refreshing their memories enabled them to reflect more coherently about changes experienced during their final year of study. The second interview, as a result, was not disjointed. Participants were eager to launch into telling their story a year later.

Interviews as Life Histories

One striking fact was that all the mature students were willing and keen to 'tell their story' to someone who was willing to listen. For Seidman (1991) this represents the core of interviewing as they are: 'stories and the details of people's lives as a way of knowing and understanding' so that, 'telling stories is a meaning-making process'(Seidman, 1991: X1). Many related their life histories and present experiences with the interviewer asking minimal questions. They perceived what was required with little direction being given. Despite being a stranger to them many openly disclosed personal aspects of their lives such as health problems, reasons for divorce, relationship problems, incidents of sexual harassment at work. Kate, a 2+2 student, talked about her deteriorating relationship with her husband who thought she should be earning a wage as a secretary, not studying. He constantly told her she did not have the ability to study for a degree. This sometimes turned to anger and violence aimed at her. After a period of childrearing she wanted to do something more fulfilling with her life; this did not include returning to secretarial work.

All of these experiences had had a deep effect upon their lives and were related in some way to their reasons for returning to education or their present situation of being a student. I had been let into their private lives after only a few minutes of knowing them. I reflected whether or not I would disclose such personal information if the roles had been reversed. Some researchers may feel narratives raise questions about the ethics of research that probe into the personal lives of participants. However, this type of method does allow the participant to map out the boundaries of which experiences to disclose.

A few participants were surprised that anyone would want to listen to their life histories and remarked: 'I am not sure that I have got anything interesting to say', or, 'I do not know if this will be helpful for your research'. This self-doubt about the value of their lives occurred with both female and male participants, although many feminists argue this is characteristic of researching women. As McRobbie (1982) expounds, 'sociology does not prepare us for the humility of powerless women, for their totally deferential attitude to the researcher, "why are you interested in me, I'm only a housewife"' (McRobbie, 1982:56,57). The men who expressed similar views in my research were working-class, part-time adult students studying for a Labour Studies degree.

Drawing on aspects of life history methodology through in-depth interviews enabled me to examine one of the key questions of my research.

Why at this particular moment in their lives did these women and men choose to study a degree at university? To answer this I needed to connect their past histories with their present contexts and future aspirations within a framework of gender and class relations. As Alheit (1994) points out, 'every event worth recounting has specific contours; it possesses a prehistory as well as a history of successive effects' (Alheit, 1994:12). Biographies are valuable research tools as they allow the sociologist to analyse the intersections of history, individual experiences and social structure. As Marx observed:

> Men make their own history, but they do not make it just as they please; they do not make it under circumstances chosen by themselves, but under circumstances directly encountered, given and transmitted from the past (Marx, 1852, 1968:96).

More recently C Wright Mills (1970) discussed the role of biography in grasping an understanding of the relationship between behaviour, history, the individual and social structure:

> By the fact of his living he contributes , however minutely, to the shaping of this society and to the course of its history, even as he is made by society and by its historical push and shove... The sociological imagination enables us to grasp history and biography and the relations between the two within society... No social study that does not come back to the problems of biography, of history, and of their intersections within a society, has completed its intellectual journey (C. Wright Mills, 1970:12).

I was interested in; how and why as adults they decided to go to university: their public and private roles and experiences as adult students, and the extent to which these were influenced by gender and class. A key concern was to relate the dialectics of individual action and structural approaches. Combining a biographical or narrative approach with two sets of in-depth interviews a year apart enabled participants to reflect upon their past, present and future lives as a situated experience:

> People live lives with meaning. Interpretive biography provides a method which looks at how subjects give subjective meaning to their life experiences (Denzin, 1989:14).

Denzin defines the interpretive biographical method as 'the studied use and collection of personal-life documents, stories, accounts, and narratives which describe the turning-point moments in individuals' lives' (Denzin, 1989:13). The virtues of this method are extolled by Jones as being:

> A unique tool through which to examine and analyse the subjective experience of individuals and their constructions of the social world. Of all research methods, it perhaps comes closest to allowing the researcher access to how individuals create and portray the world around them (Jones, 1983:147).

Interpretive biography originated with the Chicago School of Sociology in the 1920s and 30s from the work of Thomas, Burgess, Shaw and Whyte. However, the importance of 'story-telling' in defining knowledge has been central to many societies throughout history. With the swing towards positivism and the scientific approach biographical method fell into decline until the 1970s. A recent upsurge of interest by symbolic interactionists, feminists and disciplines outside of sociology is making it as popular once again. For feminists it offers the opportunity of 'giving voice' to women's lives by letting women speak for themselves (Fonow and Cook, 1991, Reinharz, 1992):

> Biographical work has always been an important part of the women's movement because it draws women out of obscurity, repairs the historical record, and provides an opportunity for the woman reader and writer to identify with the subject (Reinharz, 1992:126).

Life histories enable interviewees to reflect upon, interpret, give meaning to and construct past events and experiences within a social context. It locates participants as central to the research process in a subjective and meaningful way. Sociology is brought to life by such an approach as it is a 'commitment to the position that interpretive sociologists and anthropologists study real people who have real-life experiences in the social world' (Denzin 1989:14). A passionate plea is made by Plummer (1990) in his discussion of life histories method or 'documents of life' for a humanistic sociology which accepts the validity of subjective data in research:

> ...an important approach to understanding human life has been persistently minimised, maligned and rendered marginal by social scientists: they believe that human documents are just too subjective, too descriptive, too arbitrary to help in scientific advance... scientific advance in the social world may actually be contingent upon building a methodology that can take subjectivity and the lived life as its cornerstone... life document are an immensely valuable and vastly under-rated source (Plummer, 1990:11).

Examination of narratives frequently reveals a critical incident or a 'turning point moment in individuals' lives' (Denzin, 1989) which leads them actively to change the direction of their lives. This was the case with many of the students I interviewed. In telling their stories the adult students related incidents such as divorce, children growing up or unemployment to their decision to study for a degree. Narratives offer a powerful insight into the inner world of individuals and the meaning people give to their lives in interacting with the social world. It is important not to abuse the trust of the researched in the presentation of the research material. The application of interpretive biographies as a method has several implications for research methodology which have to be taken into account.

These relate to questions of ethics, theory, power and values as well as pragmatic ones. A fundamental issue is the need for the researcher to relinquish control in the interview process to facilitate a conversation style. How to transcribe, analyse and present data become key questions if the aim of the narrative is to enable participants to tell 'their own story'. To what extent does the sociologist interpret the life histories and hence impose values and interpretation upon the data? To what extent can particular life stories inform researchers about general social behaviour? What is the role of narratives in relation to theory?

Graham (1984) maintains that 'story-telling' has several advantages over structured interviews as, 'story-telling counteracts the tendency of surveys to fracture women's experiences' (1984:119).

We all have our own biography which we carry around with us and it is impossible to divorce this from the research process. However, far from being detrimental, this has the potential to enhance the research process, particularly if researcher and researched share similar experiences and background:

> Researchers should therefore be aware of the ways in which their own biography is a fundamental process. It is both the experiences of the researched and researchers which are important (May, 1993:14).

Feminists claim utilising biographies as a research method is a learning process for both researcher and researched. Reinharz illustrates this point: 'Once the project begins, a circular process ensues: the woman doing the study learns about herself as well as about the woman she is studying' (Reinharz, 1992: 127).

The narrative is an interpretive account on several levels and researchers need to be aware of these multiple realities. Firstly, the story told by participants is selective and an interpretive account of their lives. For Alheit (1994):

> The narrator does not simply recall the course of his life...He selects a specific autobiographical theme that is at once unmistakable and interesting. He 'organizes' the dominant lines of narrative for autobiographical recollection, creates hierarchies and competition...Whatever the narrator selects from the wealth of material that could be recounted also has something to do with himself and with the specific character of the autobiographical experiences that he has encountered (Alheit, 1994: 16,17).

In presenting the research data the researcher also selects and interprets from the narrative both in the transcribing of the interview tapes and in the writing of the research findings. Finally this process will be repeated by the reader of the text. Riessman (1993) makes the following plea:

> Precisely because they are meaning-making structures, narratives must be preserved, not fractured, by investigators, who must respect respondents' ways of constructing meaning and analyze how it is accomplished (Riessman, 1993:4).

However, later in her text, *Narrative Analysis*, Riessman recognises that 'all forms of representation of experience are limited portraits. Simply stated, we are interpreting and creating texts at every juncture' (Riessman, 1993:15). As all stories are interpretive accounts of life experience; bias will inevitably be introduced by the researched, researcher and reader. Lives and situations do not stand still. Narratives are how participants perceive their reality at a particular moment in time and within a particular social context. In reflecting upon their lives, for example, a year later, the women may choose to discuss other aspects of their lives or give a different emphasis to events.

Some of the students I interviewed, both women and men, stated upon reading their transcriptions that 'that was where they were at then', but many felt that their social situation had now changed, mostly for the better. All had grown in confidence. In particular one male 2+2 student (Mike) stands out. During the period of the first interview he was very disillusioned and depressed with studying for a degree and was contemplating leaving the degree course. Like many of the mature students I interviewed Mike was a perfectionist, wanting to read as widely as possible for essays and seminars but constricted by the pace of the curriculum programme. Pressures were building up at home; their second child was due and finances were tight. Mike felt that he could no longer cope with the course. A year later he was buoyant, lively, confident and thoroughly enjoying being a student. Strong support from a personal tutor helped him to cope with the pressures. Subject tutors had predicted he would obtain a first class degree. A tutor in sociology had approached him about studying for a PhD. This he very much wanted to do providing he was able to secure funding.

Similarly a full-time female sociology student (Sue) had also noticeably grown more confident and positive about her academic ability as pressures and problems within the family decreased. As for the 2+2 student (Mike) it was predicted that Sue might get a first. The full-time and 2+2 students were very conscious of the impending change which the end of the academic year would bring. A significant number had either been offered or had considered continuing onto graduate courses.

Another methodological issue concerns the way narrative data are presented by researchers. Phenomenologists and some feminists firmly believe that life histories need to 'speak for themselves', without interference and interpretation from the researcher. While recognising the value of this approach I would argue that without interpretation and location within a theoretical framework the data becomes merely a description. Our understanding of social life cannot move forward using such an approach. I wanted to relate the life histories of the participants to sociological concepts and theory in order to understand more fully the interaction between action and structure in people's lives. As a result I decided against presenting the life histories as a series of case studies.

My aim was to document the data from the perspective of the adult students because as Denzin advocates, 'our texts must always return to and reflect the words persons speak as they attempt to give meaning and shape to the lives they lead' (Denzin, 1989:81). I also wanted to attempt to locate the life histories within a theoretical framework without distorting the meaning participants gave to their lives. In doing this I recognise I am selecting certain aspects of their lives which relate to the conceptual and theoretical concerns I am interested in pursuing:

> Ultimately, of course, the features of an informant's narrative account an investigator chooses to write about are linked to the evolving research question, theoretical/epistemological positions the investigator values, and more often than not her personal biography (Riessman, 1993:61).

Plummer (1990) dismisses the claim that the life histories method is atheoretical and on the contrary states that reference to theory has always been part of its tradition. He highlights a contradiction with the narrative method when researchers declare that their material is 'telling it like it is' in the participants' own words: 'it is always likely to be shaped somewhat by the researcher's theory' (Plummer, 1990:123). Drawing on Glaser and Strauss's (1967) well-known work on grounded theory, Plummer (1990) suggests that theory can emerge from life histories. 'Life histories and personal documents provide rich data which can be used to cast doubt on received theories and to throw light on future directions for theoretical research' (Plummer, 1990:127,128).

Acker, Barry and Esseveld (1991), in their study of women returning to the labour market, were confronted with the dilemma of how to present life history data. The problem they faced was how to relate the material to social theory without distorting the women's perceptions of their lives. As they remark: 'in the actual task of analysis, we initially found ourselves moving back and forth between letting the data "speak for itself" and using abstracted categories' (Acker, Barry and Esseveld, 1991:143). Getting the balance right between letting the data 'speak for itself' and applying a conceptual and theoretical framework is not an easy task for the researcher to resolve. What is important to remember is that life history method 'grasps the fundamental point that interview data, ... are interactional, contextual productions' (Denzin, 1989:57). Research interviews need to be carried out in a humanistic style with researcher and researched interacting subjectively within an equal relationship.

Life histories/biographies are being increasingly used by adult education researchers (see West, 1996). In his study West (1996) also found that adult students, by choosing to go to university, were consciously attempting to change their life history.

> The people whose lives we are researching tell stories about a process at once more fundamental and humane: the struggle for meaning at times of change and fragmenatation of which occupational change is but one part (Lea and West, 1995: 172).

Interviewing: Methodological Issues and Perspectives

The adult students valued having someone listening to their life histories. In these circumstances it is not desirable to act the role of a 'distant, disinterested researcher'. With life history methodology the interview dialogue becomes a more equal two-way process as the interviewer and the interviewee interact in a conversation; it is not only the interviewer who asks the questions. Rather, the interviewer should be prepared to share life experiences with the interviewees. Throughout the interviewing process I engaged in conversations with the students I interviewed, mostly, but not exclusively with the women. I could not avoid answering their questions when they asked me about my life or requested information about studying and university life. Many of them were interested in me as a person. Morally I felt I could not expect them to talk about their lives if I was not prepared to do the same. Ethical issues have to be taken into consideration. I did not want to exploit the participants; I felt myself unable to take from them without giving back. Their questions could not be ignored or dismissed as being unimportant or irrelevant to the research process so a humanist philosophy and approach was favoured.

Throughout the course of the interview I would give examples about my life if it related to the point we were discussing. For example, a number of the women were actively changing the direction of their lives, often in relation to employment, in their late thirties or early forties. I had also decided on a career change in my thirties. Sometimes issues would be discussed further after the interview had finished. An African-Caribbean woman (Hyacinth), upon hearing that I had previously taught in a multi-cultural school wanted to talk about racism in schools and its effect upon the education of her children. This we did extensively. Adopting a non-hierarchical approach to interviewing produces a greater wealth of interview data than the traditional hierarchical method. During the course of an interview the researcher is likely to find her/himself undertaking multiple roles; as a researcher, counsellor, adviser or friend.

Acker, Barry and Esseveld (1991) experienced a similar situation when they interviewed women in their research, and extol the merits of what they consider to be a feminist approach to interviewing:

> Another part of the attempt to deal with the subject-object problem was to try to establish some reciprocity by offering, at the end of the first interview, to tell the women something about ourselves if we had not done so earlier... We always responded as honestly as we could, talking about aspects of our lives that were similar to the things we had been discussing about the experience of the interviewee - our marriage, our children, our jobs, our parents (Acker, Barry and Esseveld, 1991:141 in Fonow and Cook).

Oakley (1981) was one of the first to advocate an interviewing method which is non-hierarchical, non-exploitative, and engages the researcher in a dialogue with the interviewee. This model evolved and developed through her experiences of interviewing women for her research projects. Oakley (1981) questioned and refuted the traditional, and in her view, 'masculine' paradigm which demands disengagement from and control over the 'research object'. Within this framework: 'both interviewer and interviewee are thus depersonalised participants in the research process' (Oakley, 1981:37). Oakley (1981), in her study of pregnant women's expectations of motherhood, became highly involved with her interviewees: frequently offering them advice and reassurance. Some of them kept in contact with Oakley as friends.

To re-emphasise, research interviews should not be about exploiting those being researched. However, this may perhaps be contradictory because at the end of the day, we, as researchers are using the interview data for our particular needs although also, as feminists, hopefully, to improve the lives of those we are researching. Interactionist sociologists and feminists try to minimise the exploitation by the interviewing style they employ. Becker (1967) explicitly states that, 'researchers should ask themselves which side they are on'.

This is particularly the case when there are shared experiences between the interviewer and interviewees relating to class, gender, age, culture or history. Denzin (1978) maintains that a similar stance is necessary to achieve 'a close fit between selves of interviewer and subject'. In practice this philosophy restricts the researchers' choice of subjects for research. For many researchers, supporters of the positivistic method, a subjective approach to interviewing transgresses the boundaries of academia and professionalism as it breaks the ground rules of interviewer/interviewee relationship. Feminist researchers, according to Mies (1991), have rejected 'the methodological principle of a value-free, neutral, uninvolved approach, of an hierarchical, non-reciprocal relationship between research subject and research object' (Mies, 1991:67).

In interviews where social distance is minimal between researcher and researched the material obtained will be fuller, richer and, hopefully, more accurate. Both can relate on the same level. The majority of the students I interviewed belonged to the same generation as myself. Many of them were women, mainly from a working-class background. These three factors meant that we had shared common experiences and perceptions of the past which facilitated the interviewing process. Oakley (1992) perceives that 'where both share the same gender socialisation and critical life experiences, social distance can be minimal' (Oakley, 1992:55). Although ideal, I do not feel that researchers should limit their topics to individuals or groups from a similar background to themselves, nor should it be assumed that relevant or meaningful data can only be obtained in such a situation. Reinharz (1992), however, states a preference for women to be interviewed by women: 'For a woman to be understood in a social research project, it may be necessary for her to be interviewed by a woman' (Reinharz, 1992:23).

Finch (1993) elaborates why, as a feminist sociologist, she advocates female researchers interviewing female interviewees. For Finch the arguments are both methodological and political:

> However effective a male interviewer might be at getting women interviewees to talk, there is still necessarily an additional dimension when the interviewer is also a woman, because both parties share a subordinate structural position by virtue of their gender. This creates the possibility that a particular kind of identification will develop (Finch, 1993:170).

According to Finch (1993) women implicitly understand and trust each other in the interview process as 'a woman interviewing women is special' (1993:173). While she does not exclude the possibility of men interviewing women effectively, Finch (1993) emphasises the extra insight gained by women interviewing women. Women who have belonged to women's groups or worked in paid employment in a female team maintain that there is a bond and strength between women. My own experiences substantiate this viewpoint. However, Finch (1993) may be assuming that women are a homogeneous group and that the experiences of being a woman cut across class and ethnic divisions. Some working-class women, black or white, may feel uneasy about being interviewed by a white middle-class researcher. Methodologically, the feminist approach to interviewing raises important questions about research ethics and data gathering. Implicit in this assumption is the notion that interviewers and interviewees should ideally share the same background and experiences such as gender, class or ethnicity.

Following this argument would devalue much sociological research as it not always possible for researcher and researched to share a similar background. Many social groups would remain unstudied if this was a prerequisite for research. While accepting that commonality between researcher and researched may yield greater depth and understanding this does not preclude a researcher from a different background from understanding and studying a different social group. The difference may lie in the questions asked and perspectives adopted. What is more important is the style and approach utilised by researchers. In relation to interviewing this means employing unstructured questions in a non-exploitative manner in all situations regardless of the research topic.

Interactionists do not view interviewing a person from a different social background as problematic. Rather the art of the researcher is to 'take the perspective or role of the "acting other" and view the world from the subjects' point of view' (Denzin, 1978:21). Sociologists move between one's own world and the world of others.

Underlying this notion lies the core belief of feminism: women's lives are important and should be rendered visible through research. Advocating the need for women to be interviewed by women may derive from the feminist critique of sociology in failing to study women's lives. Sociology, from the feminist perspective, portrays a man's view of the world. Women need to redress this imbalance by studying aspects central to women's lives. Previously unknown or neglected aspects of women's lives be constructed, understood and given importance more easily by women interviewing women:

> Making the invisible visible, bringing the margin to the centre, rendering the trivial important, putting the spotlight on women as competent actors, understanding women as subjects in their own right rather than objects for men - all continue to be elements of feminist research (Reinharz, 1992: 248).

By adopting this approach a central tenet of feminism becomes significant: 'the personal is political'. Stanley and Wise (1983) develop this further:

> ...the personal is not only political, it is also the crucial variable which is absolutely present in each and every attempt to 'do research,' although it is frequently invisible in terms of the presentation of this research (Stanley and Wise, 1983:157).

Harding (1987), although a feminist, is critical of feminists who believe only women social scientists can study women. Men, according to Harding, can make 'important contributions to feminist research and scholarship' (1987:10):

> I suggest that feminists should find it inappropriate both to criticize male scholars and researchers for ignoring women and gender and also to insist that they are incapable of conducting research which satisfies feminist requirements (Harding, 1987:12).

In her critique Harding (1987) points out that, 'significant contributions to other emancipation movements have been made by thinkers who were not themselves members of the group to be emancipated' (Harding, 1987:12).

The women I interviewed openly discussed their personal lives but these experiences are also collective ones. It is fundamental to the research process that the collectivization of women's lives is made apparent through theorisation and conceptualisation of the research data. Many of their individual experiences were shared by other women in the sample; conflict with partners about studying, educational, family and work experiences. All of the women and the men were actively seeking to change their lives through education. These experiences need to be located structurally within gender, class and social relationships of society in order to render the personal more meaningful. Interpreting their lives dialectically provides a valuable medium for examining the interaction and inter-relations between action and structure in women's lives. This perspective is shared by Acker, Barry and Esseveld (1991):

> Although we view people as active agents in their own lives and as such constructors of their social worlds, we do not see that activity as isolated and subjective. Rather, we locate individual experience in society and history, embedded within a set of social relations which produce both the possibility and limitations of that experience (Acker, Barry and Essenveld, 1991:135, in Fonow and Cook).

Feminist sociologists have without doubt made a valuable contribution to research methodology and ways of raising critical awareness of the role of the interviewer and the relationship with the interviewee. In presenting an alternative model it is possible to interpret and construct the world as subjectively and collectively experienced by women. However, it may be misleading to talk about a 'feminist methodology' as expounded in the late seventies and early eighties by Bernard (1978), Roberts (1981) and Oakley (1981). The ground has shifted. Initial reactions to 'masculine', scientific research have been refined and modified in some feminist quarters. Jayratne and Stewart (1991) argue for the application of both quantitative and qualitative methods by feminists. Although this approach is not endorsed by all the feminist academic community, it is clear that a multiplicity of methods are now used by feminist sociologists. Feminists have not created new research methods but applied existing methods in a style sympathetic to feminist ideology and practices. Reinharz (1992) firmly believes that: '...there is no single "feminist way" to do research' (1992:243). She elaborates that: 'feminism is a perspective not a method' (Reinharz, 1992:240).

Linking Research and Adult Education

Interviewing my sample of adult students was an enjoyable experience, despite the number of hours spent transcribing. I know the interviews were of value to the students themselves, enabling them to reflect upon their past, present and future lives in a meaningful way. Comments expressed by participants at the second interview substantiated this as several stated it had helped them to reflect on what they were doing and why. I could only admire their enjoyment of learning and determination to succeed in a middle-class elite institution while juggling with other demands and commitments in their lives. All participants valued the opportunity to return to education and on approaching their final term, many did not want to leave.

Research does not advance in a straightforward, linear fashion as portrayed in the majority of educational and sociological literature. The study of human lives is a lived subjective experience, not a clinical one. The researcher is continually confronted by practical, political and ethical issues. Many are not easy to resolve such as the issue of sociologists exploiting those they research for their own ends. It is important for scholars to be 'up front' and declare where they are coming from without being egotistical and self-indulgent. Being honest about one's self and one's theoretical perspectives provides the reader with a better understanding and insight into the research.

Sociologists need to consider carefully why they are doing a particular piece of research and how the material will be portrayed and used. For feminists social enquiry can be employed positively and powerfully to give women a voice for altering their structural position in society. Studying adult women students in a qualitative way will, hopefully, not only result in an understanding of their lives and experiences but also improve practice for future students. Such research inevitably raises policy and organisational issues and implications for change. It also highlights a question that will be examined elsewhere; how far should adult students adapt to the organisation and how far should the organisation adapt to meet the needs of adults?

Research on adult education needs to be more theoretical and less descriptive. Theory and practice can enhance each other to bring about change. In documenting the lives of adult students the research process becomes a learning experience for the reader, researched and researcher as we are all 'lifelong learners'.

4 Warwick University: Culture, Context and Community

> I wanted to be part of a reputable establishment. Also Warwick was more in tune with the demands of their mature students (male, full-time).

Introduction

In this chapter I sketch the institutional culture and behaviour at Warwick. A contextual analysis at the meso and micro levels assists in the understanding of policy and practice in relation to the study of access and experiences of non-traditional adult students at Warwick. The meso level refers to the structure, policies and practices of the institution. The micro level, in contrast, looks at the perceptions and experiences of the actors in the institution.

Background: What type of University is Warwick?

Warwick is one of the 'plate glass' or 'green fields' universities established during the 1960s under a national programme of expansion in higher education. 'Plate glass' is rather a misnomer as Warwick's original buildings are white-tiled, dominating and contrasting with the green landscape between industrial Coventry and rural Kenilworth. The OECD (1969) study of new sixties universities in England commented about the detachment of the universities from towns compared to the civic universities.

Being a self-contained campus university has not hampered Warwick's growth. Contact with local communities has been integral to its development. The campus is surrounded by a large industrial hinterland ofCoventry and Birmingham and rural Warwickshire. Beneficial links were soon established with local companies such as Rootes and more recently Rover. The University's regional location is also enriched with multi-ethnic communities; Asian, Afro-Caribbean and a small number of Chinese, living in Coventry, Leamington Spa and Birmingham.

Warwick's first group of students (450) entered in 1965. Since then it has grown to a total degree student population in 1998-99 of 14,021; 8,195 of whom were undergraduates and 5,826 were graduates. While the gender ratio of students at undergraduate level is now fairly even, 52% male to 48% female, Warwick reflects the pattern of many 'old' universities in having a low ethnic minority intake of 12.6%. Full-time undergraduate mature students consisted of 10% of the total undergraduate students for 1997-98. Part-time undergraduate students for 1998-99 totalled 419.

Warwick's Community Links: A Brief History

Warwick's relationship with its local community has always been important to its development. Situated on green fields outside urban areas it would have been very easy for Warwick to become an 'ivory tower' isolated from surrounding communities. Historically many universities have distanced themselves from society as the Centre for Educational Research and Innovation (CERI) point out:

> The campus is an isolated, self-contained location. It is a kind of monastic refuge where knowledge and wisdom can thrive free of all constraint. The concern for knowledge - and for truth - has always led universities to seek a certain isolation (CERI, 1982:24).

From time to time throughout it's history issues related to the nature of the University's community have surfaced. Warwick, like many universities during the late 1960s and early 1970s, experienced a period of student unrest. During the late 1960s unrest centred around the question of community, specifically, the nature of the University's relationship with groups in the local community. Staff and students called into question the particular type of relationship which Warwick had at that time with its local industrial community. E. P. Thompson (1970) and other academic staff argued for a wider vision of community and the support of values which were less firmly entrenched in industrial capitalism:

> Clearly, a university cannot grow in any direction it chooses, without regard to social needs and demands; and clearly, also, relationships with the community - with industry at every level, ... with local teachers and welfare workers, with ordinary citizens, - can only enrich the University's

life and help to dig students and staff out of their somewhat introverted isolation (Thompson, 1970:160).

Defining the concept of community is complex and problematical. Thompson above is referring to community in terms of different social groups residing and working within a geographical radius of the University. There are numerous sociological definitions of community. Attempts to define community in relation to universities are few and not clear-cut (CERI, 1982). The University Grants Committee (UGC) (1990), however, stressed the importance of university involvement in local communities in a report, *A Strategy for Higher Education into the 1990s*.

In defining community geographical and sociological definitions are frequently combined. This provides a useful approach in looking at a university and its community. A community is both a geographical area or 'territory' and a social system characterised by a particular set of social relationships. Warwick's community consists of a plurality of geographical and sociological communities; urban and rural areas, business people, minority ethnic groups, middle and working-class adult students, local young students and educational institutions. For example, the inner city area of Hillfields, Coventry, is a geographical and sociological community of Warwick's with social groups, black and white, sharing similar social situations of poverty, unemployment and poor housing. The University has recently established a centre for education and research in Hillfields. Also with the development of the 2+2 degree programme strong community links have been forged with nine local FE colleges. This relationship has culminated in the establishment of a Community University Board.

Since its establishment in the 1960s Warwick has always had a high community profile and involvement. A strong policy, emanating from the top, has ensured the development of wider community links, not only with local businesses but with other sections of the community. In this sense Warwick has always been a 'community university'.

Mature Students as a Policy Issue

Over the years Warwick has established itself as a highly rated university, ranking fifth and sixth in recent national Research Assessment Exercises from 1986 to 1992. Such high research prestige, both nationally and internationally, guarantees a yearly influx of 18 year olds with good A level grades. These are overwhelmingly white and middle-class. There is no shortage of applications by well-qualified 18 year olds in most subjects to Warwick. As a research-led university Warwick makes an interesting study as it has committed itself to promoting lifelong learning opportunities for non-traditional adult students and links with the local community. Thus Warwick's 'dual mission' as both a leading research university and an institution committed to widening access for local adults makes it unique among Britain's 'old universities' as now called. This is partly attributable to the influence of the second Vice-Chancellor. As an American he brought to the University of Warwick a broader vision of a university's role and mission which in this case was distinctly Californian. Commitment to continuing education as a policy position is clearly stated in the University's Corporate Plan and other policy documents:

> Warwick is distinctive as a primarily research-led University in the high priority it has given to improving access, to developing and continuing post-16 experience education and to close collaboration with its local community. The part-time degree programme is firmly established and the 2+2 degree programme with local FE colleges has been successfully launched (University of Warwick Corporate Plan, 1992).

Having a positive statement in a corporate policy does not ensure that all organisational members are aware of it or support it. A policy can easily become mere rhetoric, ignored as just a 'bit of paper'. On the other hand, if a policy is strongly enforced from above it may meet with resistance from below:

> Change imposed from above or outside which is not believed in and 'owned' bywhat we call the 'academic community' will run into resistance - covert if not open. Innovations may fail for shadowy, barely explicable reasons (Duke and Merrill, 1993:10).

Academic autonomy still pervades as a powerful force despite the growth of decision-making 'academic politicians' (Scott, 1984) or administrators within universities. The 'academic tribalism' (Becher, 1989) enacted by some departments at Warwick encompasses resistance to widening access for local adults. Persuading colleagues from these quarters of the benefits of such a policy is difficult and time-consuming. Incorporation of commitment to its local community in the mission statement is important as it does signal support from the top. Its presence gives those seeking to broaden Warwick's role with its local community a small leverage.

Warwick has always had a tradition of accepting mature students through its doors, although until recently they mostly consisted of younger adults from outside Warwick's geographical region, entering with A level qualifications. As an undergraduate student at Warwick from 1973 until 1976 I was aware of a significant minority of mature students among the student population. Approximately one third of the students on my undergraduate course, History/Sociology, were mature students.

Over the past few years as the University has developed firmer links with its local community the mature student population at undergraduate level has increased, becoming more local and diversified. 'Local' means living within a 'travel to learn' distance from the campus. The local radius largely corresponds to the geographical area covered by the nine partnership FE colleges, stretching from Birmingham, Nuneaton, Rugby and Leamington Spa in the north and east, southwards to Stratford and westwards to rural Evesham and Worcestershire. Interestingly there is a higher number of adult students studying at graduate level than 21 year olds entering straight from completion of their first degree. Non-degree Continuing Education courses are also important in attracting local adults to Warwick. A significant number are adult students on professional updating short courses or the Open Studies programme. Open Studies Certificate courses offer a route into part-time degrees as they are credited at 60 points. Credit points can be used by students as a contribution towards advanced standing on a degree course, usually the equivalent of exemption from one course. A degree consists of 360 credits.

One of the female participants in this research (Avril) began her career back into education by taking two Open Studies Certificated courses, Women's Studies and Counselling, and used these as advanced standing towards a Social Studies part-time degree course. Studying on Open Studies courses gave her the confidence to continue onto a degree course. At that time it was possible to choose whether or not to opt for assessment which she liked because it 'gave me a way out'. After completing two Open Studies courses Avril thought that, 'it would be silly not to use them as credits towards a degree course'. Several male students on the part-time Labour Studies degree programme also entered via the Open Studies route. The latter provide a 'taster' for learning, giving adults the confidence to feel that they are capable of studying for a degree. Without this option some adults would not have entered the part-time degree programme.

Part-Time Degrees: Widening Opportunities for Local Adults

A Department of Continuing Education was established and a founding Chair appointed at Warwick in 1985. In contrast to some other universities, Continuing Education at Warwick was from the start given full departmental status within the Education Faculty, and more recently because of institutional reorganisation, within Social Studies. Continuing Education was thus given recognition as an academic subject area. The Department's role was to further continuing education as an integral part of the life of a university.

Warwick's commitment to widening access for local people is most evident in the delivery of two specific kinds of programmes: part-time and 2+2 degrees. Both are undergraduate programmes falling under the broad umbrella of 'Continuing Education'. 2+2 and part-time degrees reflect a gradual shift in the culture of the University towards a more open and accessible institution. However, cultural changes have not permeated into the structures and ethos of all departments. Innovation in academe is slow.

Resistance by some individuals and departments is couched in terms of issues concerning standards and quality. A paradigm shift has not yet been achieved. The Part-time Degree programme was launched in the academic year 1987-1988, initially offering degrees in Social Studies, Literary and Cultural Studies and Historical Studies. A part-time degree course offers a more flexible form of study for particular groups of adults. A student can take from four to ten years to complete the degree: most choose to study two courses a year. A minority later opt to go full-time in order to complete their degree more quickly. Two students in this study switched to full-time in their last year of study.

Administration and development of the programme is undertaken by the Department of Continuing Education. More specifically an academic member of the Department became Director of Part-time Degrees and a Part-time Degrees Office was established. Expansion of the Part-time Degree programme was made possible more quickly through 'pump-priming' money received from the Training, Enterprise and Education Directorate (TEED) for a development project. It was through this project that I returned to Warwick for the fourth time, not as a student, but as an employee of the Department of Continuing Education as a project development officer, initially for the last seven months of the Part-Time Degree Project.

Besides expanding the range of part-time degrees and courses, the TEED project aimed to mainstream provision into the University's regular structures and procedures. Mainstreaming part-time degrees was important to prevent the initiative from being marginalised. Departments and central administration now share responsibility for the delivery and administration of the courses and students.

Within the 'old' universities many Continuing Education Departments have taken a long time to gain and maintain credibility amongst the academic community (Titmus, Knoll and Wittpoth, 1993). Within a university hierarchy of knowledge many academics continue to hold continuing education and the education of adults in low esteem. For these academics the role of traditional universities is primarily to undertake research and educate 18-21 year olds at undergraduate level. This perspective endorses a 'front-end' model of education. Persuading academic colleagues at Warwick to participate in part-time and 2+2 degree programmes is, therefore, frequently a hard task. However, interview data indicate contradictions among some academic staff in their viewpoint of what a university should be and their practical experience of teaching adults. All the academic staff I interviewed extolled the virtues of teaching adults but some went on to express the view that they would not like access to be widened further. For this section of staff adults would be more suited at 'new' universities. 'New' universities refers to institutions that were previously called polytechnics under the binary system.

Elite University: An Outdated Concept?

Introducing and developing a part-time degree programme in a traditional university such as Warwick is also about organisational change. To be effective in implementing access strategies it is necessary to be aware of the politics of change within an organisation:

> In this project the team identified and worked with those who were already interested in supporting part-time study, who knew about and enjoyed working with older students - and with others who when the project was made known around the University 'emerged from the woodwork' (Duke and Merrill, 1993:11).

Change was encouraged through models of good practice. Financial incentives in the form of development money also helped to encourage departments, particularly those who were not ideologically committed to the access of adults, to devise new courses.

Elite is a frequently used term in relation to certain British and indeed European universities. Is this an outmoded concept in describing

Warwick and other British universities in the 1990s? Elite infers exclusivity, privileges and power for a particular social group. For as Duke stresses: 'The system is distinctly elite: hard to enter, expensive per full-time student, efficient in terms of completion rates' (Duke, 1992:3).

A distinction needs to be made between 'new' and 'old' universities. The origins and history of the former have ensured a wider distribution of black and working-class students among the population of new universities, and a broader, more vocational curriculum. Despite the age participation rate of school leavers having increased from 3.5% in the 1950s to 27% by the early 1990s the social class basis has not shifted. Since the Second World War the number of working-class university students on entry has remained around 10%. Universities have expanded to educate more middle-class young people. The gender balance is now even but it is middle-class women who are taking up the opportunity. The participation rate of ethnic minorities continues to be low. 'Old' universities remain the preserve of the white middle-class. Changes to the grant and benefits system, together with the introduction of course fees will make it increasingly difficult for working-class 18 year olds and adults to enter university (Merrill and McKie, 1998). The widening of access to adults to universities has opened the doors slightly by offering alternative entry routes thereby allowing access to a minority of non-traditional adult students.

Social elitism still exists in British universities but there are signs, particularly in the 'new' universities such as the University of North London and Thames Valley University, that the student population is now more heterogeneous and representative of British society.

Universities are also elite in terms of the academic structure, curriculum and knowledge delivered (Fowler 1979). Duke maintains that: 'most are still, typically, a preparation for the academic career to which only a tiny minority of students actually proceed' (Duke, 1992:3). In Bourdieu's (1977) terminology, 'cultural capital' is transmitted and reproduced, preserving the social and economic privileges of the dominant class. This viewpoint was echoed by academic staff in Biological Sciences at Warwick. Biology is viewed as an inappropriate subject for adults. One reason is that biologists relate teaching to preparation for an academic career. The age factor is important here as a person is considered too old for a lectureship if not in post by the age of thirty. The assumption is that a scientist's career path progresses in a linear fashion from undergraduate and postgraduate study to a lectureship.

Scott (1984), discussing the role of the modern university in the mid-1980s, maintains that producing elites was still a function of universities:

The modern university's role in the promotion of educational opportunity is not really different from the liberal university's role in the reproduction of elites. The intention has been to make access to these elites more equitable and broader, not to repudiate the university's traditional role in the formation of elites (Scott, 1984:74).

While the 'new' universities have traditionally been more open, the 'old' universities remain relatively exclusive in terms of the class background of the student population, culture and academic structure. Mature, including non-traditional, students have been let in, albeit in small numbers. Adult educators are, on a small scale, challenging the elitist culture and system within universities. Change is slow and piecemeal, confined to particular departments rather than overall institutional change. Middle-class eighteen year olds with good A level grades continue to be given priority. However, a degree is no longer an automatic passport to social and economic privilege unless it is an Oxbridge one (Brown and Scase, 1995). The currency of degrees in the market place has been undermined. A first degree plus a masters holds a better promise, and is almost a requirement for obtaining higher status employment.

Part-Time Degrees: Institutional Issues and Policy

Some academic staff initially viewed part-time adult students sceptically as they are different from 'traditional' students. Many lack A level qualifications and have been out of the education world for some time. Some academics were, and some still are, doubtful about the ability of such students to undertake an academic study and some departments were more resistant than others to participate in the programme. As Williams points out:

> The academic traditionalists place enormous emphasis upon the gold standard of A level points scores which symbolize and reinforce notions of academic merit and are presented as neutral, fair and a just selector of the suitable. A normal acceptable student is one who has undergone a quite particular form of academic socialization, designed for 16-18 year olds in schools (1997:29).

This research highlights some of the dilemmas and policy issues associated with delivering a part-time degree programme. Part-time degree courses are taught during the daytime and evening. Part-time adult students are taught as a group in seminars, particularly in the evening sessions, although Labour Studies lectures are presented jointly to both younger and part-time students. Evening teaching is essential for the accessibility of adult students in full or part-time employment. Most of the part-time degree students in my research sample were in full- or part-time employment. Although all were enjoying their degree course a commonly expressed concern was the lack of courses available in the evenings. Course choice is severely limited and some felt they had had to opt for courses in which they were not particularly interested. Dissatisfaction was expressed by some part-time students. One participant stated: 'It brings the whole issue into disrepute because if it is supposed to be part-time then why are there so many classes in the day?'

Research revealed the attitudes of academic staff in four departments at Warwick in relation to evening teaching. Evening teaching is undertaken by only a small number of departments and lecturers; daytime teaching is overwhelmingly the norm. However, 65% stated they would be prepared to teach in the evenings if it was limited to one evening a week. Others rejected the idea because it would interfere with their family and leisure lives or intrude upon their research time. '... if you are a member of staff and have a young family it is important to go home at 5.30 because if not it is an imposition on your partner' (lecturer, Law Department).

2+2 Degrees: The Beginnings of a Community University?

Acceptance and mainstreaming of part-time degrees at Warwick paved the way for another initiative; the 2+2 degree programme. Like part-time degrees it is managed and administered by the Department of Continuing Education. The 2+2 degree programme attracts a different group of adult students. Part-time degree students are mostly in full-time employment and, on the whole, more highly qualified than 2+2 students. Formal qualifications are not a prerequisite for entry onto 2+2 degrees. A small number either possess none or a few 'O' levels, Certificate of Secondary Education (CSEs) or General Certificate of Secondary Education (GCSEs). Compared to full- and part-time mature students 2+2 students possess fewer A levels. In a sample of second year mature students, 1993-94, 30% of 2+2 students had one or more A levels in contrast to 50% of part-time students and 61% of other full-time mature students.

The 2+2 degree programme was launched in 1991 initially offering degrees in Social Studies and Technology. Many 2+2 students are working-class women. A higher percentage of part-time degree students, particularly those studying Humanities courses, are middle-class compared to 2+2 students as the following table illustrates:

Adult Student Self Perception of Social Class

	2+2 %	Part-time %	Full-time %
middle-class	25.0	75.0	52.3
working-class	55.0	6.25	35.7
classless	5.0	0	4.76
unanswered	15.0	18.75	4.76
don't know	0	0	2.38

A two year Higher Education Funding Council for England (HEFCE) funded developmental project entitled, *Flexible Partnership Programme for Non-Traditional Students* began in October 1992, injecting resources into Warwick's 2+2 degree programme. This, together with a national policy favouring the expansion and widening of access of adults enabled the programme to expand rapidly in a short period of time. The project aimed to develop new degree courses in new subject areas by extending the University's partnership links with local further education colleges. During the life of the project the following new 2+2 degrees were established, thus broadening the subject base of the programme; European Studies, Sports and Leisure Studies, Environmental Studies and Labour Studies. The partnership model with FE colleges was deliberately kept local as the philosophy of 2+2 is to provide provision for local non-traditional adults. It would be difficult for students to feel part of Warwick if they were studying at a college some distance from the University.

I was the project officer for the duration of the project, working closely with the Directors of both 2+2 and Part-time Degrees. My development and research roles within the Department became intertwined and indistinguishable with each advantageously feeding the other. My intuitive knowledge as a development officer helped to inform my research. It gave me an overview of the University as a whole, providing me with a deeper understanding of the subtleties underlying access issues and institutional change. My dual role as practitioner and researcher enabled me to reflect upon the issues.   On the whole, Science Departments at Warwick are 'traditional', reluctant to admit adults in the belief that the nature of their discipline makes it difficult for adult students to apply themselves to science courses. On the other hand talking to colleagues in Social Studies Departments I knew that many welcomed applications from adults. Cultural differences between science and non-science departments at Warwick will be examined later in the chapter.

As the name implies 2+2 students spend the first two years studying for the degree in their local college and the last two years at Warwick. Years one and two are equivalent to year one of a three year degree course: year one is degree level and, therefore, not the same as an Access course. In curriculum terms it is more broadly based than the traditional three year degree. Many of the 2+2 students have been out of formal education for a number of years. This programme aims to ease them back into learning, building their confidence, in a local environment of an FE college which is less threatening and intimidating than the formal, large and impersonal institution of a university. 2+2 students are registered as Warwick University students from the beginning of their four year course:

> The programme provides new pathways into higher education for local adult students by offering an innovative degree structure tailored wherever possible to the needs of non-traditional students who may lack 'normal' entry qualifications but who are capable of studying for a degree (Merrill and Moseley, 1995: 36).

Data reveal that the majority of 2+2 students (1997-98) are in their twenties (39%) and thirties (34.2%). For various reasons, often relating to class and gender, many were unable to benefit from higher education in the past. Now, as adults, many want to 'complete their education' and prove to themselves that they are capable of achieving in higher education. This is an interesting contradiction which will be explored later. As adult educators we consider education to be continuing and lifelong but several mature students in this study viewed obtaining a degree as completing their education.

2+2 student numbers rose sharply since the inception of 2+2 in 1991, but have now consolidated largely due to changes in financial policy. The first cohort of students graduated in July 1995. Recruitment to the programme is typically late in the academic year or during the summer vacation as non-traditional adult students are reluctant to commit themselves a long time in advance of the commencement of the course.

Various characteristics of the 2+2 population (1997-98) at Warwick reveal that they are overwhelmingly female, 63% to 37%. Traditional gender patterns are reflected in the choice of 2+2 degree programmes with a higher percentage of males opting for Environmental Studies, 53.8%:46.2%; Labour Studies, 62.5%:37.5%; Sports Studies, 73.6%:26.4%; and especially Technology, 90.9%:9.1%. The average age across all programmes is 31. Although the University is situated within a multicultural community the 2+2 population is overwhelmingly white.

Partnership is the underlying philosophy of the 2+2 degree programme, unlike franchising which is built on a less equal relationship between a higher education institution and FE college. With franchising colleges do not have ownership of the curriculum: they have to deliver the curriculum as directed by the HE institution. In this kind of relationship colleges function to serve the needs of the higher education institution. Colleges experience greater autonomy in a 2+2 relationship compared to other forms of FE/HE links such as franchising and validation. Mutual benefits can be identified. For the colleges; enhancement of status through involvement in higher level work with a prestigious university, an extra dimension to staff development, a wider curriculum and general expansion and development. For the University it provides a flexible form of delivery within a traditional environment, it contributes to its mission of widening access within its local community, improves links with other educational providers and enhances inter-departmental collaboration. For both players there have to be mutual aims, objectives and benefits: without this the partnership would collapse:

> A strongly bonded and focused university will only enter into real partnership where there is a strong mutual interest - where a 'selfish' interest in both really coincides (Duke and Merrill, 1993:13).

Departments, Cultures and Mature Students

Working across departments I was aware of the variation in cultures at departmental level. 'Certain departments within the University tend to be more conservative in their attitudes, values and practices than others' (Duke and Merrill, 1993:11). Among some academic staff and departments there is concern that opening doors to non-traditional adult students lowers academic standards. Strong pockets of resistance to change therefore exist in some quarters of the University. Other academic staff and departments are supportive of initiatives to widen access for non-traditional adult students. Warwick is departmentally based:

The collegial department-based mode of decision-making is a distinctive source of strength; but the strength can be a source of resistance to change, and with the best will in the world it cannot but act as a brake on the rate of change (Duke and Merrill, 1993:11).

Knowledge of cultural differences between departments, or 'academic tribes' as referred to by Becher (1989), is essential when seeking to introduce change such as part-time and 2+2 degree programmes. 'Understanding the institutional culture and the resistances -"reasoned" or "irrational"- is an important ingredient of success. It is better -smoother and faster - to work with the grain' (Duke and Merrill, 1993:10).

The following extracts help to give a flavour of the 'academic tribes' at Warwick. Other tribal members can probably be found in other universities. In Biological Sciences there is a consensus that the subject area is unsuitable for adults, particularly those who have been out of education for a long time:

> They have to be committed to want to do a science degree. Science moves rapidly and 5 - 10 years away is a long time. In Arts this is not a problem - you don't forget how to read a book (lecturer, biological sciences).

Young (1971), in discussing knowledge and education, points out that: 'academic curricula in this country involve assumptions that some kinds of and areas of knowledge are more "worthwhile" than others' (1971:34). Science is viewed as 'high knowledge' with different sciences being placed near or at the top of the academic hierarchy within universities. Hard knowledge such as science commands a higher status than soft knowledge such as humanities. A hierarchy of knowledge exists within the sciences and biology is situated at the lower end. Biological sciences at Warwick is an exception to this rule as the Department teaches microbiology, a specialism within biology. For Becher (1989) academic cultures are related to the nature of knowledge:

> It would seem, then, that the attitudes, activities and cognitive styles of groups of academics are closely bound up with the characteristics and structures of the knowledge domains with which groups are professionally concerned (Becher, 1989:20).

Adult student numbers at undergraduate level in the mid 1990s were very few in biological sciences, rarely more than six, and the majority of these were in their twenties. There are recent signs of some changes since the availability of a few biological sciences courses to 2+2 Environmental Studies students. However, it remains hard for an adult who has not got A levels and who is over thirty to gain entry to biological sciences. Although Access is a recognised route into higher education it is rarely accepted as a mode of entry by the Department. Access and non-traditional students are considered to be more suitable for the 'new' universities:

> As far as the University is concerned, it is of course important to give equality of opportunity, but because this University is high in the Research Ratings and because it may not be able to be 'top' at everything, it should accept that in some areas of study some of the adults might be better served at another institution which is able to put on more the kind of course on which they can succeed (Admissions Tutor, Biological Sciences).

Becher (1989) observed the following behaviour amongst academics:

> The tribes of academe, one might argue, define their own identities and defend their own patches of intellectual ground by employing a variety of devices geared to the exclusion of illegal immigrants (Becher, 1989:24).

Although Becher (1989) is referring to behaviours between groups of academics the model is applicable to academic staff in relation to non-traditional adult students. The goal of Biological Sciences is to maintain and expand a high academic reputation. Teaching non-traditional adult students is not part of this strategy. Adult students are not 'real' students. Consequently Biological Sciences may be oversensitive about the presence of 'soft' adult students in the Department as they do not match comfortably with the image as a high status academic Department. Young (1971) offers another explanation. He argues that what is valued as knowledge in society is defined by those with power and that:

> those in positions of power will attempt to define what is to be taken as knowledge, how accessible to different groups any knowledge is, and what are the accepted relationships between different knowledge areas and between those who have access to them and make them available (Young, 1971:32).

Within this framework science can be viewed as a knowledge area whose access is denied at degree level to non-traditional adult students in a university like Warwick.

On the other side of campus, metaphorically and literally in terms of geography, the world is different, at least with some departments such as

Sociology, Arts Education and, surprisingly, Law. Here there is a welcoming attitude towards adult students. The Law Department at Warwick provides an interesting case. Traditionally within European universities, law has high academic status and reputation and is closely associated with the legal profession. Historically Law Departments, like Medicine, are socially exclusive and elitist in professional terms, teaching 'black letter' law. Law at Warwick does not follow this pattern as its emphasis is on social law which studies law in context. The Department has many connections with development work in the Third World countries. Law provides a good example of Becher's (1989) theory whereby the nature of knowledge shapes the culture of the department.

Academics in Sociology, Law and Arts Education were positive in their attitudes towards the participation of adults, to the point of some stating that they would like to see a larger number in their Departments. Sociology, at 21% (1994-95), had the highest undergraduate adult participation rate in the University. All three categories of part-time, 2+2 and full-time, can be found here. For these departments mature students enrich the culture as 'mature students make the whole life of the Department healthier in some sense' (sociology lecturer). This is matched by mature students' perceptions as they find these Departments welcoming and supportive. Academic staff here view the University in less exclusive terms than biological sciences. Unlike the latter, mature students are not perceived as lowering the academic standard of the Department or the University. For them widening access is an acceptable part of the mission for an 'old' university like Warwick:

> I think that Warwick would see itself as an institution that wanted to participate in a process of people having opportunities. And also because we would see ourselves as an institution that wanted to be rich and diverse and not homogeneous. We would see that fitting in to the approach to the study of law and the overall educational experience of everybody that's there (law lecturer).

Looking to the Future

Warwick has expanded rapidly since the 1960s to become one of Britain's top-rated universities, nationally and internationally, in research and teaching. In achieving a high academic standard as a top-rated University it has also maintained and strengthened its links with the local community. Local non-traditional adults have been allowed entry alongside the high-achieving 18 year olds and are proving capable of equally good academic standards. Keeping access firmly on the University policy agenda is not always an easy task. Resistance still exists amongst some 'tribes' within the institution and it is unlikely that this will decrease in the future. However, part-time and 2+2 degrees have now been 'mainstreamed' into the administrative structure of the University.

Conflict between the University's academic and community role in relation to access surfaces occasionally at departmental, University committee and senior management levels. For some these two roles are contradictory and incompatible if Warwick is to retain its high standing nationally and internationally. Access policy at Warwick is now in a period of consolidation rather than growth. This is partly due to external forces.

A significant core of academic staff, management and departments are supportive of Warwick's community mission. However, the situation is always fragile, unstable and vulnerable. Signs of a cultural shift at the top towards a still more elite university are becoming evident. Those committed to access have to work hard to maintain initiatives and establish positive working relationships against the thrust of latent internal and external opposition. Can this enclave of support at grassroots level influence the culture of the University? One positive factor is that the historical tradition of Warwick as an innovative and community oriented university is firmly embedded within the organisation's culture to the extent that access for local people will continue to survive and possibly expand.

5 Connecting the Past with the Present: The Impact of Education, Gender and Class

Girls' attitudes to school are affected by their social backgrounds, personality and ability, and the sheer implications of being female (Sharpe, 1994:93).

Class and gender factors played a significant role in preventing many of the adult students in this study from continuing in post 16 education. Many regretted not being able to stay on at school to study A levels for entry into higher education. Most, therefore, felt that their education was incomplete while others believed that they did not reach their potential at school. As adults they welcomed the opportunity of studying for a degree at university. It offered a second chance: a possibility to redress the inequalities of an education system which had failed many of them as working-class girls. As adult learners they were determined to succeed a second time round. This chapter explores the relationship between schooling, family life and learning as an adult. How do their experiences of initial education connect to their decision to study as an adult? To what extent are these experiences shared ones of gender, class and, with a small minority, race?

The decision to study for a degree as an adult is primarily rooted in her/his experience of initial schooling and the cultural and material context of family life. Most of the participants grew up in working-class families where emphasis was placed on getting a job rather than qualifications. Education was deemed unnecessary, particularly for girls whose prescribed future consisted of marriage and domesticity. Working-class culture was and is antithetical to education and middle-class institutions such as schools (Willis 1977, O'Shea and Corrigan, 1979). The desire to return and continue their education was reinforced by a series of culminative experiences and events throughout their lives in employment, marriage and family life. To understand why the women had chosen this particular moment in their lives to return to learn requires connecting their present biographies to their past ones. While a critical incident in their present lives may have acted as a catalyst, the desire to 'reach their potential in education' had been latent within the students' consciousness for several years, for many since leaving school. An examination of present influences on the lives of the women would provide only a static and partial understanding of why the women had returned to education. Schooling, family, work and marriage underpinned by gender and class relationships, interrelated and contributed significantly to the women becoming adult students. The biographies, although individual, highlight the commonalities of many aspects of family and school lives, most of who grew up as working-class girls in the 1960s and 1970s.

Gender and Schooling

The 1944 Education Act in England and Wales established a system which, in practice, was divisive in terms of social class and gender although the ideology underpinning it stressed the promotion of equal opportunity and individual potential. The tripartite system was largely replaced by the comprehensive system during the 1960s and 1970s. Comprehensive schooling purported to erode class differences and provide a more equal education system but educational inequalities were not eradicated as the lives of the students in this study illustrate. Whether they attended a grammar, secondary modern or comprehensive school the women experienced the inequalities of an education structure which promotes the life chances of children who are white, male and middle-class (Bernstein, 1973, Bourdieu, 1977, Spender, 1982). Finn explains:

> The educational system may have some degree of autonomy, but its key features of selection and hierarchy derive from the character of the social division of labour. This is achieved through complex translation of economic and social privilege into educational attainments and subsequent retranslation of those credentials into renewed forms of privilege (Finn, 1987:6).

Adding a further dimension Spender (1982) points out that: 'educational institutions play a major role in persuading people that they are unequal, but not just on the basis of class. They also persuade people they are unequal on the basis of race and sex' (Spender, 1982:24).

Schooling in the 1960s and 1970s prepared girls for their future roles as wife and mother (Deem, 1978, Payne, 1980, Sharpe, 1976, 1994). Girls internalised the sexist ideology transmitted through the curriculum and the hidden curriculum (Spender, 1982). Through the socialisation process girls learn that fulfilment lies in romance and marriage and as a consequence not to 'act clever' in front of boys (Spender, 1982). Sex role differentiation was largely manifested in the 1960s and 1970s by a curriculum which clearly defined between girls and boys subjects, hence reproducing a sexual division of labour. For girls the curriculum emphasised a dual role; preparation for paid work and domesticity. Government reports reinforced such a curriculum, particularly for working-class girls:

> Girls know that whether they marry or not, they are likely to find themselves making and running a home; moreover some quite young schoolgirls, with mothers out at work, are already shouldering considerable responsibility, a fact which needs to be taken into account in school house-craft programmes... The incentive for girls to equip themselves for marriage and homemaking is genetic (Newsom Report, 1963:135).

For Marxist feminists gender differences reflected in the curriculum stemmed from the role of the state defining the social role of women:

> The context of this imposition is that of bourgeois hegemony, of the attempt by the bourgeoisie to gain the consent of women to a definition of femininity which locates their primary role as keepers of the home with only secondary involvement in waged labour (MacDonald, 1981:161).

Middle-class girls, and a small percentage of working-class girls, who attended grammar schools, were encouraged academically but learnt that careers should be second place to marriage and motherhood. Schools in the 1960s and 1970s reproduced, and continue to reproduce, both a sexual division of labour and a social division of labour:

> The work of the school facilitates the maintenance in the long run of the work force and the social relations of production through the transmission of a set of gender relations, its association with the division between domestic and waged labour, and all the contradictions this entails (MacDonald, 1981: 161).

The above briefly sketches the schooling background of the women in this study. Experiences of schooling were, therefore, inextricably shaped by gender and class.

Reflections on Schooling and Family

Among the interview sample of thirty students the numbers were equally divided between those who were educated by the tripartite system and the comprehensive system. The high number attending comprehensive schools may appear surprising as most are in their late 30s and 40s. However, several of the participants were born in Coventry, and Coventry Local Education Authority (LEA) was one of the pioneering LEAs to introduce comprehensive schools during the 1960s.

Attitudes towards schooling varied from dislike or indifference through to enjoyment.

Among the interview sample of students eight attended grammar school, either mixed or all-girls, and eight secondary modern school. Except for Judith, those who went to grammar school disliked it. For some it was the result of a clash of culture: being working-class in a middle-class environment. Jill, from a working-class background, found herself in the bottom stream of an all-girls grammar school. Feeling a failure at being in the bottom stream she was unhappy at school and glad to leave at the age of sixteen. Being working-class in a grammar school estranged her from her friends, family and neighbourhood. Girls and boys in this situation ultimately had to choose between remaining loyal to their working-class cultural roots or cutting their ties in favour of a middle-class education and the chance of social mobility. Payne (1980) outlines this dilemma:

> ... working-class values are not readily accommodated within the middle-class culture of schools. It is not possible to incorporate both sets of values, for the conflict between them is too great. In trying to conform to the requirements of the school I ultimately had to live the ideology encompassed within the school and this meant rejecting many of the values of my home (Payne, 1980:18).

Jill compromised, opting for a business studies course and A levels at a local further education college where she felt she performed better academically. She, therefore, broke away from the traditional working-class pattern by continuing her studies but chose to do so in a less middle-class environment. Similarly another woman remarked: 'I had been in the bottom stream at grammar school, and thus felt inadequate to attempt HE' while another, a male 2+2 student stated: 'I was confined within C and D streams for four years and felt very much marginalised'. Streaming undermines the confidence of those in the lower streams, labelling pupils as 'thick' or 'stupid'. Labelling is a powerful tool which debilitates a person's self-concept (Cicourel and Kitsuse, 1971, Hargreaves, 1967). Consequently several participants perceived themselves as educational failures.

Others found the atmosphere of a grammar school too strict in terms of rules and regulations. 'I enjoyed the subjects but did not like the climate at school. It was very strict and formal' (Jean). Sue declared that the teacher-pupil relationship and teaching style did not imbue a learner with confidence:

> I hated school. I lacked a lot of confidence. I was very fearful of school. I am quite an inhibited person in many ways. When I started grammar school I became a diabetic and had to have time off school. It got me out of the system before I could get comfortable in the new school. That was really quite a problem in the end. There was a phase a couple of years into grammar school, when I just stopped going for a while and my parents could not really deal with the problem, so in essence they left me to it (Sue).

Sue was one of five children; the only one in her family to pass the 11+. Half-way through her secondary school career the grammar school was transformed to a comprehensive school. This encouraged her to return. 'The only thing which got me back was halfway through the grammar school it went mixed and became a comprehensive. We went to a different building and I was given a new chance. I was never comfortable at school' (Sue). At the grammar school she had been fearful of getting her schoolwork wrong and being made a fool of in lessons: 'I got more involved in less academic subjects because I felt safer there' (Sue). Despite the lack of confidence in her academic ability she continued into the sixth form to take a bacculaureate in social anthropology.

Another full-time student, Cathy, also felt that she did not receive any encouragement academically at grammar school. In contrast to most of the women she spent her childhood in a small rural town. She was in the top stream at grammar school and passed four O levels but feels that she underachieved because she had a negative self-image about her abilities. 'I think I could have done a lot better. I am sure I needed encouraging and did not really get it so I left' (Cathy). Most of her friends, however, stayed on at school while her parents encouraged her to take a secretarial course. This is consistent with Stanworth's (1983) research which revealed that girls, including A level students, underestimate their academic abilities.

Avril enjoyed the social side of grammar school but disliked studying. It was not, she felt, particularly strict for a grammar school but it was a large and impersonal institution. 'It was very large so it was easy to kind of disappear which was what I tended to do. I was only really interested in English and drama. I did not really bother with anything else, hence my terrible results' (Avril). She left school at the age of sixteen with two O levels. Judith initially enjoyed life at an all-girls grammar school and had intended to stay on into the sixth form and take A levels. Influenced by her peers: 'I suddenly got it into my head that I wanted to get a job' (Judith). She elaborated:

> At the age of fourteen I got in with a group of girls who were all for leaving school. I did not revise. I just suddenly went off it. I hope now that my children do not do that. I keep saying to them, look I am doing this now but I could have done it then but I did not try (Judith).

Judith left school with a few O levels and took a secretarial course which she did not enjoy. The course was academically unfulfilling and she soon regretted her decision to leave school. 'I realised straight away that I had made the wrong decision. The course was basic and not very demanding and two years is a long time. I wish now that I had carried on' (Judith). Her parents did not interfere with her decision:

> I really wish that they (her parents) had said no. At school they did try and push me. They (her parents) thought they were doing their best as they just wanted me to be happy. I think you need a push at that age to motivate you (Judith).

Two women, both part-time degree students passed the 11+ examination but had to forego a grammar school education because their parents did not value girls receiving an education. One of them, in her forties, was the eldest in the family and had to help her mother with looking after the house and the other children. The other woman, in her fifties, explained: 'It is an opportunity I missed when I was younger. I passed the 11+ but was not allowed to go to grammar school for economic and political reasons - being female etc.' (part-time degree).

Another woman (part-time degrees, sociology and education) was denied the opportunity of taking the 11+ by her father, a farmer, because he did not consider that she needed an education. For him her priority and role was to help on the farm:

> I really enjoyed learning. My primary school headmaster wondered why I would not take the 11+. I did well at a good secondary modern, although I had to keep it quiet. My father burnt most of the books in the house on a bonfire. He did not like me doing homework, studying and on occasions

going to school as it interrupted my farm work and reduced my energy for it (part-time degree).

Educational opportunities varied between secondary modern schools (the latter was for those who failed the 11+). Only a minority offered pupils the possibility of taking O level and later CSE examinations. A study by Simon argues that: 'one pupil in 22,000 proceeded from secondary modern to university' (1971:227). Secondary modern pupils who succeeded in obtaining O and A levels highlighted the inadequacies of the 11+ system. Sally enjoyed her years at secondary modern school and successfully passed her O level examinations. At this stage she did not want to continue with her education but her parents forced her to take A levels. For this Sally had to change schools and attend a grammar school. The culture of the grammar school contrasted sharply with that of the secondary modern school: it was strict and unwelcoming. She believes that if she had been able to take A levels at the secondary modern school she would have continued in education after the age of eighteen. Instead she just wanted to get out. Sally dropped one of her three A level subjects and resented being forced by her parents to stay on at school. A new value system had to be learnt and acceptance into new peer groups while coping with the stigma of being an ex-secondary modern school pupil.

The culture and ethos of most comprehensive schools is different from that of grammar and secondary modern schools although some tried to emulate the grammar school tradition. Comprehensives have a less strict regime with greater emphasis on a pupil-centred approach both academically and pastorally. Many of the participants enjoyed the academic and social life of a comprehensive school and one stressed that she 'hated' the day she left.

Dalvinder stated that the social life at school was pleasurable but admitted that the schoolwork:

> ...was OK but I was not really committed. It was routine. I just went in and did the work. I was blasé about it. I did not think about a career, my future and what all of this meant (Dalvinder).

Failing her CSE examinations forced her to reassess her situation. Dalvinder remained at school for one year in the sixth form and worked hard at resitting O levels and CSEs. Believing that she was not clever enough to study for A levels she took a business studies course at a further education college because 'everybody was doing it'. She did not find the course challenging and for its duration kept thinking that: 'I am not going to be doing this for ever. I just did it for the sake of fashion and getting on a course doing something' (Dalvinder). Most of her friends had left school at the age of sixteen; some married and had children.

Others shared a neutral attitude towards life at a comprehensive: schooling was a process which you had to endure. Jayne, who went to a single sex comprehensive, disliked the anonymity of a large secondary school. Schooling, for her:

> Just sort of happened. I cannot remember much about it. I just went through the system. I did not think there was much interest taken in you as it was a big school. It was easy to get lost and perhaps not develop everybody's potential. I was just there with a mass of other people (Jayne).

The size of a school was a factor which also affected participants either negatively or positively: 'I hated the atmosphere of a large comprehensive and the standard of my work fell to a level at which there was no point in taking examinations' (Jayne).

Joyce attributed her success and enjoyment of learning to the fact that she attended a small comprehensive enabling teachers to give pupils greater individual attention.

Two participants spent all or part of their school career at a private school. Kate left a comprehensive school at the age of thirteen to attend a private school. She much preferred this because the peer group ethos was one which stressed the importance of schoolwork : 'you did not get beaten up if you did work' (Kate). Despite this she did feel out of place at the private school. Lacking in confidence she believed that the other pupils were more intelligent than her. Only one participant, Duncan, spent his entire school career at private schools which included a top public school (Marlborough). He is now studying a BAQTS degree in arts education to become a teacher.

Reflecting upon their school experiences many of the women believed that their educational aspirations and, hence their life chances, were constrained by being female. For most this situation was compounded because they were also working-class. Throughout their early lives gender and class relationships interacted to limit educational and occupational opportunities. A traditional low-paid female job followed by marriage and motherhood were the limits of their horizon. In the interviews many revealed that their parents did not encourage them to work hard at school and actively discouraged them from staying on after the compulsory school age. Sarah, who left school with no qualifications, summarises:

> I got no encouragement from my parents. In those days from a working-class background the idea was that you worked for a few years and then got married (Sarah).

Helen who enjoyed learning at school, particularly literature and mathematics, stressed that she had to leave school at the age of sixteen because of parental attitudes and her class background:

> My parents were very much of the idea that the girls belong in the house and the boys at work. The idea was that my brother would go to college. There was never any intention that I would go. I actually started work the day I left school. We left school in the morning and I started work that afternoon. That is how it was in our family. Education has never really been highly thought of (Helen).

She elaborated that her father: 'never thought that education was worth it all' and that women should 'keep to the kitchen sink' (Helen). Her brother went to college although he did not want to go. She always resented the unfair treatment between the sexes by her parents as she had aspirations to continue her education. Similar problems were expressed by younger working-class women. Working-class attitudes and values have not significantly shifted in the 1990s. Karen, in her early twenties, obtained eight O levels and two A levels and was offered a place at a higher education institution for a Higher National Diploma (HND) in business studies. Her school, a comprehensive, encouraged its pupils to enter higher education. This conflicted with the views of her working-class parents who did not want her to go to college. To them education, particularly for a girl, was pointless. During this period her father, a miner, was made redundant and economic reasons prevented her from going to college. Karen deferred her place for a year but explained that she: 'used the circumstances as an excuse not to go'. Like many women she lacked confidence in herself. Living in a close-knit family and community she was frightened to go away to college. Karen finally decided not to leave home.

Jean successfully completed her A levels at the age of nineteen after spending a year ill with tuberculosis. Her choice of A levels, physics, mathematics and chemistry, was rare for women of her generation. Sciences, except for biology, were and still are regarded largely as male subjects. After leaving school she was compelled to go into industry because her parents could not afford for her to enter higher education. She did not resent this as she felt that she had been lucky to stay on at school into the sixth form as: 'it was quite a struggle for my parents for me to stop on at school and with being in hospital I was quite old' (Jean). At that time, she explains: 'it was quite easy to get a job with A levels in sciences. I did an Ordinary National Certificate (ONC)' (Jean). Her first choice was a sandwich course in physics but she became a victim of sex discrimination. Dunlop, her employers, would only fund males. Several years later she achieved her goal of a degree in science and technology through the Open University. Now Jean is taking a part-time degree in social science: 'to get away from engineering'.

Male Experiences of Schooling

Several of the male participants also recognised that their working-class background had impeded their educational opportunities. Working-class male youths in the 1960s and 1970s were expected to leave school because of economic necessity for a life of manual work. Leaving school with some educational qualifications opened up the possibility of obtaining an apprenticeship and a skilled job. Peter, who came from a family of six, left secondary modern school at the earliest legal age without any qualifications summarises:

> The family needed the money a wage could bring, so I did not think of staying on at school. Times were hard and we did not have any money (Peter).

Realising that without qualifications he would be limited to unskilled work for the rest of his life he started to study for O levels and other examinations. Bob, together with most of his friends, also left secondary modern school at the age of fifteen without qualifications although he had enjoyed studying English and history. Bob recalled that his headmaster asked him to stay on at school to take examinations: 'but my father soon put paid to that one'. He expressed his criticism of the tripartite education system and astutely observed that:

> The education at that time was basically geared towards producing machine fodder. Basically that was the education you had and you knew there was a job there and that there was quite a lot of money that could be earned at a young age. The whole thing about education was which factory were you going to go into. The age you were and the way that parents were you never even considered staying on (Bob).

For him the hierarchical nature of the education system which sorted pupils according to ability and future jobs was clear. His experiences of education and work closely reflected Bowles and Gintis' (1976) theory on education as a means of reproducing class relationships within capitalist society. Working-class realism resigned Bob to the fact that as a young working-class person he was powerless to change this. The relationship between working-class culture and working-class jobs is extensively explored by Willis (1977):

> One should not underestimate the degree to which 'the lads' want to escape from school - the 'transition' to work would be better termed the 'tumble' out of school - and the lure of the prospect of money and cultural membership amongst 'real men' beckons very seductively as refracted through their own culture (Willis, 1977: 100).

Another male participant was also aware of the class element in education and recalled:

> I did not reach my potential and I was unhappy at how I was treated by teachers. With hindsight I realise that I was not of the right social group to do well at that school (2+2).

The dominant attitude among male participants towards schooling was one of indifference. Paul explained: 'I neither disliked it or enjoyed it. It was something that I had to do'.

Staying On or Leaving School

Common experiences were shared by the working-class women and men in this study, in particular the lack of autonomy in deciding their own futures. Several expressed a desire to their parents to stay on at school into the sixth form. Others would have liked to enter higher education but cultural and economic reasons mitigated against this. Schools frequently conflicted with parents but it was a power struggle which teachers lost:

> I did not have a choice about staying on at school. I had to do what my parents wanted. I was told to work at the age of fourteen. It was a very sad time as school was encouraging me and it conflicted with my parents (Pamela).

Some of the women did remain in education, again at their parents' insistence, to take a vocational course at an FE college. The courses were gender-associated: secretarial, nursing, fashion modelling. Many found them boring, undemanding and unfulfilling. Cathy explicitly stated: 'I did the secretarial course like a good girl and went to work in a bank which I hated as well'. Another woman, explaining how she became a secretary recalled: 'I was just sort of pushed in that direction and my dad seemed to think it was a good thing to do, suitable for a girl'. Kate's father gave her the choice between a hairdressing or secretarial course and she opted for the latter. Like many of the women in this study she found the secretarial course boring and frequently did not attend college. She was able to do this as her parents were living and working abroad. 'There was no motivating force keeping me there so I came and went and there was not a lot they could do about it' (Kate).

Ethnicity became a factor in deciding the future of an Afro-Caribbean woman. Hyacinth's mother wanted her to become a nurse. She was accepted at a nursing college but her father intervened. He declared that, 'all black women were going in for nursing' and told her that she had to do something else. Office work was the only other choice open to her but it was not what Hyacinth would have chosen. Her relationship with her father was antagonistic. Shortly after commencing the secretarial course, which she disliked, Hyacinth became pregnant.

In the 1960s and early 1970s finding employment was not a problem for school leavers. Many young people left school at the age of 15 or 16 because they were attracted by the prospects of earning a wage and the independence it would bring. Peer group pressure was also a strong influencing factor in the decision to leave school at the end of compulsory schooling. For some families finding employment was an economic necessity. If a job became boring it was possible to leave and enter another. Finn observes:

> The attraction of leaving school enhanced after the war by vastly improved material prospects for the young working-class....early leaving was eminently sensible in the context of full employment where education was of little relevance to their actual destinies (Finn, 1987:43).

With an abundance of jobs available many young people believed that they did not need educational qualifications. As a result some drifted into jobs without considering their futures. As the eldest of three, Joyce, whose parents could not afford for her to remain at school, despite her enjoying school stated that: 'I did not consider staying on but I also did not know what I wanted to do' (Joyce). A careers teacher arranged a job interview for her at a department store to work as a member of the display team. Paul poignantly summarised the situation of working-class male youths in the 1970s:

> At school I did it because I had to. I think that as a child at that time we did it because we had to and did not think this is important because I have got

to get a job at the end of it. Getting a job then was not difficult as it is now. When I applied I went to the job centre as I had half an hour to spare and wanted something to do and I applied for the job at GEC and got it. The idea of I have got to do well, the better I do, the more chance I have got of getting a job- there was not really that in the 1970s (Paul).

Jayne explained that leaving school at the age of sixteen was the norm: 'it was just what everybody did'. She was acutely aware of how careers teachers channelled girls into limited female occupations:

You went to the careers adviser and if you had O levels you became a nurse or joined the Civil Service and if you had A levels they assumed that because you were a woman you would go and become a teacher. That was really it. You went one of two ways (Jayne).

Ann explained that she had wanted to stay on at school after the age of 16 because she wanted to enter the teaching profession but:

The type of background I came from you just did not do that. You left at 16 and went to work. I look back now and think I could have got a part-time job and put myself through college. At that time it was all or nothing. You stayed on and did that or you left and did that (Ann).

Ethnicity, Gender and Class: A Case Study of Two Women

Racism was a significant factor in the educational experiences of two women, both of whom immigrated to England in their teens: one from Barbados and the other from Hong Kong. The Afro-Caribbean woman (Hyacinth), in her forties, explained that her schooldays in Barbados contrasted sharply with those in England. In Barbados she attended a comprehensive school which she enjoyed despite the strict discipline. Education was highly valued and Hyacinth stressed that: 'my parents were anxious that we should all do well'. In contrast when she came to England at the age of 15 she explained:

I felt that I was cheated in a way with my education because I could have done better. I could have perhaps gone straight into an O level class if I had been given the opportunity and I probably could have come out with O levels and gone on to do A levels but the opportunity was not there (Hyacinth).

Lynne, from Hong Kong, arrived in England at the age of fourteen. As a child she valued education and enjoyed learning. Education was important to Lynne but this conflicted with her parents' attitudes:

> My mother thought there was no point in women being educated because they should get married. Hong Kong is a highly education oriented society but there is still the belief in society that it is not so important for women to get educated as they get married and someone looks after them (Lynne).

Like Hyacinth, Lynne was not prepared for the racism that she experienced from pupils at school in England. For the Afro-Caribbean and Chinese women gender and class inequalities were superimposed by racial inequalities. Being Afro-Caribbean or Chinese had constrained their educational opportunities in England more than being female.

Reflections on Higher Education

A minority of participants continued after the compulsory school leaving age to take A levels either in a school sixth-form or at an FE college. Some were accepted by higher education institutions but were unable to go because of economic and cultural factors. Jill worked for a year after finishing her A levels before applying for a university degree course. At the end of the first term Jill left as: 'I was unhappy there as I had been working'. She admitted that her mother was very upset when she left university and:

> she cried as they were really proud of me going to university. I was the first person in the family to go to university. They just accepted what I wanted to do and she said as long as you are happy that is it (Jill).

Changes in her family life also played a role. After university she started a nursing course training but failed to complete it:

> Then I drifted around doing all sorts of jobs. I was very confused at this time, bewildered, not happy. I wanted to travel and go to Israel. I did that and came back, worked on the coast in a hotel, met lots of friends and could not get back into studying. My parents had split up just before and I think this made me unsettled because I did not know who to live with or where to go. I just drifted around and then later on got married and had kids (Jill).

Kate was offered a place on an HND course but she failed her A levels and drifted into a secretarial course instead. Some of the women did not consider higher education at the age of 18 either because they lacked confidence in their own ability or they did not want to live away from home. Dalvinder reflected:

> I just thought that I was not clever enough for that sort of thing. I was not confident. I would never have considered something like that. I just thought that I was far too inadequate for higher education (Dalvinder).

A grammar school woman also lacked confidence in her academic ability and consequently did not consider applying for higher education courses:

> I just wanted to get out of the school environment. I had worried so long about achieving, there was no way that I was going to put myself into that situation again (Sue).

Although her parents did not put pressure on her to go to university, despite obtaining a baccalaureate, she feels that they would have been happy if she had, but as far as she was concerned it was not an option. Others wished that their parents had put more pressure on them to enter HE. Jayne, despite obtaining several O levels, decided that: 'I did not want to go away and leave home. I was quite happy just to go to work'. At that moment in her life she made the decision that she did not require A levels for a job.

A small number of the younger men in the sample had considered higher education as an option but other factors intervened. Mike, for example, from a working-class background, had intended to take A levels and enter higher education but after a summer job at the age of 16 he decided to remain in employment. He had not seriously considered university as: 'it was one of those things which people talked about' (Mike). Mike later studied A levels part-time in the evening at college.

Returning to Education as an Adult

Half of the participants returned to some form of learning before embarking on a degree course. The type of courses attended were wide-ranging: GCSEs, A levels, return to learn, Access, Open Studies, HND, Open University foundation and degrees and work-related courses. Enjoyment of learning, self-development, reaching their educational potential and the need for educational qualifications for employment/career enhancement were the main reasons expressed for re-entering education. Returning to study stimulated interest in learning as one woman stated: 'it was a new world to me'. Learning was and is a positive experience. Once they sampled learning as an adult they were keen to progress and turned their educational aspirations towards obtaining a degree. This attitude cut across gender:

> I have been a shop steward for 21 years and senior shop steward for ten years. The opportunity to look objectively at the relationship of waged labour to capital was an exciting prospect. Having completed the certificate course (Open Studies) I was hooked and enjoyed it so much that my current course was a natural progression (Bob).

Access courses are becoming a popular route of entry into universities for adult students although some admissions tutors in the old universities consider that Access credits are an inferior and inadequate mode of entry. Four students in this study chose Access courses as a route into higher education. Taking an Access course gave them confidence to build up their study skills after having been out of the education system for several years to apply to university. One participant described her Access course as 'excellent':

> It is exciting and fresh learning new things, for example, sociology. I enjoyed being with other students and a feeling of OK I missed out while at school but now I am making up for it (Sarah).

Studying can cause friction between partners and put stress on a relationship. For Kate, this began when she was studying on an Access course. Her husband informed her: 'no way I'm not having it, you have got to go out and earn some money'. Kate was forced into employment and had to complete the course by evening study. The conflict resurfaced when she began the 2+2 degree course. Another Access student, Helen, faced adversity while studying . Despite having to cope with the death of her father and the subsequent illness of her mother she managed to pass the course.

Dalvinder opted to take A levels (sociology and psychology) as this suited her employment situation, although she found it hard work combining studying with a full-time job. The A level subjects were more theoretical than she realised. Looking back, another woman, Sue, who took two A levels regretted not having opted for an Access course. Studying A levels equipped her to write essays but she believes she would have acquired a wider range of study skills through an Access course. In contrast, Sally, took a Higher National Certificate (HNC) course in business studies as a route into education as an adult but confessed: 'I do not know why I chose that. It was just that I wanted to get back into education and wanted to do something' (Sally). Later she completed an Open University foundation course in social science while working full-time.

Participants were asked if they would have preferred to go to university at the age of eighteen rather than as an adult. On reflection most were glad that they had entered university later in life. For example, one person commented: 'but in retrospect I think I have more to offer now, I am more committed and more keen and motivated'. While Sally stated: 'I am glad that I have gone to university now rather than at 18. Quite honestly I do not think I would have stuck at it at that age'. Judith initially wished that she had gone to university at the age of 18 but now having experienced being a student she enjoyed studying late in life and was not looking forward to it ending because: 'I enjoy being a student' (Judith). Some regretted being denied access to knowledge and learning earlier in their lives:

> I have not got the stamina that an 18 year old has. Its made me live with regret - why were all things hidden from me. Why did I get to 40+ before I went to university. No one before has shown me what life is about. I have learnt so much (Pamela).

As parents several were hoping that studying would encourage and motivate their children to enter higher education. A culture of learning is being embedded in families which may not have previously considered higher education as a possibility for their daughters and sons. Cathy declared that: 'besides enjoying learning I have been able to help my sons in their education,' while Pamela noticed that: 'it helps me to communicate with my teenager who is doing A levels and we have so much to talk about'. Judith stated: 'I am finding out about study skills and my daughter knows that she can talk to me about her education'. Friends are also being inspired to study for a degree, some of whom have taken positive steps in this direction. Studying as an adult has 'spin-off' effects for the family and community.

Studying for a degree was an important event in the lives of all the participants. It was an opportunity to fulfil their educational potential, a situation which many felt was denied them in initial schooling largely because of gender and class factors. As one student remarked it is: 'a chance to redress my lack of education from earlier years', while Hyacinth stated: 'there was always the idea that I could have achieved more from education'. Adult education offered them a second chance. Some were deferential in their attitude, grateful that Warwick had provided them with the chance to study:

> The opportunity to learn is such a privilege, especially to get a second chance if you did not or could not do it previously. I love the environment of the campus and feel privileged to be part of it (Cathy).

Similarly Paul expressed his thoughts:

> To be part of an institution with the reputation of Warwick. I am pleased to be part of it. To be given a second chance to achieve my goal, aims and the people I have met make it all worthwhile (Paul).

Interviews with participants in the second year of their degree course revealed that many had a narrow view of education: achieving a first degree completed their formal education. This idea stems from attitudes concerning higher education formulated while at school. Since leaving school returning to education at some point in the future had been a prime goal to prove to themselves that they are capable of studying by achieving a degree, thus completing their education:

> The opportunity to take advantage of a system which for some is taken for granted but which for me at 18 was never an option (2+2 social studies, female).

Only a minority at this stage discussed the possibility of continuing with postgraduate or professional studies although they were acutely aware that the likelihood of this was remote because of financial constraints. For adult educators this offers an interesting contradiction as they perceive education as being lifelong with no finality yet some adult students do not share this view. However, at the second interview as the degree courses were nearing conclusion some of the participants no longer viewed a first degree as completing their education. More were contemplating participating in some form of educational study.

Reproduction or Empowerment?

The education system is characterised by a theoretical and ideological paradox as education has the potential to both reproduce and change social relations. This debate centres around macro-micro sociological issues. At the macro level education acts as a means of social reproduction; reproducing class, gender and race relations and inequality within a capitalist society (Althusser, 1972, Bourdieu, 1977, Bowles and Gintis, 1976, Willis, 1977, Barrett, 1987). Schooling is not about equality of opportunity, rather, it functions to grade people required for a social division of labour within a capitalist society. Education at the micro level, however, has the potential to liberate individuals and groups from oppression, empowering them to take control and change their lives and hence break out of class and gendered roles as outlined by theories of reproduction (Freire, 1972, Lovett, 1980,

Thompson, 1983). This perspective is firmly entrenched within certain traditions of adult education, community education and feminism. Both theories are valid. Rather than separating the two theoretical approaches they need to be synthesised to understand how education both reproduces the status quo and empowers for change.

Education is a dialectical process of interaction between the micro and macro levels. For education to empower particular sets of social, ideological and structural relationships are required. For example, a democratic rather than a hierarchical structure, a student-centred approach to teaching as opposed to a didactic one. Thompson (1983) points out that adult education reproduces class and gender relationships. While acknowledging that education is a means of social reproduction and social control, Thompson (1983) also argues that adult education has the potential to liberate and uses women's education as an example. Women's studies enables working-class women to reflect upon, learn about and change their gendered position within society. Within certain contexts it could, therefore, be argued that initial education largely reproduces social relationships while adult education has a greater potential to empower and change the lives of students.

Participants in this study were constrained at school by gender, class and race inequalities. Lack of parental encouragement and support for education were also critical factors. Educational aspirations had to be curtailed as education and qualifications were deemed unnecessary for a life of unskilled/semi-skilled work, marriage and motherhood. The women, and also men, were aware that schooling, together with family cultural expectations, had prepared them for a working-class life. As young people they accepted this role. A minority chose the attraction of an immediate wage rather than the deferred gratification that qualifications could bring only to regret this step later. Others showed signs of resistance to their prescribed gender role in wanting to continue in post-compulsory education. It was an impossible struggle to break out of a culture which did not value the education of girls. As young people their lack of power meant that they ultimately had to conform. Femininity and masculinity are socially constructed by school and the family. After leaving school many were determined at some point as adults actively to change their lives by completing their education. As one male 2+2 social studies student expressed it: 'to escape, in part, from the boring drudgery of working-class life'.

Gender was also a more significant factor than class in shaping the lives of most of the small number of middle-class women in this study. While they were more likely to stay on at school and study A levels, parental expectations did not aspire to a university education. Indeed only a small percentage of women entered university during the 1970s. For the women in this study education is empowering as it is a means of self-fulfilment, something for themselves which is not related to domesticity and low-paid, boring work. Acquiring knowledge has given these women greater power over their lives. Studying has enabled them to redefine their self-concept and their gendered position in society.

The women, therefore, have high expectations of what education can do for their lives. It is a powerful view of education and learning, contrasting sharply with their experiences of initial experience. Learning and wanting to learn remained an important goal in their lives, even among those who were not positive about school. Education was always something that they wanted to return to and complete. All began their degree course with high hopes; in anticipation that education would subjectively change their lives, and hopefully, take them out of their present structural location as a working-class woman. To what extent would studying and obtaining a degree fulfil these expectations?

6 Employment, Domesticity and the Quest for Fulfilment

This period (after the Second World War) saw the development of a contradiction between the need to expand the labour force, and the need to raise the birth-rate, and tangling with this were the new anxieties about the emotional well-being of children. Women have been the battle ground of this conflict within capitalist society ever since, for what has been attempted is to retain the mother as, in practice, the individual solely in charge of the day to day care of children and yet at the same time to draw married women, the last remaining pool of reserve labour, into the workforce (Bland, Brunsdon, Hobson and Winship, 1978:52).

Background: Linking Working and Domestic Lives

Women now consist of half of the workforce in Britain but their participation in the labour market is an unequal one. In early post-war Britain a woman's place was deemed to be in the home caring for her husband and children. Such ideology has remained powerful and dominant despite changes in the economy requiring female labour. A woman's role in the labour market is linked to domestic status: unpaid and paid work is intricately interwoven (Hartmann, 1981, Adkins, 1995). Similarly Arber and Gilbert assert that, 'the nature and extent of women's participation in waged work is intimately connected with their unpaid domestic labour as mothers' (Arber and Gilbert, 1992:1).

In contrast to male waged workers, female workers experience discontinuity in their paid working lives. Periods of employment are followed by time spent in the home childrearing. In Britain only 9% of women with children under the age of five work full-time. A higher number, 23%, work part-time. Once children reach school age one-fifth of women work full-time and 44% work part-time (quoted in Arber and Gilbert, 1992). Dex (1984) claims that it is a common trend for women to change to part-time employment after childbirth and frequently this is linked to downward occupational mobility. Women provide a cheap labour force as their gendered position in society pushes many into low-paid and for some, part-time, female work. Many married women have both a paid and an unpaid job. Unpaid work in the home entails servicing the needs of men and the socio-economic system by looking after present and future workers. Delphy and Leonard maintain that:

> Marriage...gives husbands rights to the unlimited use of wives' work and wives' familial duties involve an obligation to devote whatever of their time and energy is needed to provide whatever their husbands require (Delphy and Leonard, 1992:118).

Entering the Labour Market

The working lives of the married women in this study followed a traditional gender pattern: low-paid female work interspersed by periods in the home bringing up children. Once children were of school age several women returned to the labour market as part-time workers. Upon leaving school all women, except three, entered traditional female jobs. Sharpe (1994) found a similar pattern amongst her sample of working-class female school-leavers in the 1970s:

> The jobs they chose reflected, of course, the jobs that were normally open to them: these, in turn, were usually extensions of their 'feminine' role and exploited some supposedly 'feminine' characteristic (Sharpe, 1994:167).

Changes in the economy in post-war Britain resulted in many working-class women moving away from factory to office work. A large proportion chose clerical work because of either parental pressure or lack of other options. Gender and class inequalities prevented some from launching into a professional career. Finding employment was not a problem. Work offered freedom and economic independence but many participants viewed it as a temporary state until marriage and children. Office work equipped the women with some skills such as typing, enabling them to return relatively easily to employment after having children. As Sharpe observes:

> In the early 1970s, the great popularity of secretarial and general office work was based on its considered suitability for girls, and the relative ease of entry...It is a clean and respectable job (Sharpe, 1994: 161).

Others became shop assistants, waitresses or worked in hotels. One became a postlady. Two opted for non-traditional jobs, one as a laboratory technician who later trained to become an engineer. The other accepted an apprenticeship with the Gas Board. Lynne, from Hong Kong, followed her personal ethnic interests and became a community development worker with the Chinese community.

A small minority drifted from one low-paid job to another, in some cases moving around the country. Helen, for example, moved to escape from an authoritarian father. She left school at the age of sixteen, naive about the world of work. Her first job was in Coventry as a florist assistant. After working for two months Helen realised that she was entitled to receive payment and discovered that her father had been collecting her wages. On a works holiday to Devon she decided not to return home. In Devon she worked at a holiday camp but later moved to Wales to work in a hotel. Eventually returning to Coventry she changed to manual employment to work in the same factory as her mother; a gas fitters. After a year she was made redundant but quickly found work in a bingo hall. She soon left because of health reasons. Finally she settled for office work. Sarah, a single woman in her late forties, left office work to migrate to Spain where she worked first as a nanny and then as a teacher of English in a primary school. She returned to England because of the illness and subsequent death of her mother. A few years later she worked abroad again, this time for an aid agency in Africa. Her final job before returning to study was as a senior care worker for the elderly. Sarah achieved upward mobility within the occupational structure although remained within a feminine sphere of work. The single women in this study were more focused on their work career than the married women, as work rather than the family was the dominant institution in their lives.

Entering the Labour Market From a Male Perspective

A traditional gender work pattern was also the norm for the men in this study, most of whom became manual workers. Some gained apprenticeships in engineering and car manufacturing industries. One person, Ben, who left school without qualifications, entered the army. For working-class boys this was one route open to them for learning a trade. Adam, in his sixties, explained how he became an office boy:

> Because of my father's friendship with transporters, I went in as an office boy, 'a dogsbody', in an office which was expanding because this was the beginning of the war. I was only with them for four months because my

parents had separated and I moved from one parent to the other, changing location and town (Adam).

He was later to become a draughtsman. Adrian, after leaving school having failed his A levels, worked at a summer camp in the USA and decided to stay working with disabled young people in New York until his visa expired. In contrast Duncan, who attended public school, explained that he entered banking through the 'old boy's network' as his mother's father was in banking. Lack of educational qualifications, and working-class backgrounds, constrained the occupational choices of the majority of the men in this study.

Experiences of Work: Gendered Employment

In the 1970s cultural attitudes accepted that women should work until marriage and/or motherhood. All of the married women, both working and middle-class, in this study followed this pattern. There was an unquestioning acceptance that work followed by motherhood was a woman's role in life. Paid work was not a rewarding experience for the majority of participants, particularly those who entered office work. As Arber and Gilbert point out:

> Without a change in the domestic division of labour and with women constrained to low-status, low paid, often part-time jobs, waged work may have little liberating effect for women. It may simply increase their burden and severely curtail or eliminate any 'unobligated' time (Arber and Gilbert, 1992:7).

To some extent motherhood offered an escape from an alienating existence at work. Work was perceived as boring, lacking in autonomy and low-paid. Sarah, who left school without qualifications, explained that she derived no job satisfaction from office work:

> To me it was a means to an end. You got your wage packet at the end of the week. The job was boring but at that age I did not have any ambitions or direction (Sarah).

At the age of 25 she went to live in Spain working as a nanny and later as a teacher. These two posts imbued her with a positive attitude towards employment. She elaborated:

These two jobs gave me a different outlook. I realised that I was good working with people as opposed to pushing paper but I returned to an office job in England for the next five years (Sarah).

Working in Spain made her realise that she did not want office work again although she had to temporarily accept employment in this field because of economic necessity. She discovered that her vocation resided in social work; working with people. Employment in the caring professions is also a traditional female job reflecting the caring role of women in the home. It is gendered work but Sharpe (1994) stresses that, 'being concerned with people is a very positive aspect of 'femininity'. Another participant also expressed a preference for 'contact with people rather than dealing with machines' (Helen) and this desire eventually propelled her into voluntary work.

Others also experienced alienation in clerical work. One woman, Sally, upon leaving school with one A level, joined the Treasurers' Department at a county council but only stayed for three months. She elaborated that 'I got married because that seemed like the answer to all my problems' (Sally). The post should have included a training scheme but as Sally explained:

> Work was a bit of a culture shock. I was taken on for three months for training, trying out different departments before deciding which one to work in. No supervision was given and I ended up just filing. I left after this (Sally).

After marrying at an early age she worked part-time in a newsagents until she had her first child. Marriage provided an escape from an unrewarding and undemanding job. Karen decided to work for the Department of Health and Social Security (DHSS) as a clerical assistant after rejecting a place at a higher education institution. Initially she found the job stimulating while she was in the learning stage but 'it soon became routine, boring and non-challenging' (Karen). Other participants expressed similar sentiments: 'I found it boring just sitting in an office and being called in to take dictation' (Hyacinth). Being Afro-Caribbean Hyacinth also had to contend with other factors at work: 'I can not say that I really came across a lot of racism but there were things there and you dealt with it and did not let it get to you' (Hyacinth). Another stated: 'I found office work in a bank boring. I hated sitting in an office' (Cathy). Kate moved to join her parents in Saudi Arabia after completing a secretarial course where she found that with being white she could: 'Get a job (a secretary) and be paid ridiculous amounts of money. I also got married and worked over there for five years. I did not enjoy the work but it paid a lot of money for not doing a lot' (Kate).

Three participants enjoyed clerical work. Their job satisfaction stemmed from two factors; gaining promotion or contact with people. After leaving school Jenny studied for a medical secretary diploma: a course which she found stimulating. In reflecting about her first job as a medical secretary she stated:

> I enjoyed the job immensely. The job was very satisfying and especially the involvement with children at the children's hospital. I was given a fair amount of responsibility but there was no prospect for advancement at all - that was it (Jenny).

Lack of promotion prospects led her to seek another clerical post in a solicitors' office. Jenny started legal executive training to improve her career chances but realised that for her contact with people was an important aspect of job satisfaction:

> I enjoyed that very much and found law fascinating but I missed the contact I had with people. It was very formal and all rules and regulations. I thought I do not know if I could spend all my life sitting in an office doing this (Jenny).

Pamela experienced several jobs before applying for office work. After getting married she completed a Royal Society of Arts (RSA) course. The qualification enabled her to obtain a better position where she was promoted to 'head girl' in the office until the birth of her first child. At this point in her life she declared, 'I was very happy as it fulfilled my intentions' (Pamela).

Office work was a popular choice among the women in this sample and reflected the national trend among women of this age group. However a minority did choose other occupations. Joyce explained that she drifted into becoming a member of a display team at a department store in London. Her careers teacher at school arranged the job for her. She remained there for fifteen years because she found it an 'excellent job'. Joyce gained promotion and became assistant display manager but her career in this field ended upon the birth of her first child.

Upon returning to Coventry from a nursing course in London, Lynne accepted a post at a Chinese school. This job gave a purpose to her life in England as she had not been happy since migrating to England from Hong Kong:

This gave me a clear direction. I wanted to work with people and I wanted to help disadvantaged Chinese people. I then worked as a community development officer in Coventry. It was an enjoyable work experience which opened up my mind about policy issues. I worked in this post for three years (Lynne).

Her fourth and present post, a community liaison worker at a women's unit, 'has made me more aware of the issues and difficulties which women face' (Lynne). She has become politicised as a result of working both with the Chinese community and with women, raising her awareness of inequalities in society.

Two women broke free from gender constraints and chose non-traditional jobs which in the context of the 1960s and 1970s deviated from the norm. Both encountered sexism in male dominated workplaces. Ann obtained an apprenticeship with the Gas Board. She viewed the apprenticeship instrumentally: it was a means to gain further qualifications and earn money. The work was enjoyable once she got use to it. 'It was hard and difficult being only one of two females in a male world. It was useful experience but I did experience sexism from the male students - not the lecturers' (Ann). After completing the first year of an HND she left because she did not find the work experience side interesting. Staying within the energy industry she moved to the Coal Board to become a laboratory technician where she remained until she had a family.

Jean, in contrast, left grammar school with three science A levels. She obtained an ONC while working for a large company. After marrying she changed jobs to work as a laboratory technician for an engineering firm where she discovered that engineers received higher pay than technicians. She took steps to become an engineer by studying for a science and technology degree with the Open University. Now in her late forties she continues to work as an engineer although her career has been interrupted by periods of childrearing. Over the years Jean has become accustomed to working in a male domain but remarked:

I have got use to it being male-dominated but occasionally I look round and think I am the only woman working in this area. There are not many women of my age in engineering (Jean).

She has remained in full-time employment while studying part-time for a second degree in literary studies. It was a conscious decision to move away from engineering.

Paid employment was, therefore, not a liberating experience for most women in this study. As unskilled or semi-skilled workers work offered only boredom, monotony and low wages. There was a shared sense of frustration together with a belief that they were capable of doing something better. McLaren (1985) found a similar set of attitudes among the mature women students in her study:

> It provided a wage and (in most cases) sociability, but, in general, it was not socially useful, personally meaningful, nor did it promise any future in terms of promotion, increased responsibility and better pay (McLaren, 1985:64).

This contrasted sharply with the minority of women who were in professional jobs as work did provide them with job satisfaction and self-fulfilment. Returning to study offered this group the opportunity to enhance their work prospects in their existing occupation. The married women's working lives were characterised by disjunctions in a way in which married men's working lives were not.

For the working-class women, in particular, inequalities in the labour market created economic dependence upon men in the family. Marxist feminists (Beechey, 1977, Gardiner, 1977, Barrett, 1980) maintain that oppression in the workplace and family results from the dual relationship that women have to the class structure:

> The education and training that a woman receives by virtue of her class background provide a highly significant contribution to the position she will occupy in the labour force. Yet it is equally clear that the relationship she has to the class structure by virtue of her wage labour will be substantially influenced by the mediation of this direct relationship through dependence on men and responsibility for domestic labour and childcare. For working-class women this may result in simultaneous direct exploitation by capital via their own wage-labour and indirect exploitation via vicarious dependence on the wage of a male breadwinner. For bourgeois women this may result in simultaneous ownership of, yet lack of control over, capital (Barrett, 1980:139).

The women in this study were discontented with working for low wages and later became disillusioned with domesticity and remaining in the home childrearing. Education, as Barrett points out, contributes to their class and gendered position of women yet as adults participants perceived education as a solution to the exploitation and contradictions they experienced at work and in the family.

Men and the Labour Market

The men's occupations also followed traditional class and gender patterns, ranging from unskilled to skilled work. Those in their thirties and forties worked in the traditional industries of the region; engineering and motor cars. Two, Bob and Peter, moved from the shopfloor to become trade union convenors. Others expressed a commitment to their trade union which the women did not. The women discussed work in relation to their private lives in the family while men related work to the public world. The men were more politicised in their views concerning employment and several adhered to traditional Labour Party ideology.

Bob has been a full-time trade union convenor for ten years. He began his working career in heavy engineering. He reflected that: 'My first job was enjoyable and well paid and the hours were short. My standards of living as a young man were higher than most of my friends' (Bob).

He received training during his first job and when the factory closed down he was offered a managerial post but, 'it was not acceptable with my political thoughts. They wanted me to go to South Africa, I could not do that (because of Apartheid)' (Bob). Bob was the only male who mentioned, although briefly, his domestic life while talking about his working life. He revealed: 'I was married, like most people in the period at that time. It was the thing to get married young' (Bob). Becoming a trade union convenor was a release from engineering work which he did not find enjoyable: 'being off the shopfloor for ten years does change a lot of perspectives' (Bob). He carried on a family tradition as both his father and grandfather had been trade union convenors.

Peter left secondary modern school at the age of fifteen, hoping to obtain an apprenticeship at a car factory. He did not achieve this and ended up accepting a job on the assembly line. Like the men in Beynon's (1973) study of Ford workers, Peter found working on the assembly line dehumanising. He now works full-time for the trade union; a job that he finds more fulfilling than assembly line work.

Adam achieved upward mobility in his work career by studying part-time to qualify as a mechanical engineer. He elaborated, 'I started as an apprentice, which to a certain extent in those days was cheap labour' (Adam). After six years of part-time study he achieved his goal of gaining engineering qualifications, including being made a fellow of mechanical engineering. The qualifications enabled him to obtain a senior post with a multi-national company. Despite this something was still missing in his life. He explained:

I had a very interesting working life but I always felt that I missed out in more general education and certainly I would have been a very excellent, patient university student in my younger days (Adam).

Paul completed a City and Guilds course in electronics, not for intrinsic enjoyment but to enable him to obtain a job. He found the seven years he spent working in a factory alienating:

It was a factory setting. You go in from 9 until 5, do what you are told and leave. It was very monotonous work. Same thing day in and day out. The only interest came when something went wrong with the job and you could enjoy yourself. There was not much appreciation and no chance of moving up. That was one of the reasons why I left. It became very staid. Redundancies were also looming. I decided I have had enough of this place, it is time to move on (Paul).

In complete contrast he moved on to work as a magician at a holiday camp for seven years. By his early thirties he decided that he could not continue as an entertainer for the rest of his life as the work is both seasonal and insecure. Studying for a teaching degree appeared to be a logical step as he had gained experience of working with children. Before entering the Bachelor of Arts Qualified Teacher Status (BAQTS) degree course he had to obtain GCSE mathematics and English and completed an Access course to upgrade his study skills.

A younger mature male student had to change career because of work injury. Steve left school at eighteen but continued to study for a Business and Technical Education Council (BTEC) diploma. After this he became a full-time cabinet maker until the age of 25. As a creative job he stressed that, 'it was very enjoyable and I benefited a great deal from it but I am glad I am no longer doing it' (Steve). As a single person he decided that he still had time to retrain, change career and achieve a professional qualification. He explained that it had to be, 'something that was in the real world' (Steve).

Duncan's work career and lifestyle contrasts sharply from those of the working-class participants. His family and upper middle-class background enabled him to walk into a well-paid post in banking. By the age of 34 he was an associate director of an American bank: 'I had a fabulous salary and a lovely car, a wonderful mortgage subsidy, a great office and I was in charge of a huge department but I was not happy' (Duncan). He declared that his third and current wife disliked him:

I took on the games that people play in corporate business. I was unpleasant. I thought nothing of sacking a few people or harassing them. I was very aggressive in terms of 'gold target' achievements which is what it is all about in sales. I was very good at it (Duncan).

Two of the younger men realised that they could not continue in work for the rest of their lives. Both had been expected to obtain A levels and enter higher education at the age of eighteen. Mike had been discontented with his job for five years but was trapped because he lacked qualifications and possessed no skills. He considered a range of educational options but was encouraged by his wife to apply for the 2+2 social studies degree course. Mike announced: 'It seemed like the ideal way to get back into education and you have got to grab it' (Mike).

Adrian worked in the United States of America (USA) until his visa expired. In England he accepted a post as auditor at a theme park. He recalled:

I decided I had to look for something. That is when I started looking back at education. It was a whim decision to be honest. I saw a teacher one night and I just suddenly thought this is probably going to be my way out of not working at Alton Towers for the rest of my life...the next thing I knew I was registered to go back (to school) to finish my A levels (Adrian).

Second-time round at school Adrian found that his teachers were very encouraging and 'I was prepared to stick it out'. At the age of twenty-one he just qualified for mature student status. His parents were elated as he was the first person in the family to go to university; 'my mum told just about everybody' (Adrian).

Many of the male participants shared with female participants a dislike of the world of production. Labour was viewed as unrewarding and stagnating in relation to personal development. The men had the advantages of higher pay and an uninterrupted work pattern, enabling some to undergo training at work to change their jobs in an upward direction or concentrate on a trade union career. For some of the married women their working life came second to their husband's jobs. Moving geographically because a husband changed occupations was not uncommon.

Into Domesticity: Being a Mother and Housewife

Early sociological studies viewed relationships and power inequalities in the private domain of the family as unproblematic. Arber points out:

The last twenty-five years have witnessed a paradigm shift in how sociologists conceive of relationships within the household, spurred by feminist sociological debate on gender inequalities and the private domain, previously largely invisible to sociologists (Arber, 1993:118).

Pahl's (1983) sociological study brought the issues of inequalities within the household onto the research agenda. Her study highlighted women's lack of access to and control of resources, particularly financial ones, within the family. The married women in this study were no exception. Economic power resided with their husband except in the case of two women whose husbands were unemployed.

Marriage and motherhood are important turning points in the life histories of women. These are both personal and collective experiences; ideology and structural forces define society's expectations of what constitutes being a wife and a mother. Most of the women in this study were married or lived with a partner. Those in their thirties or forties had children of varying ages. Marriage and motherhood were significant aspects in their lives as witnessed by the frequent references to both during the interviews. Discussions about family life were absent from the interviews with the male participants except for a small minority and those that did mentioned their family briefly. Family life did not impinge upon the men's lives in relation to employment and their decision to return to study as it did with the women in this sample.

Upon the birth of their first child the majority of women in this sample resigned from work. Jean, working in a professional field as an engineer, returned to work after the birth of each child. Economic factors meant that Hyacinth continued to work full-time as a secretary after the birth of her first two children. After having a third child she explained: 'I had to give up full-time work on the birth of my third child. I did not feel that I could continue with full-time work and three children' (Hyacinth). Instead she chose to become an auxiliary nurse working part-time to fit in with the schoolday. For most of the others class factors intervened. As Pam reflected: 'When I had my first child I chose, because of my upbringing, not to go back to work'.

Another participant also reached the same decision: 'I did not want to work as I wanted to be at home with my children' (Jayne). Gender socialisation is a powerful social process. Girls and women internalise the need to be a 'good mother'. As Sharpe emphasises, there:

> is the myth surrounding the importance of motherhood. Girls have long been brought up to believe that the most fulfilling thing in life

is to have children, and to be good mothers...It is taken for granted that a child needs its mother, and the mother needs to have her child (Sharpe, 1994:205).

Thus society views being a mother as natural. A woman has no room for negotiation with her partner over childcare. Motherhood is a significant factor in perpetuating inequalities and asserting male dominance within the family. Only unemployment of the husband allows women to gain economic and political power vis a vis their husbands. None of the women, middle or working-class, in this study questioned the fact that they, rather than their husbands, had to quit their jobs to look after the children. Neither did they suggest a sharing of roles with husbands. Parental responsibility remained largely one-sided. Wimbush (1987) illuminates:

> The coincidence of parental responsibility for childcare with the woman's part in childbirth has brought a tendency to 'naturalise' the social transitions that women experience in becoming a mother. Having to make sacrifices and stay at home more, are viewed as 'natural' aspects of this part of women's lives. This naturalisation of changes obscures the material and ideological forces which shape them and make gender the central relation structuring the experience of parenthood and 'family life' (Wimbush, 1987:150).

During the 1960s and 1970s powerful ideology in the mass media stressed the problems faced by 'latchkey children'; underpinned by the writings of psychologists like Bowlby (1947, 1969). Women were made to feel guilty if they were not 'good mothers and housewives'. Other factors reinforced cultural attitudes. Maternity leave was not encouraged by some firms, and as Sharpe (1994) notes, crèche facilities were and still are either non-existent or expensive. Motherhood and home dominated the lives of these married women upon the birth of their children:

> Gender inequalities remain unquestioned; women are the 'natural' carers of the home and children. If a woman's work conflicts with home-care, then she either has to give up her leisure time or her job (Arber, 1993:121).

Motherhood for some ended their work career. Jayne had worked for the Civil Service for nine years where she had been successful in gaining internal promotion. She has not undertaken any paid work since leaving the Civil Service to look after her children. However, she did complete a counselling course and became a foster parent, reinforcing further her caring role. Several other women participated in voluntary work while childrearing. Others returned to work on a part-time basis for economic reasons once children were of school age.

For two women, having a first child coincided with their partner obtaining a new job in a different part of the country. Joyce's husband, a fireman, decided to move out of London and back to his home-town in the Midlands shortly after the birth of their first child. Joyce enjoyed her job as an assistant display manager in a department store but with moving she had to sacrifice her career. After moving from London she spent six months at home with their child but claimed that, 'I was bored out of my brain, especially in a small town after London' (Joyce). In contrast Sue worked for the Employment Department in London where she had begun work as a clerical officer but soon gained promotion, eventually to become an executive officer. Her partner is a doctor and they had to move around the country for his training. There were no posts available at the Employment Department in the town they moved to so she looked after their daughter for three years. During this time she trained as a counsellor and undertook voluntary work. She had the advantage of being given special leave by the Employment Department and was able to resume her post on their return to London.

The period of time spent childrearing varied from a year to sixteen years. None had any regrets and many echoed the sentiments of Pam: 'I enjoyed this period. It was important to look after my own children. I saw this as a full-time job' (Pam). Remaining in the home gave the women space and time to reflect on their lives. In these cases reflection stirred them into acting positively about their lives. Staying at home also highlighted the contradictions of the housewife role. While childcare was viewed as enjoyable, housework and childrearing left them with no free time for themselves. Both were at times a lonely and boring experience. As Oakley points out in her classic study of housework: 'It is the isolation of women within the home and the privatized nature of the work which they perform which some women have articulated as being a site of oppression for them' (Oakley, 1974:59). The women looked for a solution to this problem. Education and, in particular, taking a degree would, it was hoped, fulfil this need.

Transitions and Turning Points: The Decision to Study for a Degree

A series of life transitions and critical incidents relating to early family life, initial schooling, work and marriage were catalysts in the decision to study for a degree. All the women shared the view that they wanted a more interesting and rewarding job. For the married women the decision was also tied up with the determination to escape a life of emptiness in the home, to spend time doing something for themselves and to make something of their lives. Intrinsic factors also played a role; the desire and enthusiasm to learn. Some adult educators (Aslanian and Bricknell, 1980, Cross, 1981) maintain that men express an instrumental view: men return to learn to improve job and promotion prospects while for women this is less important. This factor was dominant among the younger men in the study but not for those in their late forties and above. Changing and improving occupation was also cited by all the women although some maintained that it was not initially the dominant factor.

To understand why the women applied to university it is necessary to categorise them into two groups: those who are single and those who are married or who have been married with children. The need to differentiate between married and single women emerged from the women's stories as a key variable in this research. The married women took stock of their lives while childrearing and decided that it had to change direction. Jayne had not worked in paid employment since having children. Time in the home allowed her to reflect:

> I felt that I wanted to do something and I knew the children would be less dependent by the time I finish a degree and go back to full-time work. (They will be 13 and 15). My chances would be improved and it would finish at a convenient time. It is really just to improve my job prospects, whether that is going to happen or not is a different matter. I also did it because it was there; it was advertised; it was local and the first two years was convenient. Really that is why I did it because it was offered. It was just a convenient thing to do at the time (Jayne).

Her thoughts also reveal the multiple factors, both personal and structural, which shaped her and other participants' decision to return to learn. Sue, who worked for the Employment Department, stated that she had been considering a degree course for a long time:

> I think that even before I had my daughter and my partner I was beginning to get ideas that there was something I want to do with my life. I was quite interested in something like psychotherapy so I was beginning to toy with the idea of some sort of degree course. What I always thought I wanted to do was to get a degree course in something like psychology, not just in terms of the world of work but because I felt I would like to do something like that (Sue).

Sue had experience as a voluntary counsellor and now felt, in her thirties, that she had the confidence in her ability that she lacked at school. At this stage her partner was looking for a consultancy at a hospital. This factor determined which university she could apply for. 'I did not mind where he got a job as long as it was near to a university' (Sue). She was pleased when they moved close to the University of Warwick because of its reputation. Her application for a psychology degree course was unsuccessful but she did gain a place on her second choice, sociology.

Valerie also decided that her life was concentrated too much on home and work:

> It gives a different dimension to life apart from home and work. This venture is just for me, to justify me to myself if you like! You may probably describe it as a boost to one's ego (Valerie).

Housework was viewed as mindless and lacking in fulfilment. There was little evidence among respondents of a sharing of housework tasks between husband and wife. Husbands saw it as the wife's domain even if both worked and/or the wife was studying. Attitudes and practice do not appear to have changed since Oakley's early survey (1974). One participant described why she had decided to take a degree course:

> Freedom from mundane aspects of family life. Learning more about issues which affect and interest me. To increase my self-confidence and to provide a role-model for my children, especially my daughters (2+2 social studies).

Another respondent wanted to combine time for herself with childrearing:

> I decided that I did not want to spend so much time at home looking after my three and a half year old son. It was not doing either of us any good plus I just wanted to gain a degree (2+2 social studies).

Most of the married women were adamant that they did not want to return to office work. Once her children were older Hyacinth was determined to find an interesting job:

> I did not know exactly what I wanted to do. All I knew was that I did not want to go back into an office and be a secretary. There was always the idea that I could have achieved more from education but there was

the problem of how would I do it with the children being young. I did not think I could cope with it (Hyacinth).

Noticing an advertisement in a paper she applied for a place on the 2+2 social studies degree at the local college. 'I thought it sounded interesting and I have always been interested in politics etc.' (Hyacinth). One participant stressed that, 'I did not want to return to a sexist office environment' (full-time, sociology) while another stated: 'I did not want to return to a basic, boring job. I wanted to prove I could get the degree after seven years at home'.

Several women, both married and single, participated in some form of education before deciding to opt for a degree course. This both stimulated their enthusiasm for learning, making them want more, and revived thoughts that they had failed to reach their potential at school. Avril, a single parent, moved to the Midlands and obtained a job in interior design at a furniture store. Initially she viewed the job as short term but remained in this field for eight years as she found the work satisfying:

> It was always something I thought I would not be doing in two years time but I was. The job was creative and I had autonomy but I knew it was not the right thing. I needed something to stimulate me and to find out if I could do some proper studying. I thought I would give it a go (Avril).

Avril was conscious of not having worked at grammar school. To ease herself back into learning she completed an Open Studies certificated course at Warwick in Women's Studies, as she was interested in women's literature, before enrolling for a part-time degree. Financial reasons meant that she had to opt for a part-time degree course as she had to support her son. Cathy returned to part-time office work after her son started school but she 'hated sitting in an office'. However, her boss inspired her to return to learn. She explained that he was an 'educated man' who had been to Cambridge: ' He was a new breed to me. This sounds awful. I admired his mind and the way he thought about things that I never had before. It stimulated me to get keen on learning again' (Cathy).

School, Cathy felt, had not encouraged her to stay on and take A levels so she studied A level English while working part-time. Her part-time job finished and she was offered a full-time clerical post with good pay but: 'I did not like the thought of doing that for the rest of my life' (Cathy). Instead she chose an Access course and thoroughly enjoyed studying full-time. Valerie left secondary modern school at the age of fifteen where, she felt, she had been labelled a failure. Despite this she never lost the desire to learn. While looking after her children she studied part-time on various courses, GCSEs, RSA, and A level sociology, throughout the 1980s:

> This stimulated my interest in learning and I wanted to do something for myself. My children were becoming older and less dependent. I was interested in learning for its own sake and I wanted to see if I was capable of studying at degree level after being written off at the age of fifteen (Valerie).

Opening the Cracks: Marital Conflict

Returning to education contributed to marital problems for four women; leading to divorce in two cases. Others experienced a lack of support and non-co-operation once they began their studies. Leonard (1994) claims that one third of the mature women she interviewed in her study, 'met with considerable resistance from their husbands over their decision to return to education' (1994:172). The effects of women studying upon marital relationships is an area which needs further investigation within adult education. Pamela had enjoyed both working in an office and spending several years at home with the children. Both roles had given her fulfilment. Her personal contentment was undermined when she sampled a full-time course on electronics in office work at a local college. Her husband became unemployed so her objective was to upgrade her qualifications to improve her chances of getting a better clerical post. However, she was unable to complete the course as her husband obtained a job and once more assumed the role of earner in the family. Pamela was forced back into the home as the carer by her husband although at the time she accepted this role and thought 'it was the right thing to do'. Pamela's experience illustrates the potential power of education. Housework was no longer satisfying and conflict with her husband ensued:

> I no longer wanted to be the carer. I wanted learning as well. The learning had changed me and it was enjoyable. I realised that there are more opportunities in society for women. It was a whole new world to me (Pam).

Returning as a carer made her conscious that office work no longer provided her with job satisfaction. She persevered with learning and studied A level sociology in the evenings. Studying sociology awoke her gender consciousness and made her aware of the gender inequalities she had experienced throughout her life. This was a common phenomenon among several women:

I realised that I had wasted my life. I had been going down the wrong track. I never wanted to go in an office again. Sociology raised questions. I continued to look after the youngest child but it was a struggle because conflict was developing in the family. My husband wanted the wife at home with the children (Pamela).

She felt that her husband's attitudes were inevitable because of his working-class background. On reflection she explained that she felt exploited being told to go out to work by her husband when the family needed money and told to return to the home when her wages were not needed. She rationalised her situation by saying that: 'It was not his fault but that generation. I still find it a struggle but I am getting stronger at sticking at what I want' (Pamela).

Pamela responded to an advertisement in a local paper about the 2+2 social studies degree programme. The content interested her. It also had the advantage of being a daytime course which fitted in with school hours and would not disturb the servicing of her husband. Bird and West (1987) discovered similar reactions from husbands in their study of women returners:

> Much more common was the attitude of many husbands that they had no objections to their wife getting a job as long as it did not affect them in any way- in other words, as long as they did not have to cook, clean, pick up children, or stay at home if the children were ill (Bird and West, 1987:189).

A grant was a necessity as Pamela's husband refused to financially support her educational studies. Pamela and other women on the 2+2 course stated that the location of the teaching at a local college for the first two years was very influential in their decision to study for a degree.

With Kate, serious marital problems began before she applied for the 2+2 degree course. The family had lived in several geographical locations including abroad. When they moved to the Midlands she was staying at home looking after the children. Her husband wanted her to return to work for economic reasons. She decided that:

> The thought of going back to being a secretary was not wonderful and the kids were too young to leave so I reckoned that if I was going to do something I'd have to get on with it (Kate).

By this stage Kate had thought about leaving her husband and was confronted by the following comments: 'My husband would also come out with stupid comments like I could not leave anyway because I could not support myself and the children because I was not clever enough. That annoyed me' (Kate).

Returning to learn, Kate explained, 'happened without me thinking as I went to the careers office and said, right I do not want to be a secretary, suggest something'. She signed up for an Access course but her husband responded by saying: 'no way, I am not having it, you have got to go out and earn some money' (Kate). As a result she had to return to full-time employment and finish the Access course part-time in the evenings. Another 2+2 student, Joyce, demonstrated her resistance to her husband's opposition by divorcing him. She was bored as a housewife and mother and wanted to do something for herself as she succinctly explained:

> As a woman you're usually doing something that somebody else wants you to do, your mum or dad, child, husband, employer. I put my foot down and said I was doing it (a degree) (Joyce).

In response, her husband informed her that she had to choose between him or studying so she opted for the latter and left him. She reflected:

> It had a drastic effect upon my life. I moved from being a nuclear family to a single parent but I have never been happier. It really suits me. In marriage I was tied to the house and my life revolved around when my husband was there (Joyce).

Ironically divorce has resulted in her husband taking a greater responsibility in looking after their daughter at weekends and holidays. 'He is much more supportive now than when we married' (Joyce) as he took their daughter out when she was writing assessed essays. A full-time student, Sally, had been married for seven years. She disliked her part-time work intensely and had married to escape from paid employment. Sally felt she had underachieved at school, leaving with one A level. She recalled:

> When my two sons started school I started to look back on my life and thought I want to pick up the threads now and that was one of the reasons why my marriage broke down. My life and work was going nowhere. I wanted a challenge and a chance of a better future (Sally).

Before starting at Warwick she completed an HNC in business studies and an Open University foundation course in social science. A minority of women in this study had separated before contemplating returning to study:

> Once my daughter was of school age and having been a lone-parent for five years, I wanted to rebuild my life in the area of education and fulfil my ambition to work with society doing a job which was satisfying and rewarding (2+2 social studies).

These case studies illustrate the struggle which some women face in getting back into the education system. Recent evidence collected by the 2+2 Social Studies Academic Co-ordinator at Warwick highlights the increase in marital friction between female adult students and their spouses which in some cases is leading to separation. However, research is needed to investigate whether or not studying is the cause or the trigger as relationships may have been unstable before the women began their studies. Once on a degree course many married women had to study without the support of husbands. This attitude cut across class boundaries. Men appear to be threatened by 'clever women' and by the possibility that their economic power within the family may be undermined. None of the men in this study experienced resistance from their wives; they simply decided they were going to study and enrolled for a degree course.

Other Critical Factors

Several women realised that they had no desire to return to clerical work after a period at home. Two were encouraged to re-enter education by headteachers of secondary schools where they were working voluntarily. One joined a 2+2 course, the other, a single parent, a full-time sociology course. Another remarked that her decision had been an instrumental one to fulfil her aspiration of becoming a teacher, something she had wanted to do since the age of sixteen, 'but the type of background I came from you just did not do that sort of thing' (Ann). For another woman the reasons were more pragmatic:

> Three years ago my husband had a heart attack and we have got four young children. I was really frightened if he had another one and I was stuck with four kids. I needed a decent job and thought about it. I thought I would be all right as a teacher. It is not a lifelong ambition but just a means of supporting my children. I am also fed up with being a waitress (Jill).

Like many mature students she was limited geographically in her choice of universities. After obtaining mathematics GCSE she applied to Warwick as she liked the course and it was ideal because she 'could not afford to travel far' (Jill). Economic factors influenced another participant to improve her educational qualifications:

> The employment situation, that is, my husband's lifetime employment is not guaranteed. I want to be able to share financial responsibility for the family and thereby remove some pressure from my husband (full-time, arts education).

Most of the unmarried women chose to continue in employment and study part-time. This group, with the exception of one woman, were younger than the married women as they were in their twenties. However, most of the married women had been married at that age thus reflecting generational and class differences between the two groups. One of the younger females was living with her boyfriend. The unmarried women chose to study for a degree to either escape from an unrewarding job or to enhance career prospects within their existing employment. As Karen explicitly explains:

> I was fed-up at work (the Department of Health and Social Security (DHSS)). I wanted to get further qualifications so I can get a better job. I also wanted to study as it was a legitimate reason to leave work and I wanted a full-time break from work (Karen).

Dalvinder initially decided to stay in full-time employment as a tax clerk for an accountants firm. For her the work had become routine and boring; 'I could not do work like this for the rest of my life' (Dalvinder). However, to quicken the pace of obtaining a degree she resigned from her job to study full-time for her final year. One woman wanted a part-time degree course to develop her theoretical understanding of the practical issues she deals with working as a community worker at a women's unit:

> After having worked on the front-line for a few years I thought I had a good understanding of what the issues were but I needed the theory and the time to read what other people say. I am generally looking for answers. I also wanted to be in a better position to read policy-makers' minds (Lynne).

She had always planned to return and continue her education as soon as possible. Two men also chose part-time degree courses in labour studies for similar reasons to facilitate their trade union work.

Another woman, Sarah, quit a well-paid job as a senior care assistant as she decided that now was the time for her to 'finish her education': 'Over the past ten years the fact that I had not completed my education niggled me. I wanted to test myself and fulfil myself in this other area' (Sarah). Jenny worked full-time as a trainee manager in the health service but has always felt that her vocational goal was to become a teacher: 'I have always had a mission to teach in a primary school. A primary school teacher had a big effect on me as she helped me through my father's death' (Jenny). She received support from her employers; payment of fees and one day a week for studying. This factor persuaded her to study part-time rather than full-time.

Moving from Work and Domesticity to University

Discontent with their working and domestic lives and failure to reach their educational potential in school were salient factors in the decision by many women in this study to return to education. In contrast, Edwards (1993) asserts that, for the women in her study, experience in paid employment was the most important motivating factor influencing women to return to learn. I would argue that the decision to study cannot be reduced to a single factor. The economic and domestic spheres of several of the married women's lives were characterised by exploitation and oppression. Low paid, boring and undemanding employment was followed by isolation and stagnation in the home. In both institutions the women were located in structurally unequal relationships. A woman's position within the labour market has to be understood in relation to her domestic role. As Mason points out:

> ..women's relative structural disadvantage in education, the labour market and social welfare provision help to ensure that they will be responsible for domestic labour and childcare within family-households; this in turn reinforces their structural disadvantage and makes it all seem reasonable and inevitable (Mason, 1987:90).

Domesticity highlighted the contradictions, lack of power and fulfilment in their present and past lives. Although childrearing was a positive experience many women were aware that they had lost their own identity; they were either someone's wife or mother. The self was denied. Within the private sphere of the family the women had to submit to male hegemony at material and ideological levels.

The oppressive experiences within the home ironically resulted in a way forward in the women's live and provided the possibility of liberation. Domesticity encouraged the women to reflect upon their lives resulting in gender consciousness. Work, childrearing and housework had consumed their lives. Now they wanted space and time for self-development and fulfilment. The single, younger women also arrived at a realisation that they wanted more out of their lives as women and achieve, primarily, occupational mobility. In this respect age differentiation was not a significant variable, both younger and older women shared similar experiences and attitudes towards paid employment.

Education was viewed by all the women as the key to their fulfilment and autonomy. Studying for a degree, it was hoped, was one sphere of their lives where they would not feel oppressed or exploited because it was something which they had chosen to do. These women asserted their desire to learn, even at the risk of marriage break-up. Returning to education was an attempt to redress power inequalities in their private and public spheres and to gain control over their lives. The women had high expectations of the potential of education as a liberating force. To what extent did their experiences of university life live up to these expectations?

7 Learning a Mature Student Career: Adjustment and Consolidation

Actions do not thus simply follow from the norms and the role expectations associated with a particular group, but upon the interpretations made by actors of their experience within their world (Urry, 1970: 360).

Introduction

All participants in this study entered university life with high expectations of what learning, and more specifically, a university degree could potentially do to their lives in relation to personal development and employment. At the same time a university education and the role of being a student were experiences that needed to be demystified. The working-class background of the majority of participants precluded them from having such knowledge. Despite this they were convinced that a university education was now for them and wanted to prove to themselves that they were capable of studying at this level. Along with this were fears and anxieties about entering a new social world.

Both the women and the men had to take on and learn a new role. As Wheeler points out in his study of adult socialisation:

> When a person moves into a new interpersonal setting, a major problem he faces is understanding the setting and coming to terms with its demands. He must develop a workable 'definition of the situation' to guide his action (Wheeler, 1967:60).

Choosing to become a student signalled a period of change in their lives. Participants, however, entered university with their past histories and 'cultural baggages':

> The adult, therefore, brings with him into the classroom his conceptions and experience, based on extra-institutional factors and influences. On the

basis of these he interprets his role, not in terms of the normative expectations of his tutor and fellow students but in accordance with his pre-existing social norms. In turn, these provide the source of and continuing support for his interpretation of his role as a student (Harries-Jenkins, 1982: 28,29).

To what extent do previous and present roles and experiences influence and affect the role of student? The following two chapters explore how far being a student deconstructed these processes and the extent to which the self was reconstructed and redefined. How did they perceive themselves as university students? To what extent were these experiences gendered ones? In examining these questions I will draw on the work of both Becker, Geer et al.'s (1961) study of medical students and Goffman (1959, 1961).

Goffman's (1961) work, for example, on the career of inmates in total institutions offers a useful conceptual framework that can be adapted to the career of mature students in an educational institution. Goffman (1959, 1961) stresses the need to understand social behaviour within its social context which he terms as 'situational propriety'. Manning interprets Goffman's 'situational propriety' as:

> ...the meaning of our actions is linked to the context in which they arose, and that we can rarely understand behaviour without knowledge of the situation in which it occurred (Manning, 1992:10,11).

Within this analogy mature students, like inmates, are entering a new institution in an unknown social context. Although less extreme and committing than a total institution, university life does have a profound effect upon the lives of students. They leave changed persons (McLaren, 1985, Pascall and Cox, 1993, West, 1996). Goffman's concept of mortification of the self is applicable in a modified and less extreme form. The self of mature students is partially stripped on entry to a university and their identity rebuilt as they progress through their student career. The process and outcome of mortification is a liberating one for mature students. This contrasts sharply with Goffman's (1961) application as mortification is a repressive experience within total institutions.

Being a university student, however, only formed one aspect of their lives. All played a multiplicity of roles; employee, parent, wife, husband, voluntary worker, carer. Drawing on Goffman's (1974) terminology they are constantly moving from one frame to another. In this important respect, unlike 18 year olds, they were not immersed totally in student life. Only one person, a male in his early twenties, lived on campus. For the women, becoming a student provided only a partial escape from family commitments. Domesticity remained an important factor in their lives. This confirms findings from other studies, such as, Pascall and Cox (1993) and Edwards (1993). As adult students their daily lives were constructed around interaction between their public and private lives. The following chapter examines how the two spheres interrelated and conflicted. Did the women experience greater discontinuity and conflict between their public and private lives than the men? Focusing on both the macro and micro levels I was interested in exploring how the self was reshaped by both individual action and by the institution itself. How far do individual experiences of being an adult student become collective ones?

Entering the System: First Impressions

A positive initial contact is important for adults considering returning to education as they react to the messages given out by institutions (McGivney, 1993). For example, Jenny enquired about part-time degree courses at several local further and higher education institutions but discovered that they either did not offer such courses or was put through to departments who knew nothing about a part-time degree programme. When she contacted Warwick she was directed to the Part-time Degrees Office:

> I had a very good telephone response from the Part-time Degree Office. It was a very good first impression. It seemed to be well-organised and set up for it and these factors made me choose Warwick (Jenny).

Sally decided to choose Warwick after a negative interview experience at another local university: 'I walked out of the interview at X as it was so awful. The questions were really sexist. They had no interest in my academic ability. They were only concerned with how I was going to cope with my children' (Sally).

For all participants two priorities in applying to institutions were; finding a suitable course and a university that understood the learning needs of adult students. Another factor was considered crucial by the women with families; an awareness by the institution of the problems of studying and looking after a family.

Unlike 18 year olds all adult students are required to attend an interview to determine whether or not they will be offered a place.

Prospective 2+2 students are interviewed at the further education colleges by college staff and some are asked to undergo some form of written work. Nearly all participants stated that they left their admissions interview with the impression that Warwick was supportive of mature students. Helen, after interviews at Warwick and another local university felt that; 'it seemed to me that Warwick was more supportive of mature students than X university from what they were saying' (Helen). For Valerie: 'Both interviewers were mature and aware of the problems encompassed in terms of fitting study into work and family commitments. Both were sympathetic and supportive' (Valerie).

Sue recalled that she was in awe at attending an interview in 'this amazing department' (Sociology). The interviewer (female) reassured her that the department makes every effort to fit teaching within school hours for students with children. These examples highlight the importance of the role of the admissions tutor. Research demonstrates that admissions tutors sometimes act as gatekeepers, denying access to certain categories of students (Clark, 1995, Williams, 1997).

Most participants were nervous about the interview as they felt that their future rested on the outcome but several were at the same time confident about their academic ability. Some were also daunted by the prospect of entering a large academic institution. Jayne reflected: 'I was nervous but I was confident that I would be able to stay the course and that I would be able to manage it'. Paul described his interview with the Arts Education Department:

> The interview was hard. I was nervous about it because I did not want to be rejected. I was asked why I wanted to do it and why I would be dedicated to it as a mature student rather than being a school leaver (Paul).

Others were also aware that they had to demonstrate their motivation and ability for learning. A minority were relaxed and confident about the interview. Joyce went to the interview believing that she had a lot to offer and was a reasonable candidate for a degree course. 'I was good and confident at communicating' (Joyce). In contrast Sue was rejected for her first subject choice, psychology:

> Because I was so disappointed about psychology I did not give the interview any thought. I do not think that I performed terribly well so I was surprised to be offered a place (sociology) (Sue).

Duncan recounted: 'I had a very easy entrance as I had O and A levels and a diploma. I was a good salesman so I sold myself and walked in' (Duncan).

The interview process reassured participants that Warwick was the place for mature students. All began the degree course with the perception that Warwick was supportive and aware of the problems mature students faced in juggling studying with domesticity and, in some cases, employment. Would the rhetoric match reality?

Becoming a Student: Initial Experiences

As the start of the degree course approached a minority of participants began to reconsider the decision to study for a degree because of apprehension, not about studying, but about entering a large and possibly alienating institution. Sue, for example, found the prospect of starting at university alarming. Her experience highlights the need for adult educators to provide support systems at all stages of the learning process, including pre-course, to adult learners in institutions whose student population is overwhelmingly non-adult:

> I really had to make myself come to the mature students' induction day. I can remember sitting in the car park wondering, and scared, why the hell have I done this? It would have been so easy to have driven off. By the end of that day I was so relieved that I had done it. I knew a few faces. It was chaos on the Monday (start of term) and if I had walked into that I would not have survived. The induction day was useful (Sue).

Cathy also felt intimidated and was full of self-doubt:

> I found campus life absolutely daunting. That first week I could have given up because I just could not cope with it. It was too big - finding where everything was going on. The first lectures were frightening, silly really. I thought it was beyond me but I thought I would stick it out and it was fine (Cathy).

Another woman, nervous about returning to study, was reassured to find that there were other mature students at Warwick: 'The fact that there are a lot of mature students here really helped. I came to the induction day and met some people there who were on the same course and it has been OK ever since' (Jill). McLaren (1985) identified similar problems in her study of women mature students at a higher education college:

> Anyone entering a new educational institution worries about his or her academic abilities and the likelihood of their persisting in the programme. For these adult students, the level of concern and anxiety was particularly high. Right from the start, the women voiced many of their concerns in conversation with one another (McLaren, 1985:114).

For many, the first two or three weeks of student life were about survival and coping in an unfamiliar environment. The mature students had to adapt and adjust to university life quickly as the pace of ten-week terms is fast. Becker and Strauss' (1959, 1970) work on adult socialisation is useful here. Using the concept of situational adjustment Becker and Strauss (1956,1970) analyse how adults deal with the problems of change when confronted by different institutional settings. Becker and Strauss (1959, 1970) define situational adjustment in the following terms:

> The person, as he moves in and out of a variety of social situations, learns the requirements of continuing in each situation and of success in it. If he has a strong desire to continue, the ability to assess accurately what is required, the individual turns himself into the kind of person the situation demands (Becker and Strauss, 1970: 279).

The 2+2 students were faced with two situational adjustments during their university student career; year one on entry to the further education college and year three on entry to Warwick.

In *Asylums* Goffman (1961) uses a similar approach to Becker and Strauss (1959, 1970) but he develops the idea one stage further in the application of the concepts primary and secondary adjustment. On entry to a total institution inmates undergo a process of primary adjustment. During this period the inmates get used to the system. Although not a total institution the mature students had to 'learn the ropes' of their new cultural and institutional setting. My research evidence suggests that once the students had learnt the ropes they then used that knowledge both to manipulate the system to their advantage and to avoid playing all the rules. In a similar way Goffman (1961) describes how the inmates learn to get round the system through the process of secondary adjustment:

> ...secondary adjustments, defining these as any habitual arrangement by which a member of an organization employs unauthorized means, or obtains unauthorized ends, or both, thus getting around the organization's assumptions as to what he should do and get and hence what he should be (Goffman, 1961: 172).

Once participants were in the system the type of degree programme, 2+2, full-time or part-time, proved an important variable in determining how participants perceived their role as adult students. The 2+2, in years one and two, and part-time degree students were coherent and identifiable groups. They were taught as a group of mature students. This does not apply to the full-time mature students. However, on degree courses where there are larger numbers of mature students, for example, in Sociology and Arts Education Departments, my research indicates that they soon drift towards each other to form a cohesive social group.

Mature students can, therefore, be analysed as sub-cultures within the dominant student culture of a university. In defining culture I draw on the work of Clarke et al. (1976):

> We understand the word 'culture' to refer to that level at which social groups develop distinct patterns of life, and give expressive form to their social and material life-experience. Culture is the way, the forms, in which groups 'handle' the raw material of their social and material existence...A culture includes the 'maps of meaning' which make things intelligible to its members (Clarke et al, 1976:10).

A culture is a way of life whereby a group share similar experiences, values and attitudes. In this case-study two distinct sub-cultures can be identified within the mature student culture: part-time degree students as one sub-culture and 2+2 and full-time students another. I would further argue that the women mature students formed a separate sub-set; constituting a subculture within a subculture. Sub-cultures:

> ...are smaller, more localised and differentiated structures, within one or other of the larger cultural networks...A sub-culture, though differing in important ways - in its 'focal concerns', its peculiar shapes and activities - from the culture from which it derives, will also share some things in common with that 'parent' culture (Clarke et al., 1976:13).

Territorial spaces were established within the University that belonged to groups of mature students. By territorial space I mean certain areas of the University campus which were taken over and symbolically owned by mature students as a haven from younger students. These included some areas of certain coffee bars and the 2+2 and part-time degrees common room. The mature student subcultures became visible. The formation of subcultures are a response to and a way of coping with being a mature student and institutional life within a middle-class, elite university.

Induction days were held for all categories of mature students. Many expressed that the day was useful for re-introducing them to the education system. However, it did not prevent some from feeling nervous and uncertain about the decision to study once term began. For this group anxiety centred on coping with academic discourse. 'I wondered what on earth I was doing here because of the language used but I persevered and now I enjoy and understand it' (Ben). Jean explained that at first, 'lectures seemed like being on a different planet but I soon got used to the language'.

A small number expected the teaching approaches to match those of their schooldays. 'When I first came I thought it was going to be like school - teacher tells you what you do and you do it' (Helen). Jenny, in comparing Warwick to her schooldays reflected:

> At first getting used to a lecture/seminar environment was very strange. The education I had I was really spoon-fed and it's such a transition to come into a university environment and it's sort of well there's a question, go off and just do it (Jenny).

Lectures and Seminars as Approaches to Learning

Participants were asked about their attitudes towards lectures and seminars and whether or not they felt that such teaching approaches aided their learning. Attitudes were mixed. However, a critical factor that affected whether or not a student preferred lectures or seminars hinged on the teaching skills of a lecturer. 2+2 students compared their teaching experiences at the FE colleges and the University. A few studies have included adult students' perceptions on relationships with lecturers and tutor support (Edwards, 1993, Weil, 1986, and Smithers and Griffin, 1986), but there is an absence of research concerning the attitudes of mature students towards lectures and seminars as a medium for learning. For example, Edwards (1993) touches on the issues when she discusses the references to life experiences by mature women students in seminars. Bourner et al. (1991) presented a quantitative analysis of mature students' attitudes towards lectures and seminars. McPherson et al. (1994) questioned mature students about the effectiveness of teaching within continuing education. Yet lectures and seminars are a dominant part of adult student life and, therefore, an area which needs further research.

Married women, full and part-time, and other part-time students arrive on campus for their lectures and seminars and then depart as soon as they are finished. They may visit the library but the evidence from my research shows that, on the whole, these two groups have minimum participation with other facilities on campus. Seminars, in particular, constitute one of the main arenas for social interaction between mature students and lecturers and between mature students and younger students. To draw on Goffman's (1969) dramaturgical approach, seminars provide a stage for mature students to present their self to others.

Lectures

Several students, both women and men, were critical of the ability of some lecturers to teach. In critiquing lecturers' styles they were outlining their views on what constitutes good pedagogy for mature students. Paul pointed out that:

> Some lecturers seem more competent than others. They obviously know their subject but some are better at putting it across than others. Some make it more interesting and accessible. Some voices are more interesting than others (Paul).

Adrian stressed that:

> With lectures they sometimes concentrate too much on getting something across and forget about presentation. Half the time you can sit there and a lecture just goes over the top of me, simply because the way it's presented is so incoherent, so I think quite often that lectures just miss the mark (Adrian).

More poignantly Sally elaborated: 'It depends upon who the lecturer is. Some are very helpful. Some are completely hopeless. It amazes me that lecturers never acquire any teaching skills' (Sally).

A part-time student who decided to go full-time was surprised to find different teaching approaches between the two degree modes:

> Lectures and seminars did not exist in part-time degrees. You would come in for a two hour class. I had never been to a real formal lecture before. In my first law lecture I was really gobsmacked, wondering what is going on here. I was completely lost and did not know how to take notes. I would try and write everything down. Whereas now it comes as second nature. One sociology lecturer tries and crams a lot into a lecture and it can get a bit muddling but she is very good at giving out copies of her lecture notes.

Otherwise we would be stuck if she did not. I prefer lectures this way than I did coming from a two hour mish-mash of trying to get everything in. This is a lot more formal and a lot better. You have a whole hour of a good lecture and you can get all your notes down. Then you have an hour's seminar. It is a lot more clearer. You know more about the subject, whereas before I never felt that I had a grip on a module. Now I feel as if I have a good foundation of the subject (Dalvinder).

Lectures and seminars were judged in instrumental terms: they were good if they provided clear and coherent material for essays and examinations. This was particularly the case with part-time students as time for study is a critical factor for this group: 'I find lectures more useful than seminars because they outline the key points and are more helpful for writing essays and exams. It saves time especially when you are studying part-time' (Valerie). A minority of students found lectures a positive experience. As one full-time student emphasised: 'I find lectures useful but it does depend on the lecturer. Some lectures are dynamic. Some lectures I come out of them feeling really good and some seminars I enjoy' (Jill). For one part-time participant: 'Lectures present a lot of information very concisely. It is all relevant and is very useful in showing an inexperienced student precisely which areas should be given priority with regards further study. Sorting out priorities can be very difficult at first'.

2+2 students, like part-time students, were taught as a group for the first two years in the FE college. All found this a supportive learning environment but some found the structure too insular by the end of the second year. As Judith explained:

It was OK but I prefer it here (Warwick). I prefer the atmosphere. We were always together and physically separated from the rest of the college. It started to get boring, not enough people on the course. When I came here I much preferred the way they do lectures and seminars (Judith).

In comparing Warwick with the FE college Pamela summarised: 'I enjoy lectures except when the language is "over your head". These are a waste of time. College was a lot more intimate in its teaching methods - more student-centred' (Pamela).

Mike also talked about the disjunctions between college and the University:

Lectures are different to what I was used to at college. In some cases the lectures are not followed by seminars. It is not always possible to follow up points in seminars from lectures because the seminar tutor may not have attended the lecture. The lectures are very structured and are more precise than the ones we had in college but at college there was far more interaction on all tangents (Mike).

2+2 students, therefore, experienced a contrast in teaching styles from student-centred approaches in colleges to, on the whole, more didactic methods at Warwick. Part-time students faced a different set of problems.

Several part-time students mentioned the difficulty and exhaustion of rushing to two hours of evening classes after a day at work: 'The problem with that is that you are starting at six for a lecture followed by an hour and a half seminar. After a day at work you are shattered' (Peter).

Seminars

Attitudes towards seminars evoked a range of positive and negative comments by participants. All had a clear definition of what constituted a good seminar. Like lectures a good seminar depended on the teaching skill of the tutor:

> If the tutor is sensitive and responsive to the educational needs of students, seminars are very fertile in intellectual stimulation. Sometimes tutors indulge themselves in seminars in their favoured ways, values and ideas (Stephen).

For Valerie seminars were only occasionally good. 'Seminars lack direction. They do not seem relevant as the tutor sometimes goes off at a tangent and they seem like a waste of time' (Valerie). Lacking structure and meandering from key topics by either the tutor or other students were commonly voiced complaints about seminars. The variability of seminars was also expressed as a problem by Dalvinder:

> Sometimes you can come in and you need not have bothered. Sometimes you can come in and they can be really good and you can get a lot of notes. You need good notes for revision. Sometimes they are just 'waffle' (Dalvinder).

Learning with Younger Students

The most common theme discussed was the presence of younger students in seminars. Age differences are rendered visible in seminars. Seminars provide a forum for the meeting of the young and mature student subcultures. On the whole the amalgamation of the two subcultures resulted in positive experiences for both. Only a minority preferred to be in all mature seminar groups. These participants were mostly part-time students who had no experience of being with younger students in seminars.

Two commonly stated reasons for advocating mature student only seminars were that the participants found it hard to communicate with younger people and that their behaviour was immature. The women in Edwards' (1993) study expressed similar attitudes about younger students. A minority who were in mixed seminar groups were critical of younger students:

> There are mostly mature students in my seminar groups. I find this useful for support. The younger students also tend not to say anything. I find the younger women do not say as much as the younger men (Helen).

In her first year of study Helen felt intimidated by the younger students in seminar groups and this undermined her confidence as a learner:

> I use to feel that other students knew more than I did so I kept quiet. But then you realise that they do not know any more than you do. They are just more able to talk (Helen).

Another argued that younger students were not as conscientious about their work as mature students and this occasionally caused friction between the two groups:

> I find that as mature students we get our work in on time but they do not. We put more effort in to meeting deadlines but they do not seem to worry that much (Hyacinth).

A few stressed that they would not be able to cope if there were no other matures in a seminar as they would feel isolated and lonely. For Laura, a biological sciences student, this was a critical factor that affected her enjoyment of studying. She was one of three adult students in her year. Laura stated, 'I would like to learn in a mixed group as I would be able to relate to someone of my age'. Her experience of university life was qualitatively different to the mature students taking social science or humanities degrees.

The majority enjoyed the company of younger students in seminars, primarily because it produced a cross-fertilisation of ideas and perspectives and facilitated a reciprocal learning process. One woman, Cathy, described younger students as being 'lovely'. Some also stated that mixed seminars had broken down the age barriers:

> They help me to look at things slightly differently. When I first started the course I felt estranged from people of that age group. I do not feel old myself but I did when I saw the 18 year olds. It does break down the age barriers (Sue).

Valerie described how her views towards younger students changed. To her the clash of generations was a positive experience. She explained her reactions to being in a group with younger students:

> That was very strange actually. There is only one other mature. You wonder at first about the legitimacy of being there but it worked quite well. It is a bit daunting when you first go in and you feel like a mother. I do not think that it is a problem. It is just an initial problem of getting over the age gap. The shock of all these youngsters. If you are willing to go and meet them on their level and joke with them and help them in some way as I have access to photocopying. We share information. If you go in there and see yourself as different, if you are not willing to get on some rapport, some level, then you are going to get isolated (Valerie).

Sally, like others, emphasised the benefits of mixed seminars:

> I like to hear the views of mature students and the younger ones straight out of school. The mature students because their different life experiences influence their opinions and younger students because they look at things in a more straightforward way, sometimes less hampered by strong personal opinions (Sally).

Ann commented: 'The youngsters make me smile sometimes because they are so ideological. It is refreshing because it reminds you of a point of view which you would not think of' (Ann).

Life Experiences and Learning

Good teaching approaches for both adults and children encompasses the life experiences of the students (Knowles, 1990). Social science subjects are conducive to a discourse that centres on life experiences. This may be one of the appeals of social sciences to adults: the subject matter is not abstract and remote from their lives. Three men chose a part-time degree in labour studies because of the relationship of the subject to their occupation as trade union shop stewards. They were critical of any courses which they believed were too academic as they did not relate to the 'real world'. Seminars and initially essays provided platforms for expression of life experiences. The women, particularly taking law and sociology courses, were able to discuss their educational, family, work, and for a minority, racial experiences. Edwards (1993) noted the references to life experiences in seminars by the mature women students in her study. The men in my sample excluded their private lives from seminar discussions but they did refer to their employment experiences. Interviews with lecturers at Warwick revealed that many valued the contribution of life experiences to seminars by mature students. The only reservations lecturers had were that some adults were unable to cross the boundary and make the transition from anecdotal talk to a conceptualisation and theorisation of their life experiences.

Three female participants were conscious that mature students had a tendency to discuss life experiences in seminars. As Avril pointed out, 'we all tend to get into our life experiences a bit too much'. Similarly Judith commented: 'I think older people go on about what's happened to them whereas the younger ones discuss the topics more' (Judith). A comment by a younger mature female student illustrates the heterogeneity of mature students:

> Adults tend to be on a different level...Some of the really old students often talk about their family and shopping in the midst of a heavy seminar. It knocks you off course and makes you feel older than you are (Dalvinder).

However, Dalvinder in her second interview reflected positively about the relationship between her life experiences and the subject matter of sociology:

> Studying sociology has made me look more critically. Your experiences are put into theory. Maybe that was the factor for me, being able to do that more than the younger students and also with being Asian and being a woman. I have got so much knowledge of my own personal life to think about - even issues which relate to my parents (Dalvinder).

Jenny placed a high value on the learning experience which mature students bring to the learning situation:

The older people feel: I cannot do it. I have not written essays for years. I do not feel that they realise the knowledge they have. They bring knowledge to the lecture and bring it alive. I think mature students as a whole have got so many different experiences of life in general. A student who has just gone from education to education, you do not know any more than an educational setting so you cannot bring any more to it (Jenny).

Lectures and Seminars: A Summary

The daily routine of university life is, therefore, centred around lectures and seminars. Research evidence from the students reveals an awareness of a diversity of teaching styles, ranging from student-centred to didactic approaches, both within and across departments. Most preferred a combination of the traditional teaching method of a lecture with an interactive seminar. Pamela asserted the benefits of student-centred approaches:

> I like interactive teaching. Passive teaching is a waste of time as it treats people like sponges. The teacher is not always right. The teachers can learn from students just as much as students can learn from teachers (Pamela).

Some of the older mature students disliked student-centred approaches, perhaps because this did not match their school memories and images about teaching and learning. In a learning environment characterised by a multitude of teaching approaches the mature students are constantly having to adapt and change the presentation of the self to meet the needs and expectations of different tutors and departments.

Study Skills: Writing Essays and Reading

The mature students entered university with different levels and experience of studying. Those who had recently studied A levels or taken an Access course had an advantage over those who had been out of the education system for a long time. The problems are succinctly outlined by Peter:

> My daughter is at university and the way she works she is prepared for it all through the system and it is much easier but it just is not for me. I just have to keep working at it. It is very long winded. Since I started I have got myself more organised and I have got better and my marks seem to reflect it. But I have got to work at it (Peter).

Many were nervous about writing a first essay. 'It was a new thing that I had to learn from scratch' (Hyacinth). Paul explained; 'it was knowing what they wanted and the way they wanted it written'. Several admitted that the quality of their first essay was poor:

> My first essay was disastrous. I did not think about going and asking for help. I just thought that I would get on and do it. I tend to be a loner and work until it comes to my satisfaction. With one essay I was scared to go and approach the lecturer (Jean).

All, however, were unsure of the academic level expected for degree work. As Sally explained: 'In the first year I did not really know what was expected of me. I thought I was coming for an education as much as for a degree' (Sally). Participants who had recently taken A levels or whose paid employment had involved writing reports experienced fewer problems in writing essays. A part-time student commented that, 'I am learning all the time' (Lynne). Sue remarked that a study skills pack produced by the Sociology Department had aided her writing skills but revealed that, 'it is a battle but I feel that I am doing quite well and the marks are pretty good'. Interviews in the final year of study revealed that all participants felt that they had acquired and improved their essay writing skills. For example, Avril explained:

> I feel like now I can finally understand it all. It is all coming together and making sense. The way I write has grown, changed and evolved. I feel that I am writing sense and that every now and then I have a reasonably original thought. That is great watching it all (Avril).

The 2+2 students experienced a disjunction in relation to the number of essays required at Warwick compared to the colleges. Non-assessed class essays were not stipulated by most colleges. Joyce quantified this as an increase from six essays a year to seven essays a term. For many 2+2 students the transition from college to Warwick was problematical and expansion of the workload exacerbated the situation. Hyacinth explained:

> I thought that we could have done more in the second year. I did not feel as if I was pushed enough. I did not feel adequately prepared for the volume of work. There was not enough pressure put on you to do essays- you needed to be forced a bit more. I found the workload daunting in the third year at Warwick (Hyacinth).

Assessment

At Warwick assessment is by a combination of examinations and assessed work. The latter generally consists of extended essays. Participants were asked which form of assessment they preferred. Examinations evoked feelings of anxiety, fear and nerves, among both the women and the men. However, many opted for a mixture of examinations and assessment for pragmatic reasons. Other research (Bourner et al., 1991) also indicates the dislike of examinations as a form of assessment by mature students. The following attitudes about examinations were common:

> I find it difficult in exam situations as I tend to panic and forget what is to be said. Essays in this situation tend to be a garbled mess (Valerie).

> I am scared stiff quite frankly sitting there at an exam because I have not done it for years. That is one area where I would have liked a pre-run, a mock exam. That would be beneficial. I did not achieve what I thought was my potential because of my lack of skill in doing a written exam (Adam).

> My memory is terrible. If I am working on a subject area I know what I am doing but when it is exams and trying to keep all that information in is very difficult (Helen).

Helen and others pointed out that examinations are too dependent on performance on a particular day. She was ill during the examination period one year. For some examinations brought back memories of sitting in examination halls in school: 'I was absolutely terrified of doing exams for about twenty years. I did find my first exam last year, which was two hours, very exhausting. I think a lot of people find this' (Jean).

Attitudes towards assessment were frequently contradictory. Jean continued to explain the dilemmas and why, despite a dislike of examinations, most mature students prefer a mixture of assessment modes:

> The snag with assessments is that you can go on for ever trying to make sure that they are perfect. You will only end up with a few more marks for three or four more hours work. It is very complicated really. I think on the whole that I prefer assessments but there is a tendency to do just the work for assessments and not worry about the rest of your work (Jean).

Wanting to read widely and spend a long time perfecting assessed essays was perceived as a problem by most participants. Doing so increased the pressure on the workload for other courses. The hectic pace of ten week terms did not allow time for all the books on the reading lists to be read. Many, initially, found it difficult to cut down on the reading:

> I find assessed work a lot harder than exams because I never think I have done enough work. For exams there is only so much you can do. There is no point in reading hundreds of books (Avril).

By the end of her degree course Avril had sorted this problem out:

> I am much more confident and doing more assessed work than I did last year. I did not use to like assessed work because I used to feel that I could never do enough and that I could never get it right. I now realise that there is only so much you can do with 2 or 3000 words (Avril).

The adult students' culture was maturing. They were learning collectively how to get round the system: revision of examination topics became selective and fewer books were read. In Goffman's (1961) conceptual framework they were exhibiting signs of secondary adjustment to the institution.

All the participants entered university with the ideal of wanting to learn. This encompassed pursuing knowledge for knowledge's sake. By collectively cutting down on their reading the mature students were departing from this ideal. The mature student culture had learnt that to survive and be successful in assessments and obtain a degree they had to forfeit reading widely. Their prime goal became passing examinations and achieving high grades in assignments:

> You have not got enough time to perhaps do as much reading as you would like. The workload is so heavy that you have to try and balance it out. When you get to the interesting stuff, if it does not relate to your essay you feel you have been wasting time reading it. You have to concentrate on things that are just to do with your essay (Hyacinth).

The mature students were being realistic about what could and could not be achieved in the time available. As a group they were constructing the boundaries of a mature student role and setting norms. Consciously cutting down on their workload also had an important latent function: it eased the pressure on university, domestic and, in the case of part-time students, working life. Choosing not to complete all class essays was also part of this strategy. In *Boys In White*, Becker et al. (1961) observed a similar pattern of behaviour among the medical students they studied. As Becker et al. summarise: 'Students reason from their definition of the situation: if there is more to do than can be done in the time available, we can solve the problem by taking short cuts in the way we learn' (Becker et al., 1961: 117).

Like the students in Becker et al.'s study, these mature students reached a similar situation whereby the 'group reaches a consensus on how to deal with much of what is problematical in its environment' (1961:135). The mature students' culture sought other ways of minimising the work pressure; not writing class essays and not attending seminars if they have not prepared the work. Becker et al. (1961) argue that this introduces an element of autonomy into the students' lives vis a vis the institution: 'Students use autonomy in setting their levels and direction of effort. In deciding what they will study and how they will work, students have considerable autonomy' (Becker et al., 1961: 350).

Although the mature students learnt to reduce their workload to more manageable proportions, several continued to feel frustrated at having to do so: it did not match up to their expectations of learning in a university. The pace of work, and spending approximately one week on a topic, was contrary to the students' preconceptions about academic life:

> The content of some courses seems superficial - moving from one topic to another. It feels like a Cooks tour. A lot is crammed into ten weeks. There is never enough time to do all the reading and I find this infuriating. I would like to get involved in more depth in particular subjects (Joyce).

Mike experienced severe problems with his workload to the extent that he almost left university at the end of year three. He was reluctant to reduce the reading for assessed essays:

> I am thorough with my essays and I like to read widely as I can but I am struggling at Warwick because of the increase in workload. I find it difficult to cut down on the reading. It has been a major problem for me. I got behind with my work and I do not like working like this. I like to be on top of my work. I realised that this is not possible at Warwick but I did not know this beforehand. I like to be in control (Mike).

Finding the time for assessed essays was particularly difficult for part-time students in full-time employment and for women with children and husbands. One woman, who was not married, upon changing from part-time to full-time noted that she had more time to undertake preparatory and research work on assessed essays. Previously she had just been concerned with passing. Others, however, had had to opt for 100% examination for some courses. Many viewed examinations as an unfair assessment of a person's ability. Assessed essays were preferred because they were not only less stressful but enabled participants to explore a subject in greater depth:

> I personally prefer assessed essays as I believe students have a more thorough understanding of the subject studied, rather than just revising for an exam and then forgetting most of what was revised (Jenny).

A minority were critical of assessed work because they believed it to be vulnerable to cheating. Several noted a discrepancy between the marks obtained for class and assessed essays and those for examinations. One explanation offered was that some departments do not provide any information regarding topic areas to be covered by examinations:

> The marks I got in my class essays were not reflected in my exam work. That is because the department involved gave no revision advice. No exam advice whatsoever. In War and Economy I got a first for my class essay but only 50% in the exam. I was really disappointed. Basically we did not get any guidelines about what was going to be in the exam. It was a very broad topic range and you get to the stage where you are absolutely panicking, revising and going round in circles and just not revising the right things. The assessed work went OK (Joyce).

A small number made assumptions about what constituted fairness in relation to assessment. Although they disliked examinations they believed that examinations eradicated any possibility of cheating.

Thoughts on Lecturers

Many participants arrived at Warwick with stereotyped views about lecturers working in an elite university. To them being an academic meant that lecturers were on a different level from 'ordinary people', absorbed in a world of intellect and knowledge, thus making them unapproachable and elitist towards mature students. Some were in awe, holding lecturers in high esteem. In practice they discovered the images did not match reality. Only one or two lecturers were deemed to be unapproachable or unhelpful. The level of support and approachability was partly related to departmental cultures.

Individual contact with lecturers centred on help and feedback on essays and pastoral guidance from personal tutors. Support from lecturers concerning essays was perceived as being good. Dalvinder, however, noticed a difference in relationships when she changed from part-time to full-time:

> Lecturers have been very helpful, especially X. I think that he is very good. All of them go out of their way to help. They encourage you to go and see them to discuss essays. Before we did not get that. In the evening we were just given a deadline. If you wanted to come in you had to make an appointment and come in during the day. You wonder then if it is worth taking time off work (Dalvinder).

A few shared the views of Valerie: 'With essays some lecturers are more helpful than others in providing feedback such as verbal and written comments' (Valerie).

One part-time student, Avril, revealed that she always made an appointment with a lecturer if she was in doubt about an essay. She admitted that she had struggled with one course and as a result frequently met with the lecturer who 'has been really supportive' (Avril). Avril also mentioned that they are encouraged to go and collect their essays from lecturers and discuss it with them. She has found the system very useful. Valerie complained that one tutor was very slow at marking. Despite this he was very thorough and wrote extensive comments:

> You had to wait a long time to get your mark unless you really badgered him. I have sat there while he has marked it at times. He was very thorough when he did it. One compensated the other. He was very sympathetic and he knew his stuff (Valerie).

Other participants remarked that lecturers had told them to go and see them if they had any problems. Several had asked tutors for extensions to assessed essays because of serious illness or family problems. Jenny was concerned initially that lecturers would not take part-time students seriously. In practice she discovered that this was not the case. 'They always make the time to answer any questions or problems, even if it is 8.30 in the evening' (Jenny).

One 2+2 student described relationships with lecturers at Warwick as alienating compared to the informal relationships at college. As a result she felt unable to go and see tutors about her work at Warwick:

> If I left here tomorrow they would not miss me. Lecturers have so many in the group that they do not know you. I do not think that anybody would

miss me. Perhaps after six weeks they might think, oh this person does not come any more. It is so different from the college. You would not miss classes there because the teachers would know (Karen).

This interpretation of student/lecturer relationship was, however, the exception rather than the norm. Jayne expressed the opposite view to Karen by stating that: 'it has been friendlier and more intimate than we were led to believe'. Other participants were satisfied with the support and contact that they had received from tutors. For many the social distance between them and the lecturer was minimal. In some instances lecturers became friends. Interviews with lecturers revealed that they perceived mature students to be on a more equal basis with themselves than younger students because of the age similarity. The female mature students, for example, discussed issues and problems in relation to childrearing and working with female lecturers. Being female established a common bond between them. This contrasts with the findings of Edwards (1993). Most of the mature women students in her study stated that they:

> ...saw their lecturers as very different people from themselves. Lecturers could thus only be approached for help for purely academic reasons, which the women felt was, after all, what they were there for. They were not regarded as interested in other, more personal aspects of the women's lives. This was mostly seen as acceptable because the women wanted to keep the private side of their lives separate and could feel uncomfortable discussing personal problems with their tutors even where they affected their studies (Edwards, 1993: 94).

Both genders did not mind discussing personal problems with personal tutors as they were looking for ways of solving their problems and easing the pressures so that they could concentrate on their studies.

Personal Tutors

When asked about their experiences with personal tutors the majority responded that tutors had been supportive and helpful. Comments, such as the following, were very common: 'I think the tutor system is a very good idea and it works very well' (Paul), or 'he was very good. I cannot fault him' (Cathy). Consistent with the findings of other studies (Woodley et al., 1987, Edwards, 1993, Maynard and Pearsall, 1994), several of the mature students underwent varying levels of personal and study problems. In all cases the problems were successfully solved either by personal tutors or in more serious cases by the Senior Tutor's Office. Jill's reaction to her personal tutor was:

> Marvellous. I have had some problems since I started the course at home and I just came in and told my personal tutor who informed other people. They were really helpful and considerate (Jill).

Hyacinth explained that she had no hesitation in going to see her personal tutor if she had problems. 'I did have a few personal problems which I told him about and he informed my other tutors' (Hyacinth). Another student declared that he had an excellent personal tutor who was always there if you wanted advice. He expanded:

> Sometimes I think it would be nice to have a bit more interaction with personal tutors, less because of a problem but more on the subject you are doing (Adrian).

Judith regretted not having a personal tutor system at the college. She felt that, 'it is nice that there is someone you can take your problems to' (Judith). Using her knowledge and experience as a voluntary worker in the welfare services Judith declared that 'there is a lot of support here'. Karen, in contrast, chose not to go and see her personal tutor. She admitted that 'I do not want to bother them unless there is a big problem. I cannot see the point' (Karen).

Although most of the mature students in my sample had had positive experiences with the pastoral system several believed that the quality of assistance depended upon the individual tutor. Some personal tutors, they maintained, did not fulfil their role:

> There is a terrific difference in the motivation of tutors in looking after whoever they have been allocated. My tutor is excellent. She always has time to listen to my problems but I know other students who have not met their personal tutor (Sue).

Occasionally students and personal tutors were mismatched. Joyce did not meet her personal tutor until year four. He taught in the evenings and was, therefore, not on campus during the day. 'It was hit and miss concerning the support you get as it depends on your personal tutor' (Joyce). Some expressed uncertainty of what to expect from personal tutors: their role was unclear to the mature students. Several part-time students were unsure who their personal tutor was but were not concerned about this. Instead if they experienced any problems they went to see the Director of Part-Time Degrees or staff in the Part-Time Degrees Office. Similarly, one 2+2 student preferred to use the 2+2 office rather than her personal tutor if she had any difficulties.

Avril expressed a criticism of the system which other women shared. At the start of her second academic year she experienced a crisis which needed to be discussed with a personal tutor. Avril elaborated: 'I get on fine with him (personal tutor) but I wanted to talk to a woman'. Certain problems were perceived by the women mature students as being 'women's problems'; and as such were aspects of their lives which could only be disclosed to a female tutor. In these situations the women felt that only another woman could fully understand the problems they faced. In reality it is impossible to allocate a female personal tutor to all female students. The gender inequalities within the university system ensure that in the academic world women are outnumbered by men.

The mature students also highlighted another issue surrounding the personal tutor system. The age factor ensured that several of the mature students were older than their personal tutor. A few, therefore, found it difficult to receive advice from someone younger than them as they argued that the tutor's life experiences were limited. Kate remarked, 'I always feel like his mother when I am speaking to him - that is not his fault'.

Making the Transition: 2+2 Students

2+2 students collectively experienced two contrasting institutional environments during their careers as mature students; two years in FE college and two years at Warwick. In being socialised as a student they underwent two periods of situational adjustment (Becker and Strauss, 1956, 1970) or primary adjustment (Goffman, 1961). Making the transition from FE college to university was, for the majority, a difficult and stressful period in their student career. Many 2+2 students experienced anomie and alienation as they temporarily lost control and autonomy over their student lives. The definition of the self as a student had to be remade to meet the culture, structure and constrains of a new institutional setting.

In the further education colleges 2+2 students formed a strong, cohesive subculture. Their college days were spent in the company of other 2+2 students both in the classroom and socially. Relationships with lecturers were intimate and informal. The mature student subculture was dominant and, as a result they were able to command relative autonomy over their lives within the colleges. On entry to Warwick the subcultural group was, to a certain extent, split as 2+2 students slotted into existing year two degree courses. In the first few weeks of year three of their degree course the 2+2 students were preoccupied with seeking to reassert both their identity as a student, in terms of self, and as a member of a subcultural group. Both as individuals and as a group they had to find social space within a large, impersonal and informal organisation.

The following comments about the transition summarised the feelings of several 2+2 students:

> It was horrendous, a nightmare. Probably one of the worst experiences I have ever had. Effectively first year students on second year courses. It traumatized two other female students because you feel isolated as everybody has made their friends. The first couple of weeks can be really intimidating, especially with the volume of information and work. My head felt like it was going to explode with all the information and work. Everything is still going on at home, the kids etc. By the end of the second week I was prepared to quit but a friend persuaded me not to. After a while it calmed down and you got to know the routine (Joyce).

> I hated the transition it was awful. At the college you were always told exam dates etc. and everybody knew you. It was the same lecturer for the lecture and seminar. You felt a bit important. Here you are just one out of thousands. It unnerves you. I hated the first week. There was a lot more work in the third year compared to the College. I panicked at first. Several essays but no direction and I felt that I did not know what to do. The quantity of work came as a big shock (Karen).

Pamela's transition problems were added to by the fact that she had, at the same time, to cope with the death of a close friend. The transition reminded her of the trauma she had experienced in moving from primary to secondary school:

> I was not prepared for the parallels in my life. I had the same fears on leaving the safe and secure environment of junior school to this huge place where everything was going to have to be done differently. I could not believe that at my age I would have these psychological parallels. I felt like my life had come full circle. It was difficult finding practical things at Warwick like rooms. I wandered around in the first two weeks like a chicken with no head. I should have taken time out to cope with all these

things. I just found the whole experience awful. You have to absorb so much new information. It eased once I knew where everything was and I became more relaxed (Pamela).

Pamela, however was the only 2+2 student who would have preferred the whole degree course to have been taught at the FE college. Her reasons were mostly pragmatic: less travelling distance and easier on family commitments. She also argued:

> I have a fear of large institutions. I found Warwick very overwhelming and tiring going from one department to another. You can also feel very isolated at Warwick. You get to know faces in a smaller institution (Pamela).

Experiencing problems in progressing from further to higher education institutions is not confined to 2+2 students. According to studies by Pantziarka (1987), and Leonard (1994), Access students also find the transition from college to higher education a traumatic experience:

> The transition from further education to higher education is probably the most difficult that the access student has to make...and is certainly more traumatic than the initial return to education after a long period of absence (Pantziarka, 1987:33).

In contrast just under half of the 2+2 students stated that they experienced no problems. Jayne remarked that the transition was 'surprisingly straightforward'. Kate argued that the University 'went overboard in making the transition easy as everything was done for us'. All 2+2 students had had varying degrees of contact with Warwick through their colleges during the first two years of their course but those students who experienced the least problems had made more individual visits and contacts.

Summary

Gender differences were subtle and not significant in relation to attitudes and experiences towards lectures, seminar and assessment. The type of degree programme and the mature/non-mature divide were more important factors. Through the process of situational adjustment the mature students emerged as a distinct social group. The mature student culture marked a social and cultural boundary between older and younger students. They saw themselves as being different and separate to the 18-21 year olds: differentiated by age and life experiences. Social interaction between the two groups was limited except in a minority of cases.

In terms of studying, the mature students' self confidence and ability grew, changed and developed as the degree programme progressed. Some had begun their student careers questioning the legitimacy of being there, afraid that academic discourse would be beyond them. The self was initially in doubt and unsure at how to act out the student role. The presence of other mature students undergoing the same self-doubts helped to alleviate these anxieties.

Individually and collectively confidence improved as they learnt how to write essays, take notes in a lecture and present a paper in a seminar. Initiation was soon over as they settled into the routine of academic life and learnt their way around the system. The mature students became a microcosm within the world of the university. In defining their own situation the mature students had to sacrifice some of their ideals concerning learning and knowledge in a university. Time was not available to examine subjects in depth or read all the literature on reading lists. Instead the goals shifted to focus on passing assignments and examinations.

In other areas of mature student life gender issues did become significant. The career of the women mature students was qualitatively different to that of the men, particularly at the public/private interface. Institutional arrangements and organisation impinged more critically upon the women's ability to study than the men. The women experienced more constraints, both internally and externally. Being a student also challenged the way they perceived themselves as women.

8 Experiencing University Life: Intersections of Public and Private Worlds

> Many of the problems these women faced were not individual to them, but are shared by countless others who, because of their gender and class, have been forced to restrain their aspirations and to make choices within circumscribed realms of activity. Their personal problems, I would argue, are public issues (McLaren, 1985: 17).

Introduction: Probing the Public/Private Worlds

Constructing and pursuing a student career is not always an easy task, particularly for women with partners and/or children. The student world as experienced by adults in this study was partly constrained and shaped by both University organisational arrangements and outside institutions such as the family and work. Despite the structural constraints and, in some cases, relational constraints by partners, the women struggled actively to negotiate and construct their student career in ways that were more beneficial to them. In doing so they were asserting their right within the University and the family to have a space to themselves and a time when they were not just somebody's wife or mother. Studying was a sphere whereby they could gain a degree of control over their lives.

Day-to-day life was characterised by a constant juggling of roles but these women were determined to manage the demands of frequent role changes. Student life could not be divorced from family life. The public and private lives of the mature women students interacted, sometimes positively, sometimes negatively. The women had commitment and attachment (Goffman, 1961) to different institutions. Participants, therefore, had to balance the competing demands of studying, family and, in some cases, paid work.

Marxist and radical feminists (Pateman, 1987, Mitchell, 1971, Barrett, 1980, 1988) maintain that the private and public worlds are interrelated. The frequently cited observation, 'the personal is political' stems from such an argument:

> The feminist slogan, 'the personal is political', seems to imply that feminist politics is concerned with breaking down any qualitative distinction between public and private, placing personal or 'private' matters on the 'public' political agenda (McDowell and Pringle, 1994: 17).

For some feminists the separation of the public/private spheres is the root cause of the universal oppression of women (Rosaldo, 1974, Firestone, 1970). Rosaldo (1974) offers a definition of the public/private or domestic dichotomy:

> 'Domestic'... refers to those minimal institutions and modes of activity that are organized immediately around one or more mothers and their children; 'public' refers to activities, institutions, and forms of association that link, rank, organize, or subsume particular mother-child groups (Rosaldo, 1974:23).

Marxist-feminist literature has concentrated on the public/private interconnections between the economic, political and family spheres (Mitchell, 1971, Barrett, 1980, 1988). For this group of feminists the entry of women into the public world of employment has not brought about the emancipation of women as predicted by Engels (1972). Women's subordination in the family is mirrored by their subordination in paid employment. 'Feminists conclude that the "separate" liberal worlds of private and public life are actually interrelated, connected by a patriarchal structure' (Pateman, 1987: 118). This chapter extends and applies the public/private debate to the spheres of education and the family.

Edwards (1993) raises the issues of the separateness or connectedness of family and educational life for mature women students. I would argue that the two spheres are always related either positively or negatively. Studying at university was perceived by several women in this study as a positive and optimistic route for re-entering the public world after a period spent in the home. This chapter explores to what extent participation in the public world of education offered an escape from patriarchal domination in the family. How did the women's involvement in the educational sphere impinge upon relationships in the domestic sphere? To what extent did domestic responsibilities limit the women's social interaction and studies at the University?

Juggling Lives: Education, Family and Work

On becoming adult students their daily lives straddled the worlds of education, family and employment. Coping with the competing demands, and the different and sometimes conflicting roles expected by varying institutions was a dominant aspect of being a mature female student. Several participants talked extensively about the diverse pressures and struggles of trying to meet and serve the needs of partners and children while studying for a degree. The guilty mother syndrome frequently emerged in conversations:

> Time is one of the biggest factors with being a mature student because of fitting in with all of the home activities and different roles and trying so that everybody else does not feel left out. I keep trying to accommodate them as well as all the other work. It is difficult to handle and I wake up in the night sometimes and think, I have been a terrible mother lately because I have not done this or the other. It is worth it on the whole though but it is quite demanding (Cathy).

A 2+2 participant stated bluntly: 'sometimes I feel guilty when the children ask when I am going to be a proper mother again'. She continued determinedly:

> Being a student has become a major commitment in my life. Sometimes the task of studying and domestic life, that is, children, is exhausting but it is necessary in order for me to achieve my future goals (2+2 student).

Being a wife, mother, and possibly an employee made finding time to study problematical:

> It is dreadful trying to manage time for studying even with plans because families do not work like that. Families cannot fit into a framework like this especially when there are five of us. I find it very hard fitting a family into this structure (Pamela).

Joyce pointed out the problems faced by single parents:

> I am a single parent and although my ex-husband is supportive he works in London four days out of seven. All my family live in London, therefore, I have to do a juggling act with my daughter/childminder/ex-husband to ensure that she is cared for (Joyce).

However, by her final year Joyce maintained that the stress of undertaking several roles had levelled out.

To fulfil the functions of housewife and mother, studying frequently had to be undertaken at unsocial hours:

> Last night I stayed up until four in the morning to finish an assignment. It is difficult to manage the different roles but at least everybody supports me. I find it easier to work once the children have gone to bed because they forget that I am working (Judith).

Smithers and Griffin (1986) also found similar evidence among their sample of mature students.

The women in this study were having to assume dual roles as workers in the educational and family spheres in the same way as women who engage in the labour market (Adkins, 1995, Beechey, 1977, Mitchell, 1971). Studying did not offer a total escape from domesticity as responsibility for housework and childrearing still largely resided with the women. There was no evidence to suggest that domestic roles were becoming more equal between spouses as a result of the women studying. Male participants, in contrast, did not experience the burden of combining studying with domestic tasks. Hyacinth outlined her frustrations:

> I have found it very difficult to organise time for studying. It is very difficult to get them (her family) to understand how much time you need for your studies. They seem to want you to do well but at the same time they do not leave you alone or help with practical things that need to be done in the home to give you that time to get on with it. That is the problem (Hyacinth).

Hyacinth's situation had not eased by her final year of study. Family life became a focal point of discussion in her second interview as the problem had reached a crisis point. Hyacinth's plight highlights the dilemmas that women face when they attempt to break free from a life of domesticity and look for self-fulfilment:

> The family are supportive up to a point. They still do not help with the housework. It is still a big issue in our house. I am constantly screaming and yelling but they just say, 'oh mum is psycho'. Nobody listens. I just get accused of being selfish if I try to make time for myself and my studying. It is a real battle to have time to yourself. I just fall out with the kids most of the time to make my point. My eldest daughter had a baby last year. She moved out of our home after Christmas. She was coming back every weekend which I did not mind but it put pressure on me. She would turn up with the baby and come for a rest and it was giving me more

housework...In the end I had to tell her and we had a big argument. I told her that she could not keep on doing this. I have got to find time to get my studying done. She did not like it, so consequently we hardly speak to each other. In her eyes I am a bad mother. She said some awful things and I want an apology. She said that I am not there for her. It is all that sort of pressure on you and you are trying to study as well. When the kids are older I think they should realise and try and do something to help (Hyacinth).

Three women, despite the pressures of juggling roles, maintained that being a student had its rewards as it allowed them more time to spend with their children, particularly during the holidays. They also pointed out that if they were in paid employment they would also be constrained by time and roles. Judith was the most positive about this situation:

I find that I like spending time with them (the children) more than when I was at work because I would come home feeling frustrated and really dreading going tomorrow. I was in a bad mood all the time. I could not be bothered with things. At least when I am with my family I appreciate them more now. I am happier with myself. It is more quality time when we do spend time together. I can take my son to school each day, so we have a walk and a chat (Judith).

Many female part-time students have to fit studying around paid employment and unpaid employment in the home and, therefore, have to work treble shifts. Paid employment may also restrict the choice of evenings for attending classes and hence the options for courses. Valerie worked evenings at a Family Planning Clinic and frequently had to negotiate her workload and times at the clinics. For some mature students one difficult situation may end up being compounded by other factors. Valerie outlined her predicament:

My employers started out being supportive of my part-time studies - no problems. I had to work last Monday as she was getting a little fed up of accommodating me. She wants me to work alternate Monday nights. Fortunately I had a reading week last week so that took care of that. The other day when the seminar finished at five I went straight to work. It is not that easy. I need to have some more surgery this year as it did not fully work, so there is always something which gets in the way (Valerie).

A deterioration in the financial circumstances of full-time adult students due to changes in the student funding system meant that some participants had to resort to part-time work. This had a detrimental effect upon their studies. As Avril explained: 'When you have got the worry of the money you are constantly thinking about the money and not about the work. The security of having enough money leaves you time to do other things' (Avril). Karen also had to face the conflicts of studying and working part-time. She managed to find a job for four mornings a week on campus that did not coincide with the times of her lectures and seminars:

> I am trying not to think about finals next term. I have not got behind with my work but I am not working as well. To juggle a job as well as a course is extremely difficult. I knew it was going to be difficult but it was a toss-up between not being able to do the course because I did not have the money or taking the job which was really quite convenient but it is actually in my own study time. I cannot make up for that at night because of the family (Karen).

A small number discovered that they had to take on a role as carer and become 'parents' to their elderly parents. Valerie explained that looking after her elderly parents was now taking up more time than her immediate family. 'This was one factor that I did not consider when I enrolled' (Valerie). Assuming a caring role, however, was not gender specific. Peter as a part-time student managed to organise studying around his other commitments but declared:

> ...that you can plan your time but the problem comes when something goes wrong and you cannot plan for that. In the last twelve months my father-in-law was in hospital, seriously ill, so that all of my life was taken up looking after the family. The one thing that I have learnt is that you have to allow more space for slippage than I did as the family has to come first before my work (Peter).

Juggling roles and managing time for studying was made easier for the women students who received practical, moral and emotional support from husbands and partners. The amount of support given by partners varied. I would maintain, however, that the level of support was related to the relationships of power and domination within the family. On the whole the women who perceived themselves to have a good and fairly equal relationship with partners received higher levels of support. The women, however, who received little or no support were not deterred from their studies. By studying, these women were asserting control over a part of their lives for part of the day. In some cases the lack of partner support made the women all the more determined to succeed, but it did mean that they had a harder struggle to meet the needs of competing demands for their time and labour. Why were several husbands reluctant to give encouragement and support to their wife/partner?

The Struggle for Support: Patriarchy in Practice

About half of the female participants stated that they did not receive support towards their studies from their husbands/partners. A small minority maintained that their husband/partner was obstructive, occasionally hostile, and openly discouraged them from studying. Some women reported that their studies caused friction and arguments, thereby putting strain upon relationships. In one extreme case, Joyce, the situation resulted in divorce. Lack of support from partners cut across class boundaries. The issues are, therefore, gender specific. Husbands perceived that their patriarchal dominance within the family was under threat. Wives studying for a degree undermined the status quo within the family. Parallels can be drawn here with gender research in school (Stanworth, 1983). The pattern of males disliking 'clever' females is continued into adulthood.

Leonard (1994), Edwards (1993) and McLaren (1985) discuss the impact upon relationships of women studying in higher education. Leonard (1994) attributes a husband's discontent with their partner being a student to the fear that the traditional roles within the family will be eroded:

> Disapproval can be particularly acute if participation is seen to threaten gender roles. Married men in particular, fear that their partners' educational endeavours will affect the relationship and that household obligations will be traded off against university obligations (Leonard, 1994: 169,170).

I would go further than Leonard and argue that the issues are not only concerned with tasks and roles within the family. More importantly, and fundamentally, the debate is about power and male hegemony within the home. Some husbands feared that the knowledge, education and possible future employment gained by their partners would give them the power to challenge male hegemony within the family. Equalities in terms of power and roles are not viewed as appropriate and legitimate by some husbands.

The women in my study who experienced a lack of support from partners attempted to explain and to a certain extent justify why their husbands behaved in this way. Pamela pointed out: 'My husband is trying very hard to support me but he has felt very threatened and that has been difficult' (Pamela). She related his attitudes and behaviour to his working-class background that had socialised him into accepting traditional gender roles as the norm. Pamela accommodated her studies to fit in with his needs. Courses such as Return to Learn and a 2+2 degree programme were deliberately chosen in terms of their hours so that her studying 'would not disturb him' (Pamela).

Sue, a middle-class full-time student, lived with her boyfriend, a hospital consultant. Although she was achieving to a high standard Sue felt that she did not have the support of her partner:

> At home ideally there is support but often there is not. When you do not get support that causes strains. I think the reason I nearly chucked it all in was because with my partner being a consultant he does have a pressurised job. Both of us feel in the long run that if anything has to give it has got to be mine. I found that I was getting to the state where I was either feeling very angry because I could not have time to do what I wanted to do, particularly as I was doing quite well. It was frustrating because I could not do as well as I would like to do and I was feeling very angry or very guilty that I wanted time for myself... I think a lot of people share this. There is this kind of patronising feeling, well yes you can do it as long as it does not affect our lives. I will be proud of you if you get it but do not expect too much, do not expect me to be put out because it is not that important. What he found difficult is that he has a clinical mind and wants to see an end result and a clear purpose. Just to say I am going to what is almost like a whim does not seem like a good enough reason to him for everybody's lives to get disrupted. There are times when he felt well you did have a chance after school. It has changed everything at home dramatically (Sue).

Sue's boyfriend, like other partners in this study, would not assume greater responsibility for looking after their child to help Sue with her studying. Her endeavours were not considered important. As the breadwinner her boyfriend assumed economic and political power in the family. This lack of support made Sue feel guilty both about studying and for not being a 'good mother'. She felt that she was neglecting her daughter.

Domestic patterns of behaviour did not change. Sue, like other women in this study, worked two full-time shifts as a student and as a housewife. At the same time she was aware that she had allowed herself to become the person responsible for the home and the family without questioning the inequality of such a relationship. Sue elaborated and outlined the woman's burden:

I am very conscious of the fact that if I want to do something I have to arrange for our daughter to be looked after but he never has to think about that. He has someone to look after her. I sometimes feel that if I ask him to play with her he is doing me a favour. When I go to work I will make a lot more noise. It is partly my fault for colluding in this. I have allowed myself to take on this role. I find it a constant source of frustration because I am the mother and I cannot get into the course in a way I would have liked to have done (Sue).

At her second interview in her final year of study Sue stated that her partner had become more supportive although some of her comments were contradictory. However, she did confront her boyfriend about responsibilities over childcare by demanding time to herself for study:

I think he has become a lot more supportive as I have gone through the course. He says to me that I have potential but he never does anything to help me maximise it. He has seen my good marks and comments and has become progressively more supportive. From his point of view he now actually thinks well it is not me indulging in a whim to go and study. There is something coming out of this. There are often times when I do not go and talk to him about it when I am finding it difficult. I feel I cannot go and say this to him because he will just say why do you not give it up. Things have not changed massively. We still have our ups and downs. He is still not too interested to hear what I am up to, except that I am doing well. I think that to be fair he has tried to be more supportive in all sorts of ways. We had a blow up at one point and I said that I was fed up with the lack of fairness in this house. He goes off to play golf on Sundays so you have that day doing what you want to do. I want a day at the weekend to work but that day you are going to be responsible for Hannah. I said that I do not see why I have to be the one who is always there to answer all the needs twenty-four hours a day, seven days a week. He cannot understand what that demand means. I think a lot of men cannot because they have never done it. I just said, we are going to do this. I have had enough quite honestly. You are responsible for everything, including meals. I felt so much better because suddenly I had this whole day on my hands. Things seemed to settle down quite well (Sue).

Kate turned to the counselling services at Warwick when conflict with her husband verged on domestic violence:

I have not particularly enjoyed the trouble that I have had to encounter at home. It is hard work with the work and the children. My husband is not supportive. He has not got a degree, professional qualifications, but not a degree. He has always regarded me as being thick. I think that it has all come as a bit of a shock to him.. I think that he kept expecting people to throw me off the course. He can now see that I will be able to support myself and the children in the future and sees this as a threat (Kate).

Her husband continually tried to undermine her confidence and ability. The relationship did not break up but Kate thought it was probably because she did not have the self-confidence to do anything about it. At the second interview Kate revealed that her husband's attitude had worsened:

In fact it is probably slightly worse now because he realises that I will soon get a degree. He was not very happy in the summer when my examination results came through. I think he thought that once I had got here (2+2 student) I would get thrown out. He did not expect me to do as well as I did (Kate).

Kate gave examples of how her husband attempted to obstruct her studies. She chose one evening course in her final year of study as she wanted to opt for courses which would increase her chances of employment or ones that she would do well in. In order to attend the evening course she returned home from campus to look after the children and then returned for the six o'clock course. 'I go home and feed the children and take them wherever they need to go and collect them on my way back at about nine o'clock so it is a bit hectic' (Kate). Looking after the children is her responsibility:

In fact he actively goes the opposite way to make sure that he cannot help. My late night on Tuesday is a problem because I did not want to interfere with their lives (children) as both of them have athletics training. It would have been very easy for him to collect or take them but he would not do that. I have got to make arrangements for that to be done as opposed to life being made slightly easier for me (Kate).

For this group of mature women students their lives were characterised by a constant struggle to balance their degree work with the demands of domesticity. Underlying this was a strong motivation and determination to succeed. Similarly McLaren observed in her study that: 'What was particularly striking was the enormous odds against which some had to struggle to maintain their roles as students' (McLaren, 1985: 144).

The single parents with children looked to other relatives for support but did not always obtain it. Sally reflected: 'In theory my sons are supportive but in practice they still want their dinner on the table and their clothes washed'. Helen stated that her mother would not allow her the space to study at weekends. She is expected to spend Saturdays with her mother. She does not value education as it does not bring in a wage. Support for studying was also important for other groups of mature students. For many part-time students the lack of support from employers, rather than spouses was an important factor. In contrast some of the younger mature students who were still living at home valued the support they gained from parents.

Several women emphasised that they did receive support from their partner. In these cases studying had not caused tensions in marital relationships. Judith's partner understood the problems because he was also studying for an Open University degree:

> It would be difficult for me to study if I did not have support. There are others on the course whose husbands will not have the children. It is difficult to be a mature student with a family (Judith).

Valerie admitted that her husband 'is really good' and like Judith's husband he is also studying. However, Judith felt that she did not get any support from her children, parents or friends. Cathy related her husband's support to the fact that he was very involved in the business which he managed and was, therefore, independent from her. He did not rely on her for a social life. Jill's husband no longer worked full-time following an illness. As a result their roles were reversed as her husband took responsibility for housework and the cooking. In these type of situations, and for varying reasons, the husbands did not regard their wife's study as a threat.

Male Adult Students: Their Experiences of Support

Little is known about the inter-relationship of the public and private lives of male adult students. The comparative study of female and male adult students by Maynard and Pearsall (1994) is an exception. Research on mature students largely concentrates upon the lives of mature women students (Leonard, 1994, Edwards 1993, McLaren, 1985). In the absence of widespread research on male mature students two assumptions are made: male adult students are supported in their studies by female partners and marital conflict is minimal. My small sample of male mature students indicated that such a statement may be problematical, although there were gender differences in the way in which the problems were experienced.

Mike admitted that conflict arose with his wife upon the birth of their second child. He was obsessed by his degree work but also felt pressurised by it. The family were facing financial difficulties:

> Because I was in such a mess it was very difficult for my wife to support me and it got to the point when she said either get out or pull yourself together because I cannot cope with this any more. It got to that situation. If I was not doing work I was either very depressed or I was arguing with her. Everyone was losing out. That eased a lot and this year has been better because I have ignored the pressure and spent more time doing things. We are just bumbling along as most relationships do (Mike).

Mike felt he was neglecting his daughter because of the time spent studying. This concerned him:

> We are not doing the things that other families do. We do not go out very often. I feel sorry for Victoria as she is seven this month and there is a big age gap between her and Matthew. She does not really play apart from school. She is a bit on the outside looking in at times and I feel sorry for her. It would be nice to do more things with the children but it is difficult to do that (Mike).

However, Mike did recognise that many firms expect employees to work long hours and that if he was in employment the situation would be the same:

> Mind you in the work environment today, to just keep your job, you have to work more and more hours and so you are not there (home). At least I take Victoria to school and pick her up. I would not have that if I was at work. At least I am there even if we do not do a lot (Mike).

Bob noticed that he became more and more absorbed in the process and enjoyment of learning. He announced that this caused conflict with his wife:

> Predominantly I think that it is because I have got locked into myself. I think the economics course, particularly, did that. My wife thought that I was ignoring her. It did create some problems and I think that she is less supportive than she was last year. I think she likes me doing it but then she resents it because I get absorbed in something. I really do (Bob).

Another part-time student, Ben, admitted that he had difficulty managing time for studying, family, work and leisure. Ben outlined the cause of the conflict with his wife:

My wife is not supportive as I give up some of my holidays and non-work time for study although my daughter who is seventeen is supportive. Studying does cause conflict with relationships at home (Ben).

Adam, a retired person taking a part-time degree, also declared that, 'it is tricky keeping your partner's relationship'.

This evidence from my study clearly contradicts the findings of Maynard and Pearsall (1994). According to Maynard and Pearsall the mature male students in their study did not experience any conflict from their wives:

None of the married male students experienced such negative reactions: despite initial doubts and fears, their partners were more amenable to their wishes and more supportive, even though they had been excluded from participating in the ultimate decision (Maynard and Pearsall, 1994: 233).

Although some men did feel that they lacked support, and that strains were placed on marital relationships, they did not have the burden of looking after children and serving the domestic needs of family members in addition to studying. Male adult students, with the exception of Mike, were able to remain on campus to study in the library. The married women students, in contrast, had to meet children from school and undertake domestic chores. Male hegemony in the family made it easier for male students to assert their rights and state that they wanted time and space for studying. One male student, however, was aware of this qualitative difference between female and male married students:

My wife is very supportive. I recognise that I am very lucky as other mature students, particularly women, do not get that support. Women have terrible times with their husbands. I would like my wife to go to university as she would benefit from it (Duncan).

Negotiating the System

The mature students encountered, in Becker and Geer's (1961) term, 'problematic situations' both at home and at university. To deal with the problematic situations they faced participants developed group perspectives. Individual problems became collective ones. According to Becker and Geer et al. (1961) group perspectives are:

...modes of thought and action developed by a group which faces the same problematic situation. They are the customary ways members of the group think about such situations and act in them. They are the ways of thinking and acting which appear to group members as the natural and legitimate ones to use in such situations (Becker and Geer et al., 1961: 36).

Organisations, through rules and regulations, place restraints upon members. The perspectives that members bring with them may result in certain organisational rules and regulations being interpreted as a problematic situation. Group perspectives enable members to act upon the situation.

From the perspective of the mature students problematic situations arose at department level. Lecture and seminar times were key areas of concern for women students with children. Classes had to be chosen that fitted in with the school day. Frequently this limited course choices and meant that some participants had to opt for courses that they were not interested in and/or ones in which they felt they would underachieve. Several women were disappointed and angry that they were unable to pursue courses of their choice. They pointed out that although the University's policy was to encourage the access of mature students the structure did not always accommodate them:

> The only thing for me is the lack of childcare facility which feels like a lack of support for students with children. It is not a welcoming university for children. It does not actually feel like they want children here and if you are a mature student with children it is very important. I do have to come in and bring him even if it is to run into the library. Quite often I have to bring him in when I have a meeting with a lecturer. So I hurry. There needs to be somewhere where he can go and he would enjoy it (Avril).

At her interview Sue was informed by the Sociology Department that classes would fit in with school hours. She recalled:

> For the first year this seemed to be the case but the second year seemed like a free-for-all. I am not saying that there should be concessions but I think that certain things could be done that would make it somewhat easier for women with children. It is not that I do not want to be in at 9 o'clock, it is just that I cannot be in very easily by 9 o'clock. If you are going to say yes we welcome mature students then I think that you have to accept the fact there are extra difficulties and do something about that. It seems idealistic if you say yes we welcome you but we are not actually going to do an awful lot to make it a bit easier for you (Sue).

The women argued that if the University was intent upon an access policy then the institution should adapt to meet their needs. In the absence of institutional change many women took action to solve the immediate problems by negotiating with individual lecturers and departments. In doing so they learnt to manipulate the system to meet their needs. Their experiences and actions also made them aware of the different departmental cultures within the University.

Practices and policies varied among departments within the Social Studies Faculty. Some departments, such as Sociology, were positive in their response to mature students. How departments reacted to and treated mature students were important factors in the experience and quality of university life for mature students. As Becker and Geer (1961) assert:

> The ideas and actions of the faculty, residents, and interns affect the students, first of all, by setting the conditions under which students' problems arise. The rules the faculty makes, the way the faculty organizes and defines the situations in which students must perform, the way the faculty interprets and applies their rules and definitions - all these constitute a major part of the environment in which students act. The faculty and others in this way create the problems to which the perspectives of the student culture comprise some kind of solution (Becker and Geer, 1961: 48).

Interviews with Sociology lecturers revealed that some consciously organised seminar times to fit in with school hours. If seminar times were not suitable for mature students the women, individually and collectively, negotiated a new reality with the lecturer/s concerned. To draw on Cicourel's (1968) ideas, the women were, from their group perspective, negotiating justice to alter departmental rules and norms in a way that they considered to be fair. As a subcultural group they were affirming strategies within the confines of organisational regulations. The women were not displaying signs of resistance or rebellion but, from their perspective, simply asserting their rights. In Goffman's (1961) language: 'The various strategies for making out are part of the "underlife" of any institution' (Manning, 1992:112).

Two weeks before the academic year began Helen and others visited the campus to find out seminar times. On discovering that none of the sociology seminars suited their needs the women successfully negotiated with staff to change the times. For Helen as a single parent this action was a necessity. Other participants also reported that sociology staff were accommodating. However some departments were not. Pamela had wanted to major in politics but the attitudes and culture of the Politics Department forced her to change to sociology:

I think that the Politics Department at Warwick has got a lot of catching up to do. They disappointed me greatly. They are so rigid and strict in their petty rules. The Sociology Department I found so warm, affectionate and they treat you as a human being so I am very biased with Politics and Sociology. Lecturers in Sociology are more supportive (Pamela).

Joyce received a sexist response from a Politics lecturer. In making a request to change her seminar times the lecturer replied, 'we do not want to hear anything about child care arrangements. If you cannot fit in, just do not come'. Another 2+2 student commented: 'Sociology are accommodating but with Politics you would think that you were in a different university'. Jayne concluded that the Politics Department were not as helpful as the Sociology Department. 'If you go and ask about anything it is as if you should know, why are you asking us?' (Jayne). In contrast she thought that the Sociology Department was too helpful. At the second interview Sue was unsure about the practice of the Sociology Department towards married mature women students:

There is a lot of rhetoric in terms of mature student support but I am not sure how that is seen in terms of real strategies. I still feel that more could be done. Positive discrimination in a way. I do not feel like it is asking for an awful lot to try and give certain times which are easier for mothers. If you are going to have mature students and encourage them then I do think that you have to accept that they do have more constraints and try and do a few things to help (Sue).

Avril, as a single parent, noticed that the courses in her final year of study did not correspond with school hours, although in previous years there had been no problem. This caused childcare problems. 'One night a week he goes to the after school club which he really enjoys but it is very expensive; £5 a week for one night' (Avril). One of her courses was Film Studies. A course requirement was to watch two screenings of each film a week but Avril was unable to attend one of the sessions because it was after school hours. To solve the problem she asked the Department if she could borrow the video. She remarked: 'it is not ideal and they (the Department) do not like it but that is tough' (Avril). Ann commented that in terms of childcare an evening course was easier to manage than one that began at four o'clock.

Many women declared that during school holidays, half-term particularly, the only solution to childcare problems was to take children with them to lectures and seminars. Karen took her children to economics and politics classes. However, she chose her classes carefully, avoiding large lectures and two hour sessions. Sue admitted that Sociology staff were supportive in allowing children to attend seminars. Cathy acknowledged the institutional difficulties in designing a timetable to meet the needs of students with children:

> Where it is possible teaching hours should fit in with school hours. On the whole it did but I also recognise that putting together a timetable is a mammoth task as you have to get people together from different departments. On the whole I think they were as accommodating as they could be. In Education there were quite a few lectures from four to six. I managed to get round it but it was probably more difficult for other people. I have got family living nearby who can help (Cathy).

A minority of women stated that the University should not adjust its practices to suit the needs of mature students. Ann stressed:

> I am of the opinion that you choose to come here and you come here on the same terms as other students. I do not agree with providing special needs for particular groups. You cannot expect the University to organise around you (Ann).

Similarly Jayne stated that she had not found choosing classes to fit in with school hours a problem:

> On the core courses there are so many seminar classes to choose from that one will fit in. One course did not finish until 5pm but I made arrangements. You know that it is coming and you have got two years as a 2+2 student to prepare for it. I knew how old the children would be and I have got supportive parents (Jayne).

Kate was more emphatic:

> I know that there have been a lot of conversations about the University should do this and should do that but no I do not agree with that. As we are Warwick University students I think that we should behave as every other student. I do not see why they should make the exception because we knew the ground rules before we started. I think that if we want to be accepted as equals we should be. I have been very impressed with Warwick. I think that demands that I have heard from our group have been a bit ridiculous really. They think basically that the whole university should be geared towards suiting our 2+2 groups. We were getting an easy two years to be broken in and prepared for coming in to the University. All of a sudden

when we get to the point of coming all of a sudden everybody started saying why are the courses not fitting around the children? I think more adjustments have been made than I expected (Kate).

Other differences in departmental cultures were noted. Cathy studied for a joint degree in Sociology and Education. She preferred the Sociology Department to the Education Department because, 'the Education Department seems more like school and they seem to treat you like schoolchildren' (Cathy). Lynne shared similar ideas about the Centre for Education Development, Appraisal and Research (CEDAR). In comparing the Applied Social Studies Department with CEDAR she declared that:

> CEDAR is much more clinical and like being back at school again. We're not being respected as mature students. Their approach is completely wrong for mature students because people have crises and family commitments. They need to be more understanding (Lynne).

Duncan also stated that he felt that some departments, particularly the Science Education Department within the BAQTS programme, treated mature students as children, forgetting that they have life experiences and qualifications.

Participants in this study experienced and observed what Becher (1989) terms the tribes of academe. Becher notes:

> Despite their temporal shifts of character and their institutional and national diversity, we may appropriately conceive of disciplines as having recognisable identities and particular cultural attributes (Becher 1989: 22).

Summary

For many of the married women their subjective experience of the public world contrasted sharply with that of their private world. Participation in university life gave the women greater autonomy and independence over a part of their lives. Being a mature student offered a temporary escape for part of the day from patriarchy in the family. Although the two spheres were experienced subjectively differently in terms of power and autonomy the public and private worlds did interact. Domesticity frequently constrained the role of student for the women in ways in which it did not for the men. For example, finding time for study in the library on campus or at home was difficult because of the demands of being a mother.

Edwards (1993) argues that several of the women in her study chose to either consciously separate or deliberately connect their family and educational lives:

> For the women who wanted connections, education was an indivisible part of all areas of their lives, as was their family. These women did not feel they wanted to, or could, divide themselves into being students and being mothers and partners (Edwards, 1993: 123).

In contrast: 'The women who wanted separations felt that their lives were divisible into parts. They switched from being a student to being a mother/partner and back again...' (Edwards, 1993: 130).

All the married women in my study did try and make, to differing degrees, some connections between studying and family life. Discussions about their studies with partners were met with positive, negative or indifferent reactions. Women with more supportive husbands were able to discuss their studies more fully. This contrasts with Edwards (1993) who found that those who connected education and family experienced conflict with partners. Studying cannot be separated from family life. The level of support from partners, whether high or low, affected the way in which the women were able to carry out their studies. Being a mother also affected, in some cases, curriculum choice and how they were able to spend their day on campus.

The mature women students' lives engaged them in daily power struggles at home and on campus in order to make studying possible. However, they did not respond passively to the constraints that family relationships and institutional rules and regulations placed upon their lives as students. Many of the women were active agents in asserting greater equality in the home, even if it did result in conflict with partners. On campus they learnt the skills of negotiation with some departments to make seminar and lecture times more favourable to their needs. Collectively they sought ways of solving problematic situations that hindered the development of their student career. Thus their behaviour embodied a dialectical relationship between agency and structure.

The women's power struggles on campus and within the family, to use Beynon's (1973) term, can be characterised as a 'frontier of control'. In negotiating with departments and partners they were attempting to wrestle greater control over their lives. In tackling problems concerning their studies the line of control was pushed in their favour some days, for example, through changing seminar times. At other times the frontier of control was pushed back against them, for example, the lack of help from partners in sharing responsibility for children. Despite the constant power struggles all the women were determined to change their lives and complete their degree course. Greater support from partners in particular and, to a lesser extent from University departments, would have made their objectives easier to obtain and reduced conflict between their public and private lives.

9 Present and Future Biographies: Changing Lives and Future Hopes

Identity is, of course, a key element of subjective reality and, like all subjective reality, stands in a dialectical relationship with society. Identity is formed by social processes. Once crystallized, it is maintained, modified, or even reshaped by social relations. The social processes involved in both the formation and the maintenance of identity are determined by the social structure. Conversely, the identities produced by the interplay of organism, individual consciousness and social structure react upon the given social structure, maintaining it, modifying it, or even reshaping it (Berger, 1966: 194).

A Note on Identity and Self-Conception

A person's or group's identity is located within a social context. Identity is shaped by the interaction of human consciousness and social structure. As Berger elucidates: 'Identity is a phenomenon that emerges from the dialectic between individual and society' (1966:194). McCall and Simmons emphasise the historicity of a person's identity:

> We cannot fully understand interactions if we think of them only as isolated occurrences, because in many important ways they are merely the instances of sequences, the entire life histories of individuals. We cannot understand the identities and interactions of a particular moment without considering the influences of relevant life histories (McCall and Simmons, 1966: 202).

Goffman, in *Stigma* (1968), refers to three forms of identity; social, personal and ego. Manning (1992) summarises Goffman's definition of identity:

> A 'social identity' is based on relationships to other people. A 'personal identity' is tied to the individual's personal biography. Finally there is an

174

'ego identity': this refers to an individual's subjective sense of himself or herself as a result of various experiences (Manning, 1992: 98).

Social identity, therefore, enables us to understand who we are and provides us with an understanding of others. For Jenkins social identity 'is the product of agreement and disagreement, it too is negotiable' (1996: 5). In previous chapters I have stressed that the participants in my study assumed multiple roles in their daily lives as mature students. Each role was associated with a particular identity. As Turner maintains: 'social roles constitute the organising framework for the self-conception' (1968: 94). At the beginning of their student career the women and men were unsure and unclear about their mature student identity but as mature student subcultures were established individual and group student identities emerged. The self-concept became shaped by the student role-identity. Turner elaborates: 'The distinguishing content of any individual's self-conception is established during the interplay between the succession of self-images and his goals and values' (Turner, 1968: 94).

I was interested in looking at how dominant the student identity had become in their lives. What were the gender similarities and differences in how women and men perceived themselves as students? To what extent did part-time mature students regard themselves as students; or was studying merely a marginal activity in their lives? How was the 'self ' viewed by the participants themselves? How similar was this to Cooley's (1922) concept of the 'looking-glass self'?

Perceptions of Being a Student

All participants talked enthusiastically about learning, developing and widening their knowledge base. The majority used the word student or mature student to describe themselves, thus embracing the concept of being a student. A minority, particularly part-time students, were more reserved about using the term student. Jean, for example, was unsure whether or not she thought of herself as a student:

> I have not thought about it. It is nice to get away from work, even though it is a type of work. It is different from work and it does keep your brain active. It gives you fresh ideas coming to a different place (Jean).

Another part-time female student was more explicit: 'As a part-time student I feel very detached from the hustle and bustle of University life. It is difficult to make friends with full-time students as they have already formed their gangs'.

Feeling alienated and marginalised is, therefore, a problem for a small number of mature students. This group of part-time students pointed out that the campus in the evenings is a different world to the campus during daytime. There are minimal facilities open and fewer people around in the evenings. For most, being a part-time student is confined to attending the University for lectures and seminars, perhaps for three or six hours a week; possibly including a visit to the library. Dalvinder declared: 'I do not really feel part of the University. I am an outsider looking in. Being part-time can be a lonely experience' (Dalvinder). By the second interview Dalvinder had transferred status from a part-time to a full-time student. Her perception of herself as a student, therefore, changed drastically. As a result she no longer felt marginalised. Being a student rather than an employee now dominated her life enabling her to participate fully in University life. Other factors also contributed to Dalvinder's immersion in student life, both academic and social: she was in her mid-twenties and single:

> I have become more involved in Student Union activities. I am going to see a lot more bands. I went to see a few as a part-time student but I did not think much of the place. Also I never used to go and spend time in the Social Studies building. I just used to come to my seminars and just go. Whereas now you are spending days here... I have never been happier than I am now as a full-time student as I have access to everything and I feel part of the University. As a part-time student I could not say that I was a student of Warwick University as I did not think that I was with coming in for two hours but now I am. I will be happy when I have finally achieved a degree. I do not know whether I will get a decent job but I hope so (Dalvinder).

Jenny explained that she did not feel marginalised as a part-time student. Her philosophical reasoning was based on realism. 'Being part-time is just a small part of your life. You fit it in around work and families but being full-time is different as that is the centre of your life' (Jenny).

Peter shared a similar stance. 'You are going to be different from full-time students. It does not worry me and I do not feel marginalised' (Peter). Valerie also did not see herself as a student because, 'I am just somebody who comes here a couple of times a week. It is a sideline from going to work and doing the housework' (Valerie).

For Pamela, domestic responsibilities intervened and fragmented her student experience making it difficult to perceive herself as a student. 'It does not feel like being a full-time student when you are taking your child to school, doing your day there and picking your child up' (Pamela).

Age was a critical factor for two participants. For them the word student was associated with young people. Cathy explained: 'I called myself a student but I could not take it seriously. I suppose it was to do with the age. I think that it is probably better being a student when you are young without the responsibility of a home' (Cathy). Similarly another participant declared: 'The word student conjures up a young person. I do not refer to myself as a student but as someone "doing a degree". I am glad that my group (2+2) are similar in age to me' (2+2 student). Others had problems with the term 'mature student' but not with the word student. Adrian did not consider himself to be a mature student as he was in his early twenties. He was unaware that in terms of national policy and practice he was categorised as a mature student until the arrival of the questionnaire for this research:

> I have always thought of myself as a young student. I had never really considered myself any other way until I got the questionnaire and I got classified into that group. I felt about fifty when I saw it! From the beginning I have tried to fit in (Adrian).

Another young female participant stated:

> I do not regard myself as 'mature'! I was 21 when I began this degree. My friends are mainly 19-21 and so I do not feel that I am isolated or need to be fitted in.

Duncan, although in his thirties, could not cope with the term mature being attached to student in describing himself. Subjectively, like the younger participants, he rejected the objective definition of his status as a mature student:

> I do not perceive myself as a mature student. When someone says the term mature student I always think immediately that it is because of my age. I am probably more immature than the average eighteen year old (Duncan).

For the full-time students in particular the student identity and role was a dominant one in their lives. Being a mature student shaped their consciousness, how they perceived themselves and how others viewed them. The student identity was an important factor in constructing the individual's self-conception. McCall and Simmons explain that:

> A person's set of role-identities is itself organised in a complex fashion. The most distinctive aspect of this organisation is the hierarchical

arrangement of the role-identities in terms of their individual prominence in the person's thinking about himself (McCall and Simmons, 1966: 87).

The Age Factor: Younger and Older Mature Students

Younger participants, both women and men, had different expectations of what they wanted from a student life compared to the older participants. Being young and without family responsibilities meant that they wanted a 'total student experience'. This included spending a large part of the day on campus for academic and social purposes. A small minority, all men, lived on campus as their home town was outside of the University's local geographical region. Friendship groups consisted of fellow students, including younger students.

Dalvinder explained how her friendship group and social life broadened once she became a full-time student. It gave her the student experience that she had been denied whilst studying part-time in classes with mature students older than herself. Feelings of isolation were dominant because of the age barriers: some of the part-time students had children her age. As a full-time student Dalvinder found her space within the University:

> I met all these students. Everybody seemed to be on the same wavelength. It was good because there was a nice mixture of different types of people. They were not all young, they were not all old. You find your own little part. Before in the evenings it was all mature. My friend and myself thought what are we doing here? I soon made friends. You also have access to all the events. There are gigs and parties to go to. Before I would never have considered it. There were a lot of people who I thought were my age but were actually younger. I was completely shocked (Dalvinder).

Karen was one of the few 2+2 students in her early twenties. She felt marginalised within the 2+2 group especially during the college years. Although she lived with a partner they did not have any children and it was this factor which differentiated her from the other women in her 2+2 group. She felt that she had more in common with the 18 -21 year old students. At the age of eighteen she had turned down the offer of a place at a higher education institution. Now, however, she was looking for 'the student experience'. Karen explained, 'on entry to Warwick I had expected to "get the student life" but I do not feel that I have'. Friendship groups had already formed among the younger students by the time she arrived at Warwick to join year two students. Unlike Dalvinder she found it impossible to penetrate the friendship groups. On reflection she thought that she would have benefited more from taking an Access course followed by a three year degree course as this would have ensured a social as well as an academic experience as a young mature student. However, this was not practical for her at the time as she lacked a car necessary for transport.

Paul, a single full-time student in his early thirties, felt that his identity as a mature student was, in some ways, problematical as he was caught between two different groups:

> Younger students associate with their own. I get on with them and chat with them and they go to their parties at night and I go home. There is segregation between people who live on campus and those who do not. I think in many ways that I probably get on better with the younger ones than I do the matures because they are busy talking about their families. They are mostly women. There are only two mature males on this course. It is not being sexist in any way but they are talking about their children or how they dislike their husbands or something (Paul).

Paul's feelings of alienation in relation to other students was associated with both age and gender factors. Teacher training degrees, particularly those aimed at primary school teaching, attract mainly women, both as young and mature students. The nature of Paul's degree subject, therefore, meant that he felt isolated in social terms. Mode of degree course, age and marital status were, therefore, critical factors that affected the extent to which participants in this study perceived and identified themselves as students.

2+2: A Process of Labelling and Stigmatisation?

In the colleges and at Warwick those taking a 2+2 degree are generally referred to as 2+2 Social Studies students rather than Social Studies students. Several 2+2 participants questioned the need to be addressed as 2+2 students at Warwick other than for administrative purposes. The use of the term 2+2 was perceived as unnecessary, particularly as they felt that it occasionally served a negative function in labelling and stigmatising them as a distinct group of mature students. Joyce explained:

> There is still a lot of labelling of 2+2 students. I wish that there was not. Although the University uses it to simply classify a degree we are marginalised in some respects. There are signs in the library saying facilities for undergraduate 2+2s. It may be because it has only just started and we are being over-sensitive (Joyce).

As a group, 2+2 participants wanted to be integrated into the 'normal' undergraduate student population at Warwick. Integration was perceived as a common problem shared by this group stemming from the transition from the colleges to the campus. Many stated that joining year two of Warwick's degree programmes made them initially feel like outsiders within the institution.

As Ann stressed:

> I cannot understand why they still have the 2+2 label as we are no different to other students. I was under the impression, and I am disappointed that it has not happened, that we would just filter in with the other students. I can see the need for a 2+2 office at the University for the two college years but not for years three and four (Ann).

Judith also declared:

> I would like to drop the 2+2 label. It sounds simplistic. Younger students never mention it but it is just in your own mind that you are different from the others. It would be nice just to be able to integrate with the others. You feel that some lecturers might treat you differently because you have come that route and have not got A levels. I am not saying that it does happen but you feel that it could (Judith).

Aspects of labelling theory as applied to initial education and deviance (Hargreaves et al., 1975, Cicourel, 1971, Becker, 1971, 1974) are useful for examining the perceived action of labelling of 2+2 students by lecturers. Many university lecturers, like teachers in schools (Cicourel, 1971), make assumptions about the characteristics of an ideal student. At Warwick the ideal student is an eighteen year old with good A level grades, white and middle-class. Academic ability and social class are two important ingredients in the image of an ideal student. For many lecturers and certain departments, 2+2 students do not conform to the model student. Harries-Jenkins (1982) elaborates:

> ...the 'good student role' is defined solely by the tutor within a framework of educational criteria and assumptions which value cohesion rather than conflict, excellence rather than equality and achievement rather than participation...In part the problem which arises here is the result of a persistent reluctance to examine critically the extent to which the traditional interpretation of the good student role is essentially subjective. Many tutors are themselves the product of an educational system which emphasized the importance of academic achievement. Their appointment

is, in effect, their award for attainment as students (Harries-Jenkins, 1982:23).

2+2 students may be judged by some lecturers and departments as 'deviants' as they are adults, mostly working-class and lack formal qualifications. Many lecturers, particularly with the first cohort of 2+2 students, were sceptical about their academic ability and expressed reservations about them succeeding on a degree course. These fears were occasionally stated in meetings and in research interviews. As Becker (1971) argues:

> Professionals depend on their environing society to provide them with clients who meet the standards of their image of the ideal client. Social class cultures, among other factors, may operate to produce many clients who, in one way or another, fail to meet these specifications...In attacking this problem we touch on one of the basic elements of the relation between institutions and society, for the differences between ideal and reality place in high relief the implicit assumptions which institutions, through their functionaries, make about the society around them. All institutions have embedded in them some set of assumptions, and their embodiment in actual social interaction, in order fully to understand these organizations (Becker, 1971: 113).

Several 2+2 students felt that their student identity was being undermined by the use of the 2+2 label. In their perceptions, lecturers and departments were identifying, in possibly negative ways through policy and practice, 2+2 students as a separate student group. The adult students were concerned that they were not regarded as 'proper students' taking a 'proper degree course'.

Criticisms of the use of the 2+2 label were voiced mostly by those who had contact with the Politics Department. Jayne was critical of the actions of the Politics Department in separating 2+2 students from other students for teaching purposes:

> I think occasionally that the 2+2 label in the Politics Department meant that you were not taken as seriously. They group you in seminars according to which course you are on so that 2+2 are grouped together which I do not think is particularly good. It does not get me angry like some people but it is a little bit demoralising. It knocks your confidence a bit. I think that we work as hard as anybody else (Jayne).

Hyacinth explained that they were labelled as a distinct group when they arrived at the campus in year three. The labelling was compounded by the attitudes and behaviour of the Politics Department:

> It (the transition) made the 2+2 students partly isolated and labelled as a 2+2 student. For example when they sorted out the seminar groups for Political Theory they used the term 2+2. The younger students asked what 2+2 was. They should stop using that (Hyacinth).

The use of the 2+2 label was still a cause of concern for Hyacinth at her second interview:

> The 2+2 label - there is still a lot of talk about that. People are beginning to find out that there is a sort of stigma. 2+2 is seen as simplistic. I would like the label removed. On some of the Politics courses, not the one I am on, some lecturers see you as 2+2 (Hyacinth).

Kate disliked being identified as a 2+2 student by tutors in her first year at Warwick:

> I do not like being referred to as a 2+2 student which some tutors do a lot, mostly in Politics. It is used when discussing an essay on a one-to-one basis and tutors start by saying you are a 2+2 student are you not? You feel like you are going round with a beacon flashing (Kate).

However, at her second interview although Kate was still aware of the 2+2 label she did not feel that lecturers used the term in a negative way:

> I think that the lecturers still use the 2+2 label. If you are talking to a lecturer it tends to be, 'oh you are a 2+2' and I say 'yes I am'. They are not meaning to be detrimental or anything. I suppose it helps (Kate).

Participants, particularly 2+2 students, were conscious that they were perceived and labelled as being different from younger undergraduate students. They were marked out by their degree course, age, class and educational backgrounds. Pedagogically this information could be used by lecturers in a positive way to provide a learning environment which facilitates the learning needs of particular groups of students. However, the 2+2 students in this sample did not want to be singled out for special treatment or concessions in pedagogical terms. They just wanted to be integrated into the mainstream body of undergraduate students at Warwick.

Being a Mature Student: A Process of Changing Identity and Consciousness

Spending time as a mature student marked a period of transition in participants' lives. They all changed their behaviour, values and attitudes to differing degrees; some more than others. The self was redefined and reconstructed. They could not go back totally to the person they were before entering university. Pascall and Cox (1993) maintain that their research indicated that 'there had been a heightened awareness of the self, a search for a new identity, or for the "real" self that the contingencies of life had suppressed' (Pascall and Cox, 1993: 120). West stressed that adults who enter education do so in order 'to create a new identity' (1996: 25) as 'most had concluded that they simply could no longer continue as before' (1996: 25).

Although many of the women returned to domesticity temporarily while seeking employment or awaiting the start of a postgraduate course, they were more critical about their role as housewives. A gender consciousness emerged. The acquisition of knowledge, particularly in the social sciences, led many women to reflect upon their position as women in society. With the exception of one or two they did not become feminists but they were determined to strive for greater equality in both their private and public lives. McLaren (1985) noted that many of the mature women students in her study did become feminists:

> The women were on the difficult path of unlearning to be 'female', of questioning their pasts and the ways in which they had been manipulated by traditional sexist mores. This also set them questioning the current organization of society. The process of unlearning required not only that they should see themselves in different ways, but also that they should recognize the need to be given real chances to develop themselves (McLaren, 1985: 172,173).

Relating to Family and Friends

For a minority of participants becoming 'educated' established a social distance between themselves and friends and family. Helen remarked that her group of friends had changed. The topics of her conversations were different and as a result communication became difficult. Now her friends consist of fellow female students, one of whom lives near to her. Similarly Sue recalled: 'You grow apart from friends you had before being a student and your new friends are students. A lot of people in your life, friends, partners, can feel threatened by what you do' (Sue).

Mike was more explicit in his reflections about friendships and relationships with family members. Like several participants his friends are now limited to other mature students. Studying at university distanced him from his working-class background:

> The closest friends I have made are 2+2 students. There are a lot of people you talk to but do not mix with outside but those I do mix with outside are 2+2 students. I have definitely made some good friends. I now find it very difficult to talk to people, (not his new friends) but my brother and dad. We go for a steak on Sundays and I find myself sitting there in silence because I am just thinking well what do I talk about? I cannot talk about the University because they do not really understand it. You talk about different things. If we do not talk about football then we do not talk about anything. Also when I see people from where I used to work and I say things like I do not want to work they cannot understand it. They think that Mike has gone weird (Mike).

Mike did not regret the social distance he now experienced from family and previous friends. To him the access to knowledge has been of greater importance. 'It is the best thing that has ever happened to me...I think that it opens your eyes to the real world' (Mike). With many female participants social distance was experienced, to differing degrees, with partners. Culturally and academically they grew apart from peers outside of university life. As a result their lives became characterised by contradictions. Family and community life remained rooted within a working-class culture but their ideology, perspectives and attitudes were moving towards a middle-class culture. Edwards (1993) reveals similar dilemmas faced by the women in her study. Some participants recognised that the development of social distance from family and friends was an inevitable outcome of studying.

Others, like Valerie, admitted that they had a mixture of friends, those from before entering university and fellow students. However, this group of participants were encouraging their non-university friends to return to education. Some of their friends did decide to return to learn. This suggests that their friends shared similar attitudes and experiences to participants.

Changing Selves: The Influence of Academic Disciplines

Studying sociology greatly impacted upon the values, attitudes and perspectives of several students. Participants studying other disciplines did not mention to the same degree a direct link between the nature of the subject and changes to the self. Sociological knowledge and discourse enabled the mature students to reflect critically upon their lives. It heightened their awareness and consciousness about gender, class and, in some cases, racial inequalities. Sociology led them to question the 'taken for granted' in the social world. This in turn enabled them to reassess their lives and in the process change their self-conception.

For Sue:

> Sociology has really given me a lot. It is such a great subject for making you question things. You find yourself looking at things at an abstract level. We have lots of talks at home about what good is sociology. I believe it does have its uses (Sue).

A minority felt that politically they had become more left-wing as a result of studying sociology. As Sarah explained:

> I have become more flexible and more left-wing from doing sociology. Previously I might have said that being unemployed was your own fault and now I am all for the underdog. It has been a very valuable experience. It is moulding me as a human being for the better (Sarah).

Cathy, as a Christian, discovered that sociology both contradicted and challenged her religious views. She elaborated:

> Studying has changed me as a person. It has changed the way I look at things. It has made me more analytical and I am not so accepting what I see on the face of things. I was a Christian before I started. I have had my faith challenged by some of the sociological things in a big way but I am really thrilled as it has just deepened my faith as I do not see any answers in sociological theories anyway so it has deepened my faith and been challenging. I have realised that there is no answer whereas things probably seemed more simplistic before. I am beginning to see things from lots of different ways and realise that there is not a simple answer in the end (Cathy).

Peter, a Trade Union convenor in a factory, discovered that some disciplines helped him to comprehend more fully class relationships both within and outside the factory:

> I have found the two subjects, sociology and politics, interesting outside of the work situation. It has put a lot of pieces into the jigsaw so that you can understand and it is good (Peter).

Lynne also found that politics 'opened up interesting reading'. 'After doing a politics course I am now more interested in what politicians do. I am paying more attention to politics and analysing political issues. It is very stimulating' (Lynne).

For a small number of participants studying particular subjects further confirmed their ideological beliefs and gave academic credence to them. Avril, for example, was interested in gender issues before starting her studies. 'Taking courses on gender has affirmed what I have always believed' (Avril). In contrast, studying equal opportunities issues in relation to education made Paul conscious of the existence of gender and race inequalities in society.

Enjoyment of Learning and Changing

Changes to the self and learning were dialectically related. The learning process and the acquisition of knowledge broadened their perspectives about themselves and society. Their consciousness was awakened to new perspectives and new ways of perceiving and analysing the world. The learning of new knowledge brought with it a new language and discourse. As a result perceptions about the self changed. Participants, to differing degrees, redefined themselves in terms of being female, working-class and in some cases black women. In similar ways several of the male participants reassessed their lives and self-concept as a result of studying. Structure and action intersected in positive ways.

All participants were asked whether or not they had enjoyed being a student and whether or not they had changed as people as a result of being a student. The women responded that they had thoroughly enjoyed being a student despite the difficulties of studying as a mature student. All believed that they had made the right decision to return to learn. Common experiences were outlined by participants. This included feeling 'more educated', being 'more critical about the world', 'becoming a more interesting person' and feeling 'more confident' about themselves. Only a minority of men admitted to having changed as a person. They did not discuss self-change as extensively as the women. Enjoyment of learning, pursuing knowledge and self-change were inter-related factors.

The mature students became less accepting and more critical of knowledge and news as presented by the media, relations and friends. As Hyacinth explained, ' I suppose I have changed in some ways. I look at things more critically - different issues and things and not just accepting that they are given to you in the media'. Joyce felt that she had altered in several ways:

> I think I have changed as a person. I have become a lot less irritable. I have a lot more patience. I am a lot more questioning. You see conspiracy theory wherever you go! I am just generally more aware. It does give you confidence and a good education as the University is so well recognised (Joyce).

Like others Jayne believed that gaining knowledge had improved the quality of her life. 'It makes a tremendous difference even when you read the newspaper, everything you do. It is just widening your knowledge on everything' (Jayne). Sue acknowledged that participating in a university institution had transformed her in multiple ways:

> I feel more educated as a general comment. I know a lot about the areas which sociology touches but I do not know about anything else. I think I thought that when I came I would know more about general knowledge but sociology does draw on a lot of areas anyway. I feel better able to express an educated opinion. I am conscious that a lot of my opinion has been shaped by here. I hope that it has made me quite sort of critically aware. I think I accept things on face value a lot less than I used to. I suppose it has made me aware that I have got some skill that I did not realise I had such as writing skills. That has been a good thing (Sue).

Cathy was over-awed by the knowledge that she had acquired through studying sociology:

> I have enjoyed learning. I have had my eyes open to the so many things which go on. Sociology in particular. I am staggered at the things that I have learnt and I just want to keep learning (Cathy).

Jenny noticed that studying for a degree has addicted her to learning. Consequently she stressed the value of continuing education:

> Studying has widened my horizons. It has helped me to develop my personality as there are things that you are totally ignorant of and it is amazing the things you learn and you go through life and do not know anything about. It is interesting how it develops and your craving for learning continues. I think that without any continued education you get blinkered in life - just do your job and anything else you do not need to know a thing about. Part of your brain just dies. There are a lot of people

who say what on earth do you want to put yourself through doing that and I find that a strange attitude. Learning gives you confidence as a person. I think it is very good (Jenny).

Similarly other participants maintained that learning had liberated them from sheltered lives and a naivety about the world. Valerie, for example, reflected:

I probably have changed as a person as you are evolving all the time but I do not think that my basic personality has changed. It has made me more confident. The learning process does wonders for your ego. I do analyse situations a lot more now. It is making me look deeper into things. I am always saying to myself what is going on here? I think that sums it up really. Is everything as it seems? Probably the influence of studying sociology and counselling (Valerie).

For Sue the benefits and enjoyment of being a student have been both social and academic:

I have enjoyed feeling like something special here. I have found that I can come to a place like this and fit in, make connections with people and be comfortable with them and find that people want to know me as I am not a great socialiser. At times, in certain courses, certain subjects I have really enjoyed learning about it and wanted to learn about it and really get into it and understand why things are the way they are (Sue).

Others remarked that they had become more tolerant of people different to themselves. Ann stated, 'being a student has made me more tolerant of other people's opinions. At home you are insulated and think that what you think everybody thinks' (Ann). Ben was explicit:

Studying has changed me as a person as I have gained knowledge and am now more willing to listen and accept other people's ideas. For example, when I was in the army we were told that communism was our enemy and at that time I would not have talked to a Marxist. But now I talk and listen to a Marxist student in one of our groups and we find that we have a lot in common (Ben).

For the women in this study gaining confidence was a major factor identified in terms of self-change. Their roles as daughters, mothers and wives had subjected them to male dominance throughout their lives, resulting in low self-esteem. Feminists have highlighted this problem (Jaggar, 1983).

Being confident gave the women a stronger identity; a new femininity which enabled several to question and challenge male hegemony in the family and at work. Dalvinder, for example, as an Asian woman felt that learning had given her a sense of power. Several women declared that they felt more fulfilled as a person because they are doing something for themselves. For Joyce, whose studying resulted in a divorce, fulfilment was an important outcome of learning. She also felt more independent, freer and more in control of her life.

Avril, another single parent remarked when asked if she had changed as a person:

> Definitely. It has made me more confident. It has changed the way I think about change itself. I am a lot more positive about myself and about the years I have got ahead of me. I am not as materialistic. I do things differently (Avril).

Sue also reflected about how she had developed. Like several other participants Sue noticed that she had become a more confident person. However, she was uncertain whether she would continue to feel confident once she had left the security of campus life and entered the world of work:

> I am a more well-rounded person. I feel like I have become more substantive. I am very aware of the fact that I am saying that while I am here (at the second interview). Because I have done well in this Department (Sociology) it gives me a lot of confidence. It feels like I am being head-hunted. When I step out into the outside world I am just going to be Joe Bloggs. I do not know if it will last when I go out there. It just feels like a sheltered experience, a very sheltered life. I think going out there is going to be quite intimidating. I like to think that it has done something to increase my self-confidence but I almost feel that I will not know about that until I have left here (Sue).

For Duncan, a former corporate executive, student life offered a significant but positive change:

> It has basically made my life what I thought it should be. It is perhaps the case that I always wanted to do it and it is more my style. Perhaps it is my own statement to myself. It has changed my life by loosening up and losing the claustrophobic corporate life. I have gained an enormous amount being a student (Duncan).

Hopes for the Future

Escaping domesticity and boring traditional female employment were critical factors for several women in deciding to return to education. Gaining a degree would, it was hoped, provide a pathway to obtaining a more fulfilling occupation. Once participants began their degree courses some of the women became less optimistic about securing a career. In thinking more seriously about their futures they became aware of the age barriers in relation to career prospects. Many employers are reluctant to employ older graduates (Graham, 1992, Brown and Webb, 1990). Others recognised the declining value of a first degree on the labour market. Karen pointed out: 'I feel that it would be better to have a Master of Arts (MA) from an employer's point of view as so many people have degrees' (Karen).

A minority were unclear about which career to enter because of the age factor and a lack of knowledge about certain occupations and entry requirements. Judith, for example, when asked about her future replied: 'I do not really know. I think that I will have to see what is available because there is a problem with being older and a mature student' (Judith). Hyacinth was also concerned about her age discriminating against her career prospects:

> I think that I would have preferred to have done it (a degree) when I was a lot younger because I think that at this age it is very difficult to go into a career now. You have got age against you. There are only certain areas that are accessible, such as social work and teaching. I suppose they prefer to take people a lot younger. I was going to take a degree when I was younger but one of my daughters was taken ill and I had to leave it. I have got no regrets that I have done it (Hyacinth).

Hyacinth became more concerned about obtaining a career as her studies progressed:

> When I first started I was not worried about getting a job. I just wanted to learn things; politics and social policy. I was just quite happy to have this information and know how things work. I did not really think about what I was going to do with it but I would like to put it to use and get a job (Hyacinth).

At the same time Hyacinth was becoming nervous about attending job interviews. 'I know that they will be different and harder to previous secretarial ones. I am also aware that I will probably have to go to several interviews'. Towards the end of her final year of study, at the second interview, Hyacinth stated that ideally she would like to become a careers adviser and work with children in school. She was also considering studying for a social work qualification in order to work with black groups.

Occupational preferences were for posts in the public rather than the private sector. Social work and community work were popular career choices among the women. As most were studying social sciences these choices of careers were not surprising. However, they would be changing from one female job, such as secretarial work, to another that reflects the caring role of women. Three women wanted to enter social work for more radical reasons to enable them to work with women and black groups. Lynne's long-term aim, as a Chinese woman, is to return to the Far East to use her degree and promote education to improve the social situation of women in China. She remarked: 'Women are very vulnerable there. It is still a very harsh regime' (Lynne).

Dalvinder was considering working in the USA at some point in the future but her more immediate plan is to obtain a community work qualification:

> First of all I would like to do community work. I would like to do something in the legal world, maybe work for a law centre or some advisory centre or a race relations council. I would rather do that than go back to where I was before working for an accountant who earns loads of money for nothing. I would just fall back into that negative way of thinking (Dalvinder).

Before entering Warwick Sarah had worked as a residential care worker and had entered university with the aim of achieving a social work qualification to improve her promotion prospects. On reflection she felt that she had chosen the wrong degree course (2+2) for remaining in social work:

> At Warwick it is a two-year MA/Certificate and Qualification in Social Work (CQSW). I do not see the point in going back into residential care work without the qualification. I have spoken to a careers officer but a two year course is financially impossible. I do not know what I will do. I have thought about teaching. I hope that the degree will not be wasted but I do feel stuck. I could be philosophical and say that it does not matter without the CQSW (Sarah).

Jayne realised that the employment she obtains may not relate to the subject area of her degree. 'I do not expect to walk into a job which I will necessarily be needing my degree for but I expect it to come in useful in the longer term' (Jayne).

Those studying for a BAQTS degree had opted for a particular career at an earlier stage than other participants. Jill hoped to obtain a teaching post. She explained that, 'I think I will be able to cope with it (teaching) more and more as the course goes on' (Jill). However, Jill continued, 'we have been told that we might not get jobs at the end of the course. I have got a lot of life experience. Who knows what might turn up' (Jill). The male BAQTS participants were clearer about their future aspirations. For example Paul stated:

> At the moment the foremost thing in my mind is getting a 2:1 which should set me up reasonably well for interviews. I would like to get a teaching job in Coventry for a few years, then move out and possibly emigrate. Basically I do not want to be stuck in Coventry for the rest of my life. I have lived in Coventry all my life.

Duncan was clear about the type of school that he wanted to teach in but was also considering emigrating with his family to Canada:

> I am looking for a teaching job that has got 'quality of life'. I would not go for a job in an inner city. I would not feel guilty about not helping such children as I am supposed to. If I could get a very small school in the middle of Cornwall teaching middle-class children I would be very happy (Duncan).

A small number of non-BAQTS students were considering applying for a Post Graduate Certificate in Education (PGCE) course. Initially they had been unaware of a PGCE qualification as a route into teaching. By the second interview Ann, for example, had been accepted onto the PGCE course at Warwick. A minority were undecided about the type of career they wanted and sought advice from the Careers Office at Warwick. However, they felt that they were confronted with prejudiced attitudes from careers officers because they were mature students. As Joyce outlined:

> I went to see careers as I was not sure what I wanted to do. It is a symptom of my personality. I am totally vacant. I have no driving ambition. I had wanted to see a certain person in careers but careers make the decision about who you see. I felt that the careers adviser I saw was very negative towards mature students. It was awful. I found out that two other 2+2 students had had the same response. When you are mature and you are not very confident about going back into the workplace you need somebody who is more positive and gives you ideas (Joyce).

Joyce persisted with the Careers Office and went to see another careers officer. This time she received a more positive response and discussed several options. This included contacting her previous employer about graduate training and information about teaching and local authority work. She was unaware of the existence of post-graduate teacher-training courses. Initially she had wanted to enter into local authority work in a housing department until the careers adviser told her that she would have to think about how she would feel implementing policies that she might not agree with. As a single parent she had decided to move back to London and her family as this would provide a network of support for her daughter while she was working. 'I feel that the work prospects will also be greater in London especially for women. Around here it is manufacturing and engineering. It is so isolating here' (Joyce). Like many other participants Joyce would also like to do postgraduate study but financial reasons deterred her. 'Really I want to find work as I am fed up of being broke' (Joyce).

Cathy's second interview occurred immediately after she had taken her finals and when she was at the stage of applying for employment. She had sent off for details for a range of jobs but was becoming disillusioned:

> Every job I am interested in I have something missing - experience, skills. I will keep applying. I am thinking of going to the Careers Service in Leamington as they have someone who deals with mature students. If I do not get a job I might do voluntary work or a certificate course. I would like a job in advice work but quite a lot want a counselling qualification. I have also got an application for a marketing researcher at the University. I feel that I could do the job but it wants qualitative and quantitative research experience. I am also interested in teaching on Access courses in FE but I am not sure whether or not you need teaching experience (Cathy).

Adrian, a law degree student, aspired to becoming a solicitor but was experiencing class discrimination when applying for posts. As a result he was considering returning to the USA:

> I think that the state of law over here, the difficulties of getting in are just so phenomenal that I sometimes wonder is it worth it? It is cliquey. I got an application form from a solicitors firm the other week but it essentially said that if you are not from Oxford or Cambridge, do not apply (Adrian).

Two women, both in their forties, did not view obtaining a degree in instrumental terms. They were not, therefore, planning their future in relation to employment. Valerie assessed her situation:

I do not look long-term. I do not have any ambitions. There has been so much illness and death around me recently that I just take every day as it comes. I am also realistic about my age - late 40s in terms of employment. My main priority is getting the two children through the degree. The degree is just something that I have done that I thought I could not do. It is not the glittering prize. Your perspectives change when you are in your mid-forties. You really want to enjoy life when you have been constrained for 20 years bringing your kids up and I am not going to constrain myself with a full-time job (Valerie).

Similarly Pamela declared that getting a degree was, 'a completeness of completing an education. I do not look at it as a means to an end'.

On entering university participants were convinced that achieving a degree would open doors to more interesting and satisfying careers. Towards the end of their studies they began to realise that employment opportunities for mature graduates were not as plentiful as they had initially assumed. Many lacked knowledge and information about certain professions and qualifications, indicating the need for mature student support and guidance in relation to employment. Some who did seek guidance from the Careers Office found it a negative and unhelpful experience. By the end of this research a small number had been offered places on various postgraduate courses at Warwick. The other full-time students were applying for jobs, some had had interviews but none had been successful. Edwards noted that the women in her study 'sometimes found it difficult to gain employment' (1993:148). Only a minority found employment that they considered 'a suitable reward for doing a degree' (1993: 149). In contrast Pascall and Cox (1993) revealed that the majority of their participants did become upwardly mobile and economically secure as a result of obtaining a degree.

However positive the experience of studying for a degree was, it does beg a question for adult educators to consider. In widening access to higher education what are we widening access to? Are false hopes being set if one of the reasons for adults returning to study is to improve their employment prospects, or is the experience of learning sufficient in itself? As Kate remarked: 'Widening access for adults is only a good idea if there are jobs afterwards to go to. If they get more matures it could end up being a waste of money' (Kate).

Postgraduate Study as a Future Option

Several women expressed an interest in continuing their studies to postgraduate level but in practice they were restricted by the financial cost.

Avril applied for an MA course at Warwick in Women's Studies and Film. As a single parent studying for a master's degree would be dependent on obtaining funding. However, she elaborated:

> I am not actually sure that I am going to do it because the plan is that we go to New Zealand in September. This is an option depending on my partner's work. I am working on a book for creative writing. I would like to spend the first year in New Zealand doing that and doing some part-time training work and once I have done that and we are settled then I would have a look at studying. My partner is a New Zealander. We have talked about other places but it makes much more sense to go there. We have got all his family support. I have got friends there too. It is a wonderful place (Avril).

At the first interview Sue was considering counselling work as a career as she had worked voluntarily as a counsellor. Her ideas had altered by the second interview. A sociology tutor encouraged her to either apply for a master's course or register for a PhD. Sue commented:

> I was very much of the opinion that I would stop now after my first degree because I felt that I could not really ask people to put up with me carrying on. It has cost a lot to them, particularly my daughter. I used to fantasise about carrying on particularly as by the end of year 2 I had all these positive messages about how I was doing. And in a department you start to get people asking you because they clearly mark out the people they feel they would like to continue here. One tutor gave me a real vote of confidence and expressed quite clearly his belief in me. That spurred me on to thinking that I really would like to do this (Sue).

As her partner had not been very supportive of her studies she felt that she had to get his agreement about continuing her studies:

> I went home and talked to my boyfriend about it. In his rather less admirable way he often becomes very enthusiastic about what I can do when he sees it in other people's eyes. When I was telling him about all these positive remarks I have had he got quite interested in the idea of me carrying on. When we were talking seriously about the child issue he was really saying that in actual fact he feels like the time is passed for another child. So he was not completely against it in a way that I thought perhaps he would be. We said that we would talk again about it. I have been trying to find a suitable MA course at Warwick. I did toy with the idea of going straight to a PhD but quite frankly the pressure to just get through the third year is such that I did not feel in a position to get a decent research project together and also applying for funding. Although that was a really nice idea I said no (Sue).

Sue recognised that financially she was in an advantageous position compared to other mature students as her partner is a doctor. Whether or not she would study for a MA would be dependent upon her partner's agreement:

> It will come down to the crunch of how important my boyfriend sees or how supportive he is going to be. If I could not do it full-time I would like to do it part-time so I could do a really great MA. It is also cheaper. My boyfriend is very traditional in many ways and if I was at home doing all the housewifey sort of things it would be much easier for me to do a part-time MA. He would feel much happier about it (Sue).

In contrast Mike did not feel the need to discuss the possibility of continuing his studies with his wife. Like Sue, a tutor in the Sociology Department persuaded him to register for a PhD. Initially he was unsure what the tutor meant because of the language he used:

> I did not know what he meant by personal research but I pretended I knew what he meant. I said, 'oh not really'. He said that I ought to think about it. I said, 'oh right I will' not knowing what the hell he was talking about because he never said the words MA or PhD. If he had said those particular words I would have known. I went away and talked to people and asked them what they thought he meant. Basically he meant a PhD. I went back and saw him and said that I wanted to do research about inequalities in health but I need funding. I have got supervisors sorted and references and I am applying for funding. I am putting all my eggs in one basket because I am not really looking for a real job (Mike).

Reflecting upon their Experiences and making Recommendations

All participants valued the opportunity of a second chance in education to complete their educational goals and reach their potential. The experience of being a mature student marked an important watershed in their life. Whatever the future holds the women felt that their lives had changed for the better. As one participant explained: 'I feel that this is a very exciting time in my life and that my life is and will continue to change as a result of my studies'.

For the married women knowledge and studying offered a liberation from domesticity. They had gained a space and territory in the social world for themselves, something that their lives had previously lacked. Lifelong learning was valued highly:

> Knowledge is wonderful. I am questioning things. Why did I get to 40 before I went to university? I have learnt so much. Whatever happens no

one can take the three years away. It has been like gold. I have really enjoyed it (Pamela).

Throughout their mature student career participants accumulated a wealth of knowledge about coping as a non-traditional student within a traditional elite university. Warwick was perceived as being a middle-class institution by several participants. Valerie, for example, observed:

> It is full of people with professional qualifications, middle-class people. The Part-time Degree brochure is off-putting for people like me. It needs some case studies of people like me who left school at 15 and are working-class. It must be even more off-putting for black women (Valerie).

Criticisms of Warwick were mostly practical ones but important issues to mature students. These included the shortage of books in the library, the lack of childcare facilities, access to part-time degree staff and the inflexibility of part-time degree courses. All participants felt that on the whole the University did cater for mature students in providing a positive and enjoyable learning experience. Kate exclaimed, 'I just think that the whole University has coped with us pretty well. I think that it adapts to mature students very well' (Kate). Similarly Duncan announced: 'I think that Warwick does a good job in terms of mature students. I do not feel I am a mature student, I am a student' (Duncan).

Institutionalisation: A Sense of Belonging and a Fear of Leaving

Towards the end of their student career several participants, particularly the women, expressed their regret and sadness that the degree course would soon be completed. This group of mature students, to use Goffman's (1961) terminology had become 'institutionalised'. For the past three or four years a central and important part of their lives had revolved around campus life and being a student. The women were reluctant to leave the academic culture and lifestyle. For many women university life offered a retreat from domesticity and an arena where they could act out what they perceived as their 'real self' rather than being a mother or wife. At the same time they were becoming dependent upon the security, stability and familiarity of institutional life. As Avril remarked, 'I do not want to go back to the real world'. The time at Warwick passed too quickly for some:

> You start day one, year one and suddenly it is the last day, year three. I cannot believe that I am nearly at the end of it now. I have gone from that

naive person not knowing anyone to swanning in as if I own the place. When I do stop there is going to be an awful lot of sadness. I am not looking forward to the day when I say well that is it and now I must go back to being a housewife (Sue).

Cathy explained that she felt both empty and elated when the three years finished. 'It is all what is next? I feel sad in a way that I will not be going back there. I am really thrilled that I have done it and when I heard that I had got a 2:1 I could not stop crying' (Cathy). The desire by many participants to continue with postgraduate studies resulted from both an enjoyment of learning and to delay re-entering the outside world. Goffman in *Asylums* (1961) and *Relations in Public* (1972) discusses the construction of the self in relation to a social organisation. As Goffman (1961) indicates:

> Without something to belong to, we have no stable self, and yet total commitment and attachment to any social unit implies a kind of selflessness. Our sense of being a person can come from being drawn into a wider social unit; our sense of selfhood can arise through the little ways in which we resist the pull. Our status is backed by the solid buildings of the world, while our sense of personal identity often resides in the cracks (Goffman, 1961: 280).

Leaving Warwick marked another transition in the lives of the mature students. Only a minority will continue with postgraduate studies. The mature student role will be deconstructed but the student experience may continue to impact upon their lives. The new knowledge gained has enabled participants to view the social world more critically from different perspectives. Spending time in an academic institution enabled the women to find the space to reassess themselves and their lives as women and leave changed persons. A new self-conception will have to be constructed on entry to a work organisation. As McCall and Simmons point out:

> As a result of these ties to specific persons and institutional contexts, the content of a given role-identity continually changes as alters and institutions enter and pass out of the person's life-stream (McCall and Simmons, 1966: 68-69).

However, the self-conception constructed in the new institution and in the family will be shaped by the mature student experience.

10 Transforming Women's Lives: Education as Empowerment?

> Knowledge that was 'really useful', we believed, would raise awareness; provide ways of analysing and understanding how oppressions were structured and sustained; and would lead to educational and social action for change that was informed by theories derived from collective experience (Thompson, 1995: 125).

Since the 1980s radical adult education, left-wing sociology and feminism in Britain have been in decline, replaced by the ideology of the 'New Right' developed from the ideas of Thatcherism (Hutton, 1995). In academic circles postmodernism has become the dominant paradigm. Drawing on the work of Foucault and Derrida, for example, supporters of postmodernism claim that it provides a more appropriate understanding of our fragmented contemporary society than theories grounded in a materialist explanation. Postmodernism has further fractured the theoretical strands of feminism. As Thompson (1995) points out even former Marxist feminists such as Michele Barrett have switched their allegiances to postmodernism. However, within the world of adult education the tradition of radical adult education is being re-established through the work of a small group of academics such as Thompson, Steele, Johnston, Allman and O'Rourke. Thompson, for example, maintains that: 'the time might well be apposite to reclaim the radical initiative. Maybe others feel the same?...And to find some ways of putting the politics of resistance and transformation back onto the agenda of adult and continuing education' (Thompson, 1993: 244). For as Giroux (1983) stresses:

> ...the task of radical educators must be organized around establishing the ideological and material conditions that would enable men and women from oppressed classes to claim their own voices (Giroux, 1983: 116).

This study attempts to identify, clarify, re-assert and draw on the radical traditions within sociology, feminism and adult education as an approach to understanding the experiences of mature women students in universities. Certain social groups, working-class women and men, black people, continue to be excluded from adult education and, in particular higher education, because of inequalities in initial schooling. In some ways I was looking at the success stories of second chance education, those from socially excluded groups who made it to university as an adult. Achieving a place at Warwick, however, was a struggle for many participants. To obtain their goal of making it to university the women had to contend with gender and class inequalities, for example, a lack of support from partners, feelings of guilt about not being a good mother, and financial shortage.

Changing Institutions

Despite the policy of widening access, most universities like Warwick remain overwhelmingly white and middle-class. Non-traditional adult students continue to be a minority at undergraduate level. Mature students in many 'old' universities experience an organisational structure that is better suited to the needs and designs of eighteen year olds. Mature students have to adjust to the institution and culture rather than the institution changing to meet their needs. A recent survey by McGivney (1996) revealed that:

> Although further and higher education now have large numbers of mature students, there is evidence that staff attitudes and institutional practices have not entirely caught up with the needs of this clientele. The research literature suggests that while there has been action to encourage applications from non-traditional student groups, in some institutions the reception they receive is not always sympathetic and comparatively few measures have been introduced to assist them to cope with any problems they may experience (McGivney, 1996:131).

Without change, however, disjunctions may arise between 'learners' expectations and experiences of higher education' (Weil, 1986: 219).

Maintaining a traditional institutional hierarchy and framework may place adult students at a disadvantage in terms of their student experiences. Such a structure may perpetuate inequalities in terms of, for example, attitudes of lecturers and departments, access to the library and other facilities. The mature married women students and part-time students at

Warwick were more constrained by institutional inflexibility than full-time adult male students. Seminar times outside school hours and lack of playgroup/crèche facilities were constant sources of complaint. Many of the women felt that if Warwick wanted mature women students then playgroup/crèche facilities should be provided which would make the lives of female students with children easier. Within the institution the need for improved childcare is not given a high priority, perhaps because women are largely excluded from the decision-making process. University life and policy-making at Warwick are dominated by the perspectives of male managers. Rigid systems and inflexible rules make it more difficult for adults to function as undergraduate students in the same way as younger students. Adult educators need to seek out, identify and study these issues within their institutions and challenge them.

Classifying Mature Students

The definition of mature or non-traditional adult students is oversimplified in some studies, for example, Bourner et al., 1991, Woodley et al. and Knowles 1984, 1990. Such studies largely assume that adult students are a homogeneous group. This approach hides the complexities of the concept 'mature student'. In this research group differences among adult students proved to be important variables and formed the basis for the formation of subcultural groups. These differences are reflected in terms of mode of study (part-or full-time, 2+2), age, gender and class. Like Barrett (1988) I did not want to follow the path of many feminists and treat women as a homogeneous group. As earlier chapters illustrate married female students experienced life at Warwick as qualitatively different from the experiences of young mature female students. The issues and problems faced by married women are distinct.

Younger female adult students felt that they did not share anything in common with older women whose lives and conversations centred on children and the home. As Dalvinder and Karen explained they were looking for the full student experience. The married women had to employ more complex coping strategies than the younger women or men students. Domesticity together with, in some university departments, an inflexible system intervened to make constructing a student career more arduous for married women students. University and family life were juxtaposed for many of the women. Confronted by conflicting and competing demands the women had to work out ways of resolving the situation that allowed them to continue with their studies while causing minimum disruption to family life.

Part-time degree students have a more marginal student experience than full-time mature students. Being a student occupies a smaller fraction of their daily lives although it is spread out over a longer time span. Campus life is very different in the evenings from the hustle and bustle of the daytime. Several part-time students became increasingly critical of the University's part-time provision as they found that subject choices for evening sessions were restricted. The mature women on part-time courses organised their lives around housework, looking after children, working in paid employment and studying in order to fulfil their ambitions. Life was a continual adjustment to competing pressures upon their time. Thus, the connotation of being a student was perceived differently by part-time students and full-time students.

Integrating Sociological and Feminist Theory and Methodology

The voices of women reflecting upon their lives provides a powerful research tool. Talking to the women in this study about why they chose to return to learn and how they perceived themselves as university students revealed the complexities, interconnections and contradictions in their lives. The dynamics of structure and human agency became apparent. Above all the intersections of gender and class dominated their life histories. Using the life history method enabled me to render visible the dominant processes in the women's lives. 'The life history, more than any other technique except perhaps participant observation, can give meaning to the overworked notion of processes' (Becker, 1970: 69). Drawing on Mead's work Becker elaborates:

> The formation of the individual act is a process in which conduct is continually reshaped to take account of the expectations of others, as they may come to be expressed in the immediate situation and as the actor supposes they may come to be expressed. Collective activity, of this kind pointed to by concepts like 'organization' or 'social structure', arises out of a continuous process of mutual adjustment of the actions of all the actors involved. Social process, then, is not an imagined interplay of invisible forces or a vector made up of the interaction of multiple social factors, but an observable process of symbolically mediated interaction (Becker, 1970: 69).

The processes of change were apparent in this study. By the second interview participants, even the part-time students, had become firmly immersed in the student role. Values, attitudes and behaviour changed as the student career progressed. Institutionalisation (Goffman, 1961) was one outcome of this process. The women did not want to leave the haven of the University where they had acquired an element of control over their lives.

Agency and structure interacted to shape the behaviour and consciousness of the mature students in this study. Combining macro and micro theories illuminates the intricacies of the actors' lives; lives that are both reproduced by patriarchal and class structures and acted upon by human agency in an attempt to transcend structural constraints. Interactionist theory, particularly the works of Goffman and Becker, helps adult educators to make sense of and understand the mature student career in universities. Despite the differing contexts of total institutions and medical school the theoretical approaches are, I would argue, highly relevant. Life within the institutional world becomes meaningful as it is portrayed from the perspectives of the actors.

On entering Warwick many participants were unsure what the role of student entailed. It was outside their experience. To survive, the mature students formed subcultural groups by mode of study, gender and age, and claimed their social and territorial space within the university. As individuals and as a group, to draw on Goffman (1959), the mature students soon managed to present the self in front of other students and lecturers in order to meet their needs in the social situation of academe.

The students had in common being mature in years. This united them as a group and helped them initially to make sense of their new social world. Group identities were re-formed within the mature student subculture to create subcultures within a subculture. The mature women students with children, some of whom were single parents, formed a dominant subculture. In doing this they also gained power as a group of women. This enabled them to challenge and manipulate the system, particularly departments, to meet their needs as both students and mothers. The one area where they gained success was in changing seminar times.

Enthusiasm for learning was something all the mature students shared. Belonging to mature student subcultures helped them to survive the rigours of learning and the constraint of a ten week university term. In many cases there was a mismatch in terms of their expectations about learning at degree level and what, in practice, they had to do to get through the demands of a course. The mature students wanted to explore subjects in more depth than time allowed. Several found it hard to accept that they could not read widely for each topic. Assessment and class essay deadlines made this virtually impossible. This was part of the learning process in their student career. Cutting down the workload to more manageable proportions was an imperative, especially for the women with children. Adjustment to the institution had to be made but within the women's frame of reference.

Gendered Lives

From childhood to adulthood the women's lives had been shaped by the forces of gender and class. In some situations gender cuts across class boundaries with degrees of difference in relation to educational aspirations, expectations of marriage and relationships with partners. This group of mature students was not, on the whole, disaffected at school. It was gender and class cultural expectations which prevented them from continuing in post-school education rather than a dislike of school. Most participants left school feeling that they had not achieved their educational potential and this was a powerful factor in their decision to return to learn as adults.

The mature student experience has to be placed within the wider context of their biographies. A study confined to participants' educational career at university would offer only a partial insight into the mature student experience. Instead a holistic approach to lives, past and present, is required. Past experiences of family, schooling and employment closely connected with their decision to study as adults. Similarly, as a student the impact of being a mother, wife and possibly employee could not be ignored. As Antikainen et al. (1996) explain; ' we attempt to situate people's learning experiences in the context of long-term societal learning processes. We look at the meaning of education on three levels: life-course, identity and significant learning experience' (Antikainen et al., 1996:7).

Studying for a degree represented an active decision to take greater control, to break free from gender and class constraints and to transform individual lives. All felt that they did achieve this in varying ways. It would be too simplistic to argue that the women were liberated from a false gender consciousness, but their gender identity was reconstructed as a result of learning. Experiences of low paid, boring female work and time spent in the home childrearing enabled the women to assess their past lives and futures. All realised that being female and, in most cases working-class, had limited their aspirations and horizons. Something was missing; life had become alienating. Education was seen as a way out of this trap, offering the possibility of self-realisation and career enhancement. A high value was placed on education as a mechanism for personal change and self-development.

Breaking out from the private sphere and asserting themselves in the public world was not always easy, particularly as it meant challenging male hegemony within the home. Marxist feminist analysis of the family provides a theoretical framework for understanding the oppression experienced by the women in this study:

> The family-household constitutes both the ideological ground on which gender difference and women's oppression are constructed, and the material relations in which men and women are differentially engaged in wage labour and the class structure. Women's dependence on men is reproduced ideologically, but also in material relations, and there is a mutually strengthening relationship between them (Barrett, 1988: 211).

Women have a dual relationship to the class structure in society (Gardiner, 1977) as both wage labourer and domestic labourer. 'An aspect of women's relationship to the class structure is that it is mediated, to some extent at least, by the configuration of the family, dependence on men, and domestic labour' (Barrett, 1988:135). Life at university ended one aspect of the dual exploitation experienced by the women; that of the labour market. Domestic oppression, however, continued.

The women found that studying did not produce a more equal distribution of tasks within the home; they remained domestic labourers. They also continued to have dual roles, and in the case of part-time students, three roles. For full-time married students the role of wage labourer was replaced by 'student labourer' although, unlike the role of wage labourer, being a student was an enjoyable experience. However, coping with the workload of studying while still serving the needs of partners caused stress. For most, private lives impinged negatively upon public lives in university. Marital conflict and divorce resulted in some cases, while many more experienced a lack of support from partners in their studies. Only a minority received practical and emotional support. This was not experienced on the whole by male students. For many women the decision to go to university was the first occasion when they had ever really asserted themselves and put their individual needs first.

University life did give the women in this study time and space in their lives to develop, and change their self and identity. In doing so they redefined themselves as women. They no longer wanted to be dominated by domesticity. Studying social science subjects, and sociology in particular, imbued them with a critical perspective. They wanted a more equal role within the home and the workplace but, with one or two exceptions, this was a move towards a liberal rather than a radical or Marxist feminist awareness:

As women learned to validate their own experience, values and relationships, they were demonstrating that there were alternative ways of being and knowing than those legitimated by the masculinist visions of modernity (Seidler, 1994: 93).

Studying gave the women, collectively and individually, a measure of power and control over their lives. By the end of their studies they had become 'new women'.

The inclusion of male mature students in this study helped to clarify the extent to which student experiences were gendered ones. The women's experiences of university were influenced by both the intersections of class and gender and the intersections of public and private lives. While the women and men shared many learning experiences in common, for example, a dislike of examinations and lack of confidence in writing first essays, the women's student lives were characterised by greater pressures and demands as a result of women's oppression in the family. The men, in contrast, rarely talked about their private lives. There was an unspoken assumption, on the whole, that their university studies were unproblematic for their partner. One factor the women and men did share in common was the realisation that moving into an academic world had distanced them culturally and socially from friends, parents and partners. None regretted this and accepted it as an inevitable outcome of learning.

Learning: A Means of Reproduction or Empowerment?

To what extent are the women's experiences of education as an adult student emancipatory or empowering? The answer may differ according to whose frame of reference is used: the participants' or the researcher's. First the term empowerment needs to be clarified. It is frequently used politically and ideologically by those on the left within community education, adult education and sociology without, on the whole, an elaboration of its meaning. More recently, as Troyna (1994) points out, empowerment has been 'hijacked' by the New Right. Empowering and changing women's lives has been at the heart of feminist discourse and research. Gore (1993) clarifies the meaning of empowerment within her feminist discourse:

> Empowerment carries with it an agent of empowerment (someone, or something, doing the empowering), a notion of power as property (to empower implies to give or confer power), and a vision or desired end state (some vision of what it is to be empowered and the possibility of a state of empowerment) (Gore, 1993:73-74).

Antikainen et al. (1996) in their study of adult education and learning draw upon Mezirow's (1981) concept of 'critical reflectivity' in defining empowerment. For them empowerment refers 'to an experience that changes an individual's understanding of him/herself and/or of the world' (Antikainen et al., 1996: 70-71). Two indicators of empowerment are identified by Antikainen et al. (1996):

> - the expansion of the world view or cultural understanding - the strengthening of one's 'voice' so that he or she is encouraged to participate in dialogue or even break down the dominant discursive forms, and, the broadening of the field of social identities and roles (Antikainen et al., 1996: 82).

Empowerment, however, must embody a redistribution of power within society to emancipate those who previously lacked power. It also implies that through the acquisition of power individuals and groups are able to act upon and change their lives, and liberate themselves from oppression. Empowerment is defined here in a political and collective sense rather than a psychological or individualistic one. Within education empowerment enables individuals and groups to view their lives and the world from a critical perspective. Empowerment also implies changing ideology, social relationships and structural constraints in society. This brings us back to the importance of human agency and social structures in the understanding of human behaviour.

Initial schooling is experienced in reproductive terms. Gender and class relationships are reinforced by the process of schooling, preparing women in this study for domesticity and unskilled work (MacDonald, 1980, Spender, 1982, Bowles and Gintis, 1976). Participants in this research spoke about learning at university as an empowering experience. For the women it was empowering in terms of the acquisition of knowledge which enabled them to view the world in a different and critical way. Learning did bring about personal empowerment but the women were not liberated from gender and class inequalities within the family and society as a whole. Despite this, the women were changed persons. Collectively they were able to reflect upon their past lives, recognise the constraints that gender and class had imposed upon them and demand greater, albeit limited, equality in their future lives.

Learning as an adult was, from the perspective of the participants, emancipatory. Schooling, by comparison, prepared them for lives as working-class women. Education, it must be remembered, is contradictory as it has the potential both to reproduce social inequalities and to transform social life:

there is no such thing as a neutral education process. Education either functions as an instrument which is used to facilitate the integration of generations into the logic of present system and bring about conformity to it, or it becomes the 'practice of freedom', the means by which men and women deal critically with reality and discover how to participate in the transformation of their world (Thompson, 1980: 26).

Education institutions provide an arena in which the interaction of human agency and structural forces are visible, each engaged in a constant struggle for dominance.

Mature Students as Agents of Institutional Change

Learning at Warwick impacted greatly upon the mature students in this research. Change, however, was not a one-way process. The presence of mature students in certain departments does have implications for small-scale institutional change. Teaching times are accommodated in some departments like sociology to meet the needs of mature women students with children. The UK/Belgian research revealed that some lecturers had modified teaching approaches as a result of teaching adults. In such cases teaching has become more student-centred. Staff have been identified with specific 2+2 and part-time degree responsibilities. The management of 2+2 and part-time degrees is embedded within the University's organisational structure through, for example, the Board of Flexible and Continuing Studies. Overall, however, the pace of institutional change is minimal despite the fact that mature students, undergraduate and graduate, are clearly visible around the campus.

Life After Study: What Next?

Education as an adult was a meaningful experience in the lives of the women and men in this study. The acquisition of knowledge and academic discourse was given a high value by participants. Knowledge emanating from the institution was internalised but not passively. The women reflected upon the knowledge presented to them, reassessing their self-identity and re-interpreting the world around them. It was a dialectical relationship between action and structure. Within a Marxist framework participants were both creators of their social world and produced by it.

As the degree course drew to a close most participants, particularly those studying full-time, did not want to leave Warwick. The student identity became a dominant aspect of their life-story. Leaving Warwick marked another transition and turning point in the participants' lives. A new identity would have to be found. As Antikainen et al. stress: 'a person's identity is composed of the meaningful parts of his or her life-story. Identity is the individual's socially constructed definition, formulated by using available cultural meanings' (Antikainen et al., 1996: 53).

Employment at graduate level may not be easy to find in a period of economic transition and recession. A new economic environment is emerging. The labour market is no longer stable. Rifkin (1995) predicts that the changing nature of work will result in the end of full-time employment. The women will also have to contend with the prejudices of many employers towards employing older graduates. Some may end up returning to the low paid female jobs that they were desperately trying to escape from. Whatever the future holds the student experience will have a lasting effect upon their attitudes, values and behaviour both within the family and employment. The student self-concept will not be totally deconstructed but will help to formulate the new self-concept within the institution of work in the next stage of the women's life-stories.

This study is in many ways an optimistic one. Despite these struggles and hectic lives the women managed through their determination and resilience to complete degree studies and achieve lifetime ambitions. As one 2+2 student who lived in an inner city area explained, learning as an adult was: 'the chance to do something that I never thought I would ever do, the chance to learn and to move on from this place where I now live'. None regretted the decision to study for a degree. All the participants enjoyed the process of learning. Knowledge opened up a powerful and new way of viewing the world. The value of education was transmitted to children and friends, who, participants hoped, would enter higher education. All advocated that opportunities for second chance education and lifelong learning should be widened. However, many feared that current policy changes to student grants and benefits system would increasingly curtail the possibilities for adults to study full-time for a degree in the future. The fears of participants may be well grounded. National policy now favours consolidation rather than expansion. A survey of mature students at Warwick revealed that changes to the grants and benefits system has resulted in a deteriorating economic situation for adults (Merrill and McKie, 1998). This situation is reflected by the declining number of 2+2 degree applications as adults become less willing to commit themselves to a four year degree course. Governmental policy continues to support widening access and social inclusion (Dearing and Fryer Reports and the Green Paper) yet financial constraints are not being addressed.

Both the women and the men in this research successfully demystified degree studies. All declared that lives had changed qualitatively for the better. As Giroux reminds us:

> The achievements of critical theorists are their refusal to abandon the dialectic of agency and structure and their development of theoretical perspectives that treat seriously the claim that history can be changed, that the potential for radical transformation exists (Giroux, 1983: 5).

Bibliography

Abrams, P. (1982), *Historical Sociology*, Open Books, Shepton Mallett.

Acker, J. (1989), 'Making Gender Visible', in Wallace, R. *Feminism and Sociology Theory*, Sage, Beverley Hills, California pp65-81.

Acker, J., Barry, K. and Esseveld, J. (1991), 'Objectivity and Truth: Problems in Doing Feminist Research', in Fonow, M. A. and Cook, J. A. (ed), *Beyond Methodology, Feminist Scholarship as Lived Research*, Indiana University Press, Indianapolis, pp133-153.

Acker, S. (1984), *Women in HE: what is the problem?*, Survey, SRHE/NFER.

Acker, S. (1994), *Gendered Education*, Open University Press, Buckingham.

Acker, S. and Warren-Piper, D. W. (1984), *Is HE Fair to Women?*, SRHE/NFER, Nelson, Guildford.

Adkins, L. (1995), *Gendered Work, Sexuality, Family and the Labour Market*, Open University Press, Buckingham.

Alexander, J. (1987), 'Action and its environments', in Alexander, J., Gieson, B., Munch, R. and Smelser, N. (eds), *The Micro-Macro Link*, University of California Press, Berkeley.

Alheit, P. (1994), *Taking the Knocks*, Cassell, London.

Allman, P. and Wallis, J. (1995), 'Challenging the Postmodern Condition: Radical Adult Education for Critical Intelligence', in Mayo, M. and Thompson, J. (eds), *Adult Learning Critical Intelligence and Social Change*, NIACE, Leicester, pp18-33.

Althusser, L. (1972), 'Ideology and Ideological State Apparatuses', in Cosin, B. (ed), *Education: Structure and Society*, Penguin, Harmondsworth.

Antikainen, A., Houtsonen, J., Kauppila, J. and Huotelin, H. (1996), *Living in a Learning Society*, Falmer Press, London.

Arber, S. (1993), 'Inequalities within the Household', in Morgan, D. and Stanley, L. (eds), *Debates in Sociology*, Manchester University Press, Manchester, pp118-139.

Arber, S. and Gilbert, N. (1992), 'Reassessing Women's Working Lives: An Introductory Essay', in Arber, S. and Gilbert, N. (eds), *Women and Working Lives*, Macmillan, London.

Archer, M. (1998), 'Social Theory and the Analysis of Society', in May, T. and Williams, M. (eds), *Knowing the Social World*, Open University Press, Buckingham, pp69-85.

Arksey, H., Marchant, I. and Simmill, C. (1994), *Juggling for a Degree, Mature Students' Experience of University Life*, Lancaster University Unit for Innovation in Higher Education, Lancaster.

Arnot, M. (ed) (1985), *Race and Gender: Equal Opportunities Policies in Education*, Pergamon, Oxford.

Arnot, M. and Weiner, G. (eds) (1987), *Gender and the Politics of Schooling*, Hutchinson, London.

Aslanian, C. and Bricknell, H. (1980), *Americans in Transition: Life Changes as Reasons for Adult Learning*, College Entrance Examination Board, New York.

Barrett, M. (1980 and 1988), *Women's Oppression Today: Problems in Marxist Feminist Analysis*, Verso, London.

Barrett, M. (1987), 'Gender and Class: Marxist feminist perspectives on education', in Arnot, M. and Weiner, G. (eds), *Gender and the Politics of Schooling*, Open University Press, Milton Keynes.

Barton, L., Meighan, R. and Walker, S. (eds) (1981), *Schooling, Ideology and the Curriculum*, Falmer Press, Barcombe.

Becher, T. (1989), *Academic Tribes*, SRHE/Open University Press, Buckingham.

Becker, H. S. (1963), *Outsiders*, Free Press, New York.

Becker, H. S. (1964), 'Personal Change in Adult Life', in Becker H. S. (1970), *Sociological Work*, Aldine Publishing Company, Chicago.

Becker, H. S. (1967), 'Whose Side Are you On?', *Sociological Problems*, 14.

Becker, H. S. (1970), 'Life History and the Scientific Mosaic', in Becker, H. *Sociological Work*, Aldine Publishing Company, Chicago.

Becker, H. S. (1971), 'Social-class variations in the teacher-pupil relationship', in Cosin, B., Dale, I., Esland, G. et al. (eds), *School and Society*, Routledge/Open University Press, London, pp107-113.

Becker, H. S. (1974), 'Labelling theory reconsidered', in Rock, P. and McIntosh, M. (eds), *Deviance and Social Control*, Tavistock, London, pp41-66.

Becker, H. S., Geer, B., Strauss, A. and Hughes, E. (1961), *Boys in White: Student Culture in Medical School*, University of Chicago Press, Chicago.

Becker, H. S. and Strauss, A. (1959), 'Careers, Personality and Adult Socialisation', in Becker, H. (1970), *Sociological Work*, Aldine, Chicago.

Beechey, V. (1977), 'Some Notes on Female Wage Labour in the Capitalist Mode of Production', *Capital and Class*, Autumn, No. 3.

Benn, R., Elliot, J. and Whaley, P. (1998), *Educating Rita*, NIACE, Leicester.

Berger, P. (1963), *Invitation to Sociology*, Penguin, Harmondsworth.

Berger, P. and Luckman, T. (1966), *The Social Construction of Reality*, Penguin, Harmondsworth.

Bernard, J. (1978), 'My Four Revolutions: An Autobiographical History of the ASA', in Huber, J. (ed), *Changing Women in a Changing Society*, The University of Chicago Press, Chicago.

Bernstein, B. (1971), 'On the classification and framing of educational knowledge', in Young, M. (ed), *Knowledge and Control*, Macmillan, London, pp47-69.

Bernstein, B. (1973), *Class, Codes and Control*, Vol. 1, Routledge and Kegan Paul, London.

Bernstein, B. (1979), *The Restructuring of Social Political Theory*, Methuen, London.

Beynon, H. (1973), *Working For Ford*, Penguin, Harmondsworth.

Birch, W. (1988), *The Challenge to Higher Education*, SRHE/Open University Press, Buckingham.

Bird, E. and West, J. (1987), 'Interrupted Lives: A Study of Women Returners', in Allat, P. and Keil, T. (eds), *Women and the Life Cycle, Transitions and Turning Points*, Macmillan, Basingstoke.

Birkett, I. (1991), 'The Self in Everyday Communication', *Current Sociology*, Vol. 39, No. 3, Winter, Social Selves - Theories of the Social Formation of Personality, pp55-82.

Bland, L., Brunsdon, C., Hobson, D. and Winship, J. (1978), 'Women "inside and outside" the relations of production', in *Women Take Issue. Aspects of Women's Subordination*, Centre for Contemporary Cultural Studies, Hutchinson/University of Birmingham, London.

Blumer, H. (1956), 'Sociological Analysis and the Variable', *American Sociological Review*, 21 December, pp683-690.

Blumer, H. (1964), 'Society as Symbolic Interaction', in Rose, A. (ed), *Human Behaviour and Social Processes*, Houghton, Mifflin.

Boudon, R. (1973), *Education, Opportunity and Social Inequality*, Wiley, New York.

Bourdieu, P. and Passeron, J. (1977), *Reproduction in Education, Society and Culture*, Sage, London.

Bourner, T., Reynolds, A., Hamed, M. and Barnett, R. (1991), *Part-time Students and their Experience of Higher Education*, SRHE/Open University Press, Buckingham.

Bowlby, J. (1953), *Child Care and the Growth of Love*, Penguin, Harmondsworth.

Bowlby, J. (1969), *Attachment and Loss, Vol. 1: Attachment*, Penguin, Harmondsworth.

Bowles, S. and Gintis, H. (1976), *Schooling in Capitalist America*, Routledge and Kegan Paul, London.

Brannen, J. (1992), 'Combining Qualitative and Quantitative Approaches: An Overview', in Brannen, J. (ed), *Mixing Methods: Qualitative and Quantitative Research*, Avebury, Aldershot.

Brown, A. and Webb, J. (1990), 'The higher education route to the labour market for mature students', *British Journal of Education and Work*, Vol. 4, No 1, pp5-21.

Brown, P. and Scase, R. (1995), *Higher Education and Corporate Realities: Class, Culture and the Decline of Graduate Careers*, UCL Press, London.

Bryman, A. (1992), 'Qualitative and Quantitative Research: Further Reflections on their Integration', in Brannen, J. (ed), *Mixing Methods: Qualitative and Quantitative Research*, Avebury, Aldershot.

Bryne, E. (1978), *Women and Education*, Tavistock, London.

Bulmer, M. (ed) (1977), *Sociological Research Methods - An Introduction*, Macmillan, London.

Carby, H. (1982), 'White Women Listen! Black feminism and the boundaries of sisterhood', in *The Empire Strikes Back*, Centre for Contemporary Cultural Studies, University of Birmingham, London, pp212-235.

Cicourel, A. V. (1968), *The Social Organisation of Juvenile Justice*, Wiley, New York.

Cicourel, A. V. (1972), 'Basic and Normative Rules in the Negotiation of Statistics and Role', in Sudnow, D. (ed), *Studies in Social Interaction*, Free Press, New York.

Cicourel, A. V. (1976), *The Social Organisation of Juvenile Justice*, Heinemann, London.

Cicourel, A. V. (1982), *Quantity and Quality in Social Research*, Routledge, London.

Cicourel, A. V. and Kitsuse, J. (1971), 'The social organisation of the high school and deviant and adolescent careers', in Cosin et al. (eds), *School and Society*, Routledge and Kegan Paul/Open University Press, London, pp114-121.

Clark, S. (1995), 'Access and Admissions: current bottleneck and the transition to a democratic higher education', *Journal of Access Studies*, Vol. 10, Autumn (2), pp137-155.

Clarke, J., Hall, S., Jefferson, T. and Roberts, B. (1976), 'Subcultures, Cultures and Class', in Hall, S. and Jefferson, T. (eds), *Resistance Through Rituals*, Hutchinson, London, pp9-74.

Coates, M. (1994), *Women's Education*, SRHE/Open University Press, Buckingham.

Cohen, L. and Manion, L. (1980), *Research Methods in Education*, Routledge, London.

Connelly, B. (1992), 'A Critical Overview of the Sociology of Adult Education', *International Journal of Lifelong Education*, Vol. 11, No. 1, July-September, pp235-253.

Cooley, C. H. (1922), *Human Nature and the Social Order*, Schribner and Sons, New York.

Corrigan, P. (1979), *Schooling the Smash Street Kids*, Macmillan Press, London.

Cross, K. P. (1981), *Adults as Learners*, Jossey-Bass, London.

Davies, S., Lubelska, C. and Quinn, J. (1994), *Women in Higher Education*, Taylor and Francis, London.

Dawe, A. (1970), 'The Two Sociologies - British Journal of Sociology', in Thompson, K. and Tunstall, J. (eds), *Sociological Perspectives*, Penguin/Open University Press, Harmondsworth , pp542-554.

Deem, R. (1978), *Women and Schooling*, Routledge and Kegan Paul, London.

Deem, R. (1980), *Schooling for Women's Work*, Routledge and Kegan Paul, London.

Delphy, C. and Leonard, D. (1992), *Familiar Exploitation: A New Analysis of Marriage in Contemporary Western Societies*, Polity Press, Cambridge.

Denzin, N. (1971), 'The Logic of Naturalistic Inquiry', *Social Forces*, 50.

Denzin, N. (1974), 'Symbolic interactionism and ethnomethodology', in Denisoff, S., Callahan, O. and Levine, M., *Theories and Paradigms in Contemporary Sociology*, Peacock, Itasca, Illinois.

Denzin, N. (1978), *The Research Act*, McGraw Hill, London.

Denzin, N. (1989), *Interpretive Biography*, Qualitative Research Methods Series 17, Sage University Paper, California.

Dex, S. (1984), *Women's Work Histories: An Analysis of the Women and Employment Survey*, Department of Employment Research, Paper No. 46, London, HMSO.

Douglas, J. D. (ed) (1970), *Understanding Everyday Life*, Aldine, Chicago.

Duke, C. (1992), *The Learning University. Towards a new paradigm*, SRHE/Open University Press, Buckingham.

Duke, C. and Merrill, B. (1993), *The Winding Road: Widening Opportunities for HE*, Department of Continuing Education, University of Warwick/Employment Department.

Durkheim, E. (1938), *The Rules of Sociological Method*, Collier-Macmillan, Toronto.

Edwards, R. (1993), 'The University', and 'The University of Life: Boundaries between Ways of Knowing', in David, M., Edwards, R., Hughes, M. and Ribbens, J. (eds) *Mothers and education: inside out? Exploring family - education, policy and experience*, Macmillan, London.

Edwards, R. (1993), *Mature Women Students: Separating or Connecting Family and Education*, Taylor and Francis, London.

Elsey, B. (1986), *Social Theory, Perspectives on Adult Education*, Department of Adult Education, University of Nottingham, Nottingham.

Engels, F. (1884), 'The Origin of the Family, Private Property and the State', in Marx, K. and Engels, F., *Selected Works (1970 Edition)*, Lawrence & Wishart Limited, London.

Filstead, W. J. (ed) (1970), *Qualitative Methodology, First hand involvement with the social world*, Markham, Chicago.

Filstead, W. J. (1979), 'Qualitative Methods: a needed perspective in evaluation research', in Cook, T. P. and Reichardt, C. S. (eds), *Qualitative and Quantitative Methods in Evaluation Research*, Sage, Beverly Hills, California.

Finch, J. (1984), 'It's great to have someone to talk to: the ethics and politics of interviewing women', in Bell, C. and Roberts, H. (eds), *Social Researching: Politics, Problems and Practice*, Routledge and Kegan Paul, London.

Finch, J. (1993), 'Conceptualising Gender', in Morgan, D. and Stanley, L. (eds), *Debates in Sociology*, Manchester University Press, Manchester.

Finn, D. (1987), *Training Without Jobs*, Macmillan Education, London.

Firestone, S. (1970, 1972), *The Dialectics of Sex*, Paladin, London.

Fletcher, R. (1966), *The Family and Marriage in Britain*, Penguin, Harmondsworth.

Fogarty, M.,Rapoport, R. and Rapoport, R. (1971), *Sex, Career and Family*, Allen & Unwin, London.

Fonow, M. A. and Cook, J. A. (ed) (1991), *Beyond Methodology, Feminist Scholarship As Lived Research*, Indiana University Press, Indianapolis.

Fowler, G. (1979), 'A Labour View', in Roderick G and Stephens, M (eds), *Higher Education for All?*, Falmer Press, London.

Freire, P. (1972), *Pedagogy of the Oppressed*, Penguin, Harmondsworth.

Freire, P. (1972), *Cultural Action for Freedom*, Penguin, Harmondsworth.

Friedan, B. (1963), *The Feminine Mystique*, Penguin, Harmondsworth.

Fulton, O. (ed) (1989), *Access and Institutional Change*, SRHE/Open University Press, Buckingham.

Gardiner, J. (1977), *Women in the Labour Process and Class Structure*, Lawrence and Wishart, London.

Garfinkel, H. (1967), *Studies in Ethnomethodology*, Englewood-Cliffs (re-issued, Polity 1984), Cambridge.

Giddens, A. (1971), *Capitalism and Modern Social Theory*, Cambridge University Press, Cambridge.

Giddens, A. (1976), *New Rules of Sociological Method*, Hutchinson, London.

Giddens, A. (1983), *Sociology: A Brief but Critical Introduction*, Macmillan Press, London.

Giroux, H. A. (1983), *Theory and Resistance in Education*, Heinemann, London.

Glaser, B. G. and Strauss, A. (1967), *The Discovery of Grounded Theory*, Aldine, Chicago.

Goffman, E. (1959), *The Presentation of Self in Everyday Life*, Penguin, Harmondsworth.

Goffman, E. (1961), *Asylums*, Penguin, Harmondsworth.

Goffman, E. (1968), *Stigma, Notes on the Management of Spoiled Identity*, Pelican, Harmondsworth.

Goffman, E. (1972), *Relations in Public, microstudies of the public order*, Harper and Row, London.

Goffmann, E. (1974), *Frame Analysis: An Essay on the Organisation of Experience*, Harper and Row, New York.

Goffman, E. (1979), *Gender Advertisements*, Macmillan, London.

Goffman, E. (1983), 'The Interaction Order', *American Sociological Review*, Vol. 48, pp1-17.

Gooderham, P. (1993), 'A Conceptual Framework of Sociological Perspectives on the Pursuit by Adults of Access to Higher Education', *International Journal of Lifelong Education*, Vol. 12, No. 1, January-March, pp27-39.

Gore, J. (1993), *The Struggle for Pedagogies*, Routledge, London.

Gouldner, A. W. (1971), *The Coming Crisis of Western Sociology*, Heinemann, London.

Graham, B. (1992), *Messages from Mature Graduates*, Association of Graduate Careers Advisory Service.

Graham, H. (1984), 'Surveying through Stories', in Bell, C. and Roberts, H., *Social Researching*, Routledge and Kegan Paul, London.

Hammersley, M. (1992), 'Deconstructing the Qualitative-Quantitative Divide', in Brannen, J. (ed), *Mixing Methods: Qualitative and Quantitative Research*, Avebury, Aldershot.

Hammersley, M. (ed) (1993), *Social Research, Philosophy, Politics and Practice*, Open University/Sage, London.

Hammersley, M. and Atkinson, P. (1983), *Ethnography, Principles in Practice*, Tavistock, London.

Harding, S. (ed) (1987), *Feminism and Methodology*, Open University Press, Milton Keynes.

Harding, S. (1991), *Whose Science, Whose Knowledge?* Open University Press, Milton Keynes.

Hargreaves, D. H. (1967), *Social Relations in a Secondary School*, Routledge and Kegan Paul, London.

Hargreaves, D., Hestar, S. and Mellor, F. (1975), *Deviance in the Classrooms*, Routledge and Kegan Paul, London.

Harries-Jenkins, G. (1982), 'The Role of the Adult Student', *International Journal of Lifelong Education*, Vol. 1, No. 1, pp19-39.

Hartmann, H. (1981), 'The unhappy marriage of Marxism and Feminism: toward a more progressive union', in Sargent, L. (ed), *Women and Revolution: A discussion of the unhappy marriage of Marxism and Feminism*, Pluto Press, London.

Hopper, E. and Osborn, M. (1975), *Adult Students: Education Selection and Social Control*, Frances Pinter, London.

Hughes, M. and Kennedy, M. (1985), *New Futures Changing Women's Education*, Routledge and Kegan Paul, London.

Hutton, W. (1995), *The State We're In*, Vintage, London.

Ignatieff, M. (1983), 'Life at Degree Zero', *New Society*, 20 January 1983, pp95-97.

Jaggar, A. (1983), *Feminist Politics and Human Nature*, Rowman and Allenhead, Totowa.

Jarvis, P. (1985), *The Sociology of Adult and Continuing Education*, Croom Helm, London.

Jayratne, T. (1993), 'The Value of Quantitative Methodology for Feminist Research', in Hammersley, M. (eds), *Social Research, Philosophy, Politics and Practice*, Open University/Sage, London.

Jayratne, T. and Stewart, A. (1991), 'Quantitative and Qualitative Methods in the Social Sciences', in Fonow, M. and Cook, J. A. (ed), *Beyond Methodology, Feminist Socharlarship as Lived Research*, Indiana University Press, Indianapolis.

Jones, G. R. (1983), 'Life History Methodology', in Morgan, G. (ed), *Beyond Method*, Sage, California.

Jones, R. K. (1984), *Sociology of Adult Education*, Gower, Aldershot.

Kanter, R. M. (1977), *Men and Women of the Corporation*, Basic Books, New York.

Keddie, N. (1986), 'Book review of the Sociology of Continuing Adult Education', by Jarvis, P., *Studies in the Education of Adults*, Vol. 18, No. 1, pp54-56.

Kelly, H. H. and Thibault, J. W. (1978), *Interpersonal Relations: A Theory of Interdependence*, Wiley, New York.

Kennedy, E. (1987), 'Labouring to learn', in McNeil, M. (ed), *Gender and Expertise*, Free Association Books, London.

Knorr-Cetina, K. (1988), 'The micro-social order', in Fielding, N. (ed), *Actions and Structure*, Sage, London.

Knowles, M. (1990, 1984), *The Adult Learner, a neglected species*, Gulf Publishing Company, London.

Labov, W. (1973), 'The Logic of Non-standard English', in Keddie, N., *Tinker, Tailor, The Myth of Cultural Deprivation*, Penguin, Harmondsworth.

Layder, D. (1998), 'The reality of social domains: implications for theory and method', in May, T. and Williams, M. (eds), *Knowing the Social World*, Open University Press, Buckingham, pp86-102.

Lea, M. and West, L. (1995), 'On biographies and institutions - Changing selves, fragmentation and the struggle for meaning' in Alheit, P., Bron-Wojciechowska, A., Brugger, E. and Dominicé, P. (eds), *The Biographical Approach in European Adult Education*, Verband Wiener Volksbildung, Wien, pp172-187.

Leonard, M. (1994), 'Transforming the Household: Mature women students and Access to Higher Education', in Davies, S., Lubelska, C. and Quinn, J. *Changing the Subject: Women in HE*, Taylor and Francis, London.

Lewis, J. (1972), *The Marxism of Marx*, Lawrence and Wishart, London.

Lovett, T. (1980), 'Adult Education and Community Action', in Thompson, J. (ed), *Adult Education for a Change*, Hutchinson, London.

Lunnebourg, P. (1994), *Undoing Educational Obstacles*, Cassell, London.

McCall, G. and Simmons, J. (1966), *Identities and Interaction*, The Free Press, New York.

McCall, M. and Becker, H. (1990), *Symbolic Interaction and Cultural Studies*, University of Chicago Press, Chicago.

McClaren, A. (1985), *Ambitions and Realisations - Women in Adult Education*, Peter Owen, London.

MacDonald, M. (1980), 'Socio-cultural reproduction and women's education', in Deem, R. (ed), *Schooling for Women's Work*, Routledge and Kegan Paul, London.

MacDonald, M. (1981), 'Schooling and the Reproduction of Class and Gender Relations', in Dals, R. et al. (eds), *Politics, Patriarchy and Practice*, Falmer/Open University Press, London.

McDowell, L. and Pringle, R. (1994), *Defining Women, Social Institutions and Gender Divisions*, Polity Press and Open University Press, Cambridge.

McGivney, V. (1992), *Tracking Adult Learning Routes*, NIACE, Leicester.

McGivney, V. (1993), 'Participation and Non-Participation: a review of the literature', in Edwards, R., Sieminski, S. and Zeldin, D. (eds), *Adult Learners, Education and Training*, Routledge, London, pp11-30.

McGivney, V. (1996), *Staying or Leaving the Course: Non-completion and retention of mature students in further and higher education*, NIACE, Leicester.

McPherson, J., Hadfield, M. and Day, C. (1994), 'Student Perspectives and the Effectiveness of Continuing Education', in Haselgrove, S. (ed), *The Student Experience*, SRHE/Open University Press, Buckingham, pp117-124.

McRobbie, A. (1978), 'Working-class girls and the culture of femininity', in Centre for Contemporary Cultural Studies Women's Group (eds), *Women Take Issue*, Hutchinson, London.

McRobbie, A. (1982), 'The Politics of Feminist Research: between talk, text and action, *Feminist Review*, 12, pp46-58.

Manning, P. (1992), *Erving Goffman and Modern Sociology*, Polity Press, Cambridge.

Marx, K. (1844), *Economic and Philosophic Manuscripts*, Lawrence & Wishart, London.

Marx, K. (1852), 'The 18th Brumaire of Louis Bonaparte', in Fischer, E. (1973), *Marx in His Own Words*, Penguin, Harmondsworth.

Marx, K. (1856), 'The Holy Family', in Fischer, E. (1973), *Marx in His Own Words*, Penguin, Harmondsworth.

Marx, K. (1971), 'The German Ideology 1845-46', in Jordan, Z., *Karl Marx*, Nelson, London, pp52-54.

Marx, K. and Engels, F. (1848, 1967), *The Communist Manifesto*, Penguin, Harmondsworth.

Mason, J. (1987), 'A Bed of Roses: Women, Marriage and Inequality in Later Life', in Allatt, P., Keil, T. and Bryman, A. (ed), Macmillan, Basingstoke.

May, T. (1993), *Social Research, Issues, Methods and Process*, Open University Press, Buckingham.

Maynard, E. and Pearsall, S. (1994), 'What about male mature students? A comparison of men and women students', *Journal of Access Studies*, Vol. 9, pp229-240.

Maynard, M. (1990), 'The re-shaping of sociology? Trends in the study of gender', *Sociology*, 24, 269-90.

Mead, G. H. (1934), *Mind, Self and Society*, University of Chicago Press, Chicago.

Merrill, B. and McKie, J. (1998) 'Money and the Mature Student', *Adults Learning* February, Vol. 9, No. 6.

Merrill, B. and Moseley, R. (1995), 'Access and Partnership: the 2+2 degree programme at the University of Warwick', *Seda Paper 92: Franchising, Flexibility and Fruitful Partnerships*, SEDA Publications, Birmingham.

Mezirow, J. (1981), 'A Critical Theory of Adult Learning and Education', *Adult Education*, 32, pp3-24.

Mies, M. (1991), 'Women's Research or Feminist Research? The Debate Surrounding Feminist Science and Methodology', in Fonow, M. and Cook, J. A. (eds), *Beyond Methodology, Feminist Scholarship as Lived Research*, Indiana University Press, Indianapolis, pp60-84.

Miliband, R. (1969), *The State in Capitalist Society*, Quartet Books, London.

Millett, K. (1970), *Sexual Politics*, Garden City, New York.

Mitchell, J. (1971), *Women's Estate*, Penguin, Harmondsworth.

Morley, L. and Walsh, V. (1995), *Feminist Academics*, Taylor and Francis, London.

Moser, C. A. (1958), *Survey Methods in Social Investigation*, Heinemann, London.

Musolf, G. R. (1992), 'Structure, institutions, power and ideology: new directions within symbolic interactionism', *The Sociological Quarterly*, Vol. 33, No. 2, pp171-189.

Newsom Report (1963), *Half Our Future*, Report of the Central Advisory Council for Education (England), HMSO, para 390, p135.

O'Shea, J. and Corrigan, P. (1979), 'Surviving Adult Education', *Adult Education*, 52 (4), pp229-235.

Oakley, A. (1974), *The Sociology of Housework*, Martin Robertson, London.

Oakley, A. (1981,1992), 'Interviewing women: a contradiction in terms', in Roberts, H. (ed), *Doing Feminist Research*, Routledge and Kegan Paul, London, pp30-61.

OECD (1969), *Innovation in Higher Education: New Universities in the United Kingdom*, OECD, Paris.

OECD (1982), *The University and the Community. The Problems of Changing Relationships*, Centre for Educational Research and Innovation, OECD, Paris.

Pahl, J. (1993), 'The Allocation of Money and Structuring of Inequality within Marriage', Sociological Review, 13, pp237-62.

Pantziarka, P. (1987), 'The Step from Further to Higher Education', *Journal of Access Studies*, (2), Fast, London, pp102-105.

Parry, G. (1997), Preface in Williams, J. (ed), *Negotiating Access to Higher Education*, SRHE/Open University Press, Buckingham.

Parry, G. and Wake, C. (eds) (1990), *Access and Alternative Futures for Higher Education*, Hodder and Stoughton, London.

Pascall, G. and Cox, R. (1993), *Women returning to HE*, SRHE/Open University Press, Buckingham.

Pateman, C. (1987), 'Feminist Critiques of the Public/Private Dichotomy', in Phillips, A. (ed), *Feminism and Equality*, Basil Blackwell, Oxford.

Payne, I. (1988, 1980), 'Sexist Ideology and Education', in Spender, D. and Sarah, E. (eds), *Learning to Lose, Sexism and Education*, The Women's Press, London, pp12-21.

Percy, K. (1988), 'Opening Access to a Modern University', in Eggins, H. (ed), *Restructuring Higher Education*, SRHE/Open University Press, Buckingham.

Phillips, D. (1973), *Abandoning Method*, Jossey Bass, San Francisco.

Plummer, K. (1990), *Documents of Life*, Unwin Hyman Ltd., London.

Pollert, A. (1981), *Girls, Wives, Factory Lives*, Macmillan, London.

Reinharz, S. (1983), 'Experimental Analysis and Contribution to Feminist Research', in Bowles, G. and Duelli Klein, R. (eds) *Theories of Women's Studies*, Routledge and Kegan Paul, London.

Reinharz, S. (1992) *Feminist Methods in Social Research*, Oxford University Press, Oxford.

Reiss, A. J. (1968), 'Stuff and Nonsense about social surveys and participant observation', in Becker, H. S., Geer, B., Reisman, P. and Weiss, R. S. (eds), *Institutions and Persons*, Aldine Publishing Company, Chicago, pp1-23.

Ribbens, J. and Edwards, R. (1998), 'Living on the Edges: Public Knowledge, Private Lives, Personal Experience', in Ribbens, J. and Edwards, R. (eds), *Feminist Dilemmas in Qualitative Research*, Sage Publications, London.

Rich, A. (1979), 'Towards a woman-centred university', in *On Lies, Secrets, Silence*, Virago, London.

Riessman, C. (1993), *Narrative Analysis*, Qualitative Research Methods Series 30, Sage University Paper, California.

Rifkin, J. (1995), *The end of work, the decline of the global labour force and the dawn of the post-market era*, G P Putnam's Sons, New York.

Roberts, H. (1981), 'Some of the Boys Won't Play Any More: The impact of feminism on sociology', in Spender, D. *Men's Studies Modified*, Pergamon, Oxford.

Roberts, H. (ed) (1982, 1988), *Doing Feminist Research*, Routledge, London.

Rock, P. (1979), *The Making of Symbolic Interactionism*, Macmillan, London.

Rogers, M. (1980), 'Goffman on Power, Hierarchy and Status', in Ditton, J. (ed), *The View from Goffman*, Macmillan, London.

Rosoldo, M. Z. (1974), 'Women, Culture and Society: a Theoretical Overview', in Rosalde, M. and Lamphere, L. (eds), *Women, Culture and Society*, Stanford University Press, Stanford.

Rossi, I. (1983), *From the Sociology of Symbols to the Sociology of Signs, towards a dialectical sociology*, Columbia University Press, New York.

Ruddock, R. (1971), 'The Sociology of Adult Education; A plea for humanism', *Studies in Adult Education*, 3(1) May, pp15-27.

Sanderson, K. and French, M. (1993), *From Sainsbury's to Sartre: mature women undergraduates at university*, British Sociological Association, Conference Paper.

Schaff, A. (1970), *Marxism and the Human Individual*, McGraw-Hill, New York.

Schutz, A. (1954), 'Concept and Theory Formation in the Social Sciences', excerpt in Thompson, K. and Turnstall, J. (1971), *Sociological Perspectives*, Penguin, Harmondsworth.

Schutz, A. (1962), 'The Problem of Social Reality', in *Collected Papers Vol. 1*, Martinus Nijaff, The Hague.

Scott, P. (1984), *The Crisis of the University*, Croom Helm, Beckenham.

Seidler, V. J. (1994), *Unreasonable Men, Masculinity and Social Theory*, Routledge, London.

Seidman, I. E. (1991), *Interviewing As Qualitative Research*, Teachers College, Columbia University, New York.

Sharpe, S. (1976, 1994), *Just Like a Girl*, Penguin, Harmondsworth.

Sheridan, L. (1992), 'Women returners to FE: employment and gender relations in the home', *Gender and Education*, Vol. 42, No. 4, Autumn, pp213-228.

Simon, B. (1971), *Classification and Streaming: A Study of Grouping in English Schools 1860-1960*, Lawrence and Wishart, London.

Slowey, M. (1995), *Implementing Change From Within Universities and Colleges*, Kogan-Page, London.

Smart, B. (1976), *Sociology, Phenomenology and Marxian Analysis*, Routledge and Kegan Paul, London.

Smith, D. (1978), 'A peculiar eclipsing: Women's exclusion from man's culture', *Women's Studies International Quarterly*, Vol. 1, No. 4, pp281-96.

Smith, D. (1987), 'Women's Perspective as a Radical Critique of Sociology', in Harding, S. (ed), *Feminism and Methodology*, Open University Press, Milton Keynes, pp84-96.

Smith, D. (1989), 'Sociological Theory: Methods of Writing Patriarchy', in Wallace, R., *Feminism and Social Theory*, Sage, California, pp34-64.

Smithers, A. and Griffin, A. (1986), 'Mature Students at University: entry, experience and outcomes', *Studies in Higher Education*, Vol. 11, No. 3, pp257-268.

Smithers, A. and Robinson, P. (1989), *Increasing Participation in Higher Education*, BP Educational Service, London.

Spender, D. (1981), *Men's Studies Modified*, Pergamon, Oxford.

Spender, D. (1982), *Invisible Women, The Schooling Scandal*, The Women's Press, Reading.

Sperling, L. (1991), 'Can the Barriers be Breached? Mature Women's Access to Higher Education', *Gender and Education*, Vol. 3, No. 2, pp199-213.

Stacey, J. and Thorne, B. (1985), 'The missing feminist revolution in sociology', *Social Problems*, 32 (4), pp301-16.

Standing, K. (1998), 'Writing the Voices of the Less Powerful: Research on Lone Mothers', in Ribbens, J. and Edwards, R. (eds), *Feminist Dilemmas in Qualitative Research*, Sage Publications, London, pp186-202.

Stanley, L. (1992), 'The Impact of Feminism in Sociology', in Spender, D., (eds), *The Knowledge Explosion*, Teachers' College Press, New York.

Stanley, L. and Wise, S. (1983, 1993), *Breaking Out Again, Feminist Ontology and Epistemology*, Routledge, London.

Stanworth, M. (1983), *Gender and Schooling: A Study of Sexual Divisions in the Classroom*, Hutchinson (revised edition), London.

Statistical Bulletin (June 1993), *Student Numbers in HE - Great Britain 1981/82 to 1991/92*, Issue No. 17/93, DFE, HMSO, London.

Thomas, J. (1984), 'Some aspects of negotiated order, loose coupling and mesostructure in maximum security prisons', *Symbolic Interactionism*, 7, pp213-231.

Thomas, W. I. (1928), *The Child in America*, Knopf, New York.

Thompson, E. P. (1970), *Warwick University Limited*, Penguin, Harmondsworth.

Thompson, J. (1980), *Adult Education for a Change*, Hutchinson, London.

Thompson, J. (1982), *Women, Class and Adult Education*, University of Southampton, Department of Continuing Education, Southampton.

Thompson, J. (1983), 'Women and Adult Education', in Tight, M., *Opportunities for Adult Education*, Croom-Helm, London.

Thompson, J. (1983), *Learning Liberation: Women's response to men's education*, Croom-Helm, London.

Thompson, J. (1993), 'Learning, Liberation and Maturity, An Open to Whoever's Left', *Adults Learning*, Vol. 4, No. 9, May, p244.

Thompson, J. (1995), 'Feminism and Women's Education', in Mayo, M. and Thompson, J. (eds), *Adult Learning Critical Intelligence and Social Change*, NIACE, Leicester, pp124-136.

Titmus, C., Knoll, J. H. and Wittpoth, J. (1993), *Continuing Education in Higher Education*, University of Leeds, Leeds.

Troyna, B. (1994), 'Blind Faith? Empowerment and Educational Research', *Educational Studies in Sociology of Education*, Vol. 4, No. 1, pp3-22.

Turner, R. (1968), 'The Self-Conception in Social Interaction', in Gordon, C. and Gergen, K., *The Self in Social Interaction*, John Wiley and Sons, New York.

UGC (1984), *A Strategy for Higher Education into the 1990s*, HMSO.

Universities Funding Council (1993), *University Statistics 1991-92. Vol. 1: Students and Staff*, Universities Statistical Record, Cheltenham.

University Grants Committee (1990), *A Strategy for Higher Education*, HMSO, London.

University of Warwick, *Corporate Plan 1992*.

Urry, J. (1970), 'Role analysis and the sociological enterprise', *The Sociological Review*, 18 (3).

Usher, P. (1982), 'Women and University Extension', in *Women, Class and Adult Education*, University of Southampton, Department of Continuing Education, Southampton.

Wagner, L. (1990), 'Adults in Higher Education: the next five years', *Adults Learning*, Vol. 2, No. 4, pp94-96.

Wallace, R. (1989), *Feminism and Sociological Theory*, Sage, Beverly Hills, California.

Weber, M. (1964), *Basic Concepts in Sociology*, Citadel Press, New York.

Weil, S. (1986), 'Non-traditional learners within HE institutions: Discovery and disappointment', *Studies in HE*, Vol. 11, No. 3, pp219-235.

Weil, S. (1989), 'From a language of observation to a language of experience: studying the prospectives of diverse adults in higher education', *Journal of Access Studies*, 3 (1), pp17-43.

Weiner, G. (ed) (1985), *Just a Bunch of Girls: Feminist Approaches to Schooling*, Open University Press, Milton Keynes.

West, L. (1996), *Beyond Fragments*, Taylor and Francis, London.

Westwood, S. (1980), 'Adult Education and the Sociology of Education: an Exploration', in Thompson, J., *Adult Education for a Change*, Hutchinson, London.

Wheeler, S. (1967), 'The Structure of Formally Organised Socialization Settings', in Brim, O. and Wheeler, S., *Socialization After Childhood - Two Essays*, John Wiley and Sons, New York.

Williams J. (1997), 'The Discourse of Access: The Legitimation of Selectivity' in Williams, J. (ed), *Negotiating Access to Higher Education*, SRHE/Open University Press, Buckingham, pp24-46.

Willis, P. (1977), *Learning to Labour*, Saxon House, Westmead.

Wimbush, E. (1987), 'Transitions: Changing work, leisure and health experiences among mothers with young children', in Allatt, P. and Keil, T. (eds), *Women and the Life Cycle: Transitions and Turning Points*, Macmillan, Basingstoke.

Wolpe, A. M. (1977), *Some Processes in Sexist Education*, Women's Research and Resources Centre Publications, London.

Woodley, A., Wagner, L., Slowey, M., Fulton, O. and Bowner, T. (1987), *Choosing to Learn*, SRHE/Open University Press, Buckingham.

Woodrow, M. (1988), 'The access course route to higher education', *Higher Education Quarterly*, 42 (4), pp317-34.

Wright Mills, C. (1970), *The Sociological Imagination*, Penguin, Harmondsworth.

Young, I. (1980), 'Socialist Feminism and the limits of dual systems theory', *Socialist Review*, 10, Nos 2-3, March/June, 174.

Young, I. (1981), 'Beyond the Unhappy Marriage: A Critique of the Dual Systems Theory', in Sargent, L. (ed), *Women and Revolution*, Pluto Press, London.

Young, M. (ed) (1971), *Knowledge and Control*, Macmillan, London.

Youngman, F. (1986), *Adult Education and Socialist Pedagogy*, Croom-Helm, London.

Index